DERRIDA AND THE INHERITANCE OF DEMOCRACY

DERRIDA AND THE INHERITANCE OF DEMOCRACY

Samir Haddad

Indiana University Press

Bloomington and Indianapolis

This book is a publication of

Indiana University Press
Office of Scholarly Publishing
Herman B Wells Library 350
1320 East 10th Street
Bloomington, Indiana 47405 USA

iupress.indiana.edu

Telephone orders   800-842-6796
Fax orders   812-855-7931

© 2013 by Samir Haddad

Library of Congress Cataloging-in-Publication Data

Haddad, Samir.
    Derrida's inheritance of democracy / Samir Haddad.
    pages cm. — (Studies in continental thought)
    Includes bibliographical references and index.
    ISBN 978-0-253-00836-7 (cloth : alk. paper) — ISBN 978-0-253-
00841-1 (pbk. : alk. paper) — ISBN 978-0-253-00843-5 (ebook) 1.
Derrida, Jacques. 2. Democracy—Philosophy. 3. Political science—
Philosophy. I. Title.
    B2430.D484H325 2013
    320.092—dc23

                        2013002397

1 2 3 4 5 18 17 16 15 14 13

For my father,
in thanks and admiration

Contents

Abbreviations

The following abbreviations have been used in the text for frequently cited works by Jacques Derrida.

A/AP   *Aporias: Dying—Awaiting (One Another at) the "Limits of Truth."* Translated by Thomas Dutoit. Stanford: Stanford University Press, 1993. Published in French as *Apories* (Paris: Galilée, 1996).

AV   "Avances." Preface to *Le tombeau de dieu artisan—sur Platon*, by Serge Margel, 9–43. Paris: Minuit, 1995.

FK/FS   "Faith and Knowledge: The Two Souces of 'Religion' at the Limits of Reason Alone." Translated by Samuel Weber. In *Acts of Religion*, edited by Gil Anidjar, 42–101. New York: Routledge, 2002. Originally published as "Foi et savoir," in *Foi et savoir, suivi de Le siècle et le pardon* (Paris: Le Seuil, 2000), 9–100.

FOL/FDL   "Force of Law: The 'Mystical Foundation of Authority.'" Translated by Mary Quaintance. In *Acts of Religion*, edited by Gil Anidjar, 230–98. New York: Routledge, 2002. Originally published as *Force de loi* (Paris: Galilée, 1994).

FW/DQ   *For What Tomorrow . . . A Dialogue.* Coauthored with Elisabeth Roudinesco. Translated by Jeff Fort. Stanford: Stanford University Press, 2004. Originally published as *De quoi demain . . . Dialogue* (Paris: Fayard/Galilée, 2001).

NW/LV   "The Night Watch (over 'the book of himself')." Translated by Pascale-Anne Brault and Michael Naas. In *Derrida and Joyce: Texts and Contexts,* edited by Andrew J. Mitchell and Sam Slote, 87–108. Albany: State University of New York Press, 2013. Originally published as "La veilleuse (' . . au livre de lui-même')." Preface to *James Joyce ou l'écriture matricide*, by Jacques Trilling (Belfort: Circé, 2001), 7–32.

OH/DH   *Of Hospitality.* Coauthored with Anne Dufourmantelle. Translated by Rachel Bowlby. Stanford: Stanford University Press, 2000. Originally published as *De l'hospitalité* (Paris: Calmann-Levy, 1997).

PF/PA   *Politics of Friendship*. Translated by George Collins. London: Verso, 1997. Originally published as *Politiques de l'amitié* (Paris: Galilée, 1994).

R/V   *Rogues: Two Essays on Reason*. Translated by Pascale-Anne Brault and Michael Naas. Stanford: Stanford University Press, 2005. Originally published as *Voyous: Deux essais sur la raison* (Paris: Galilée, 2003).

SOM/SDM   *Specters of Marx: The State of the Debt, the Work of Mourning, and the New International*. Translated by Peggy Kamuf. New York: Routledge, 1994. Originally published as *Spectres de Marx: L'état de la dette, le travail du deuil et la Nouvelle Internationale* (Paris: Galilée, 1993).

Throughout the text all references to works by Derrida that are available in both English and French refer first to the English pagination, then to the French. Unless stated otherwise, translations of works that are available only in French are mine.

Acknowledgments

THIS BOOK WAS written over a number of years, and I have many people to thank for the inspiration, conversations, and help that were essential to its production.

First, thanks to David Michael Kleinberg-Levin, who, from the very beginning, provided excellent guidance and support, giving extensive feedback on everything he read. I owe an enormous amount to Penelope Deutscher, an inspiring philosopher whose influence on me is hard to measure. I'm very lucky to have first encountered European philosophy in Penny's lecture hall, and to have received her help ever since, not in the least across the whole process of the writing of this book. I am also grateful to Bonnie Honig and Sam Weber for their expertise and advice during the project's early stages. Their input was key in shaping the core argument.

I am privileged to have had Martin Hägglund as a friend and interlocutor over the past decade. I thank him for countless hours of conversation and argument, as well as for his feedback on the manuscript as a whole. Geoffrey Bennington and Johanna Oksala also read a draft of the manuscript, and their suggestions for improvement were invaluable. I thank Michael Naas for his generosity and insight the many times we talked—his clarity and knowledge never failed to illuminate the more difficult ideas that I sought to understand. And thanks also to Ann Murphy and Jeffrey Flynn, exemplary colleagues and friends with whom I've discussed so much that is in these pages.

I've benefited from a strong community of scholars who helped me work through the ideas in this book at various stages in discussion and correspondence. Thanks to Joshua Andresen, Pleshette DeArmitt, Matthias Fritsch, Allan Hazlett, Leonard Lawlor, Paul Patton, Gayle Salamon, Alan Schrift, Daniel Smith, Jill Stauffer, Nicholas Tampio, and Patrick Weil for their time and input.

At Fordham University I owe much to two of my senior colleagues, John Drummond and Merold Westphal, for their support in the early stages of my career. I also received valuable financial support from Fordham in the form of a Faculty Research Grant in 2009, a Summer Faculty Research Grant in 2011, and a Faculty Fellowship in 2011, which aided in the writing of this book.

At Indiana University Press, Dee Mortensen, Sarah Jacobi, and Tim Roberts were an excellent editorial team, providing expert knowledge and advice that went a long way to improving the book. I also thank Paolo Pecchi for the permission to use his wonderful painting for the cover.

Finally, I thank my parents for all they have done to support me across a lifetime of learning. And thank you to Luisa, my light, for everything.

Earlier versions of some of the arguments in this book appeared in the following publications: "Derrida and Democracy at Risk," *Contretemps* 4 (2004): 29–44; "Inheriting Democracy to Come," *Theory & Event* 8, no. 1 (2005); "Reading Derrida Reading Derrida: Deconstruction as Self-Inheritance," *International Journal of Philosophical Studies*, 14, no. 4 (2006): 505–20; "A Genealogy of Violence, from Light to the Autoimmune," *Diacritics* 38, no. 1–2 (2008): 121–42; "Language Remains," *CR: The New Centennial Review* 9, no. 1 (2009): 127–46; "Jacques Derrida," in *History of Continental Philosophy*, vol. 6: *Poststructuralism and Critical Theory's Second Generation*, edited by Alan D. Schrift (Chicago: University of Chicago Press, 2010), 111–32; and "Citizenship and the Ambivalence of Birth," *Derrida Today* 4, no. 2 (2011): 173–93. In all cases the arguments have been modified.

Introduction

Derrida's Legacies

Upon Jacques Derrida's death in October 2004, obituaries appeared, memorials were held, conferences were convened, and at least twenty-eight academic journals in disciplines across the humanities published special issues dedicated to his memory. Surveying the published record, one is struck by two dominant themes. The first is that of Derrida's legacy. This theme is not surprising, since raising the question of legacy is a common reaction to a public figure's death. But it was amplified in Derrida's case, no doubt owing first to the fact that his work as a whole is characterized by a constant engagement with the legacies of others. "Deconstruction," the word he used consistently across decades of publishing to describe what he was doing (despite the occasional lamentation of its more popular associations), names an approach to inheriting from the work of others. As Derrida once claimed, "This is one of the possible definitions of deconstruction—as inheritance."[1] Further, throughout his work Derrida also explicitly reflects on inheritance and related phenomena. From his early texts arguing for an essential relation between writing and death, to his final interview in which he considers what will happen to his work after his own death, one finds discussions of the themes of legacy and inheritance, and of what it is to be an heir. When Derrida died, these analyses provided a resource for those who had learned so much from his writings, seeming to speak directly to the current experience of inheriting from a thinker whose life had now ended, but whose work lives on. Thus, despite Derrida's claim in that final interview that he "never *learned-to-live* [appris-à-vivre]" (a phrase which he points out can mean equally "*taught to live*"), it was as if he had managed to accomplish the latter after his death, finally teaching his readers how to read his work and thus live as heirs to this work.[2]

The second dominant theme that one finds in the many texts written in response to Derrida's death is that of politics. Although not as typical a response to the death of a thinker, the choice of this topic too has a ready explanation. In the last fifteen years of his publishing career, Derrida turned his attention increasingly to politics, analyzing at length concepts central to political thought and writing extensively on contemporary political issues. As has often been remarked, by Derrida himself and many of his commentators, this need not imply that his writings were ever apolitical to begin with. But it is the case that politics is treated more explicitly in the later work than in the earlier, with long and detailed explorations of issues such as state violence, the legitimacy of law, immigration, reconciliation, cosmopolitanism, sovereignty, and the nature of democracy. In "The Reason of the Strongest (Are There Rogue States?)," in *Rogues*, the last major work published in his lifetime, Derrida brings all of these themes together, providing an extended analysis of democracy in the context of the post–September 11 world and elaborating on the rather enigmatic notion of "democracy to come [*démocratie à venir*]."[3] Given the desire to speak of something new, together with the massive turn to political thinking that took place in continental philosophy and theory after September 11, it is thus to be expected that so many of those responding to Derrida's death would highlight the political dimensions of his work, with special mention made of "democracy to come."

Thus taking the initial reaction to his death as a guide, two of Derrida's most important legacies concern politics, on the one hand, and the thought of legacy, on the other. In this book my aim is to demonstrate that these two themes are fundamentally related. My central claim is that inheritance, understood in a very precise manner, plays a crucial role in Derrida's theorization of democracy. Now I am not alone in noting the connection between Derrida's understanding of democracy and a certain relation to the past. Geoffrey Bennington claims that in every deconstruction "the point is to exploit other resources in the inheritance" and that "the case of 'democracy' would in that case be exemplary."[4] Matthias Fritsch argues that for Derrida democracy's futurity is linked to "the promise of repetition," a link "achieved by the notion of history, and [which] seems to rely on modern forms of historical consciousness: as opposed to other political formations, democracy is aware of its perfectibility (and, we would have to add, the possibilities of its degeneracy) in history, thus opening and exposing itself to the future to come."[5] Pheng Cheah speaks of the "paleonymy of democracy . . . an essential historicity [that] gives it a to-come, sends it into a future to-come beyond any positive forms of democracy."[6] And Judith Butler notes that "'democracy to come' is a presupposition of any existing democracy, and we err if we think that it belongs only to a future that is somehow dissociated from the past and present."[7] There is thus acknowledgment in the literature of an important relation between the past and "democracy to come."

However, just what this relation is and what it entails are not so clear. This is apparent when considering two recent books that go far beyond just mentioning this relation, using Derrida's work precisely to intervene in debates on democracy and inheritance. In *Aversive Democracy*, Aletta Norval draws Derrida's understanding of democracy to come into close proximity to Stanley Cavell's perfectionism. Her aim is to articulate a democratic subjectivity that is normative without being teleological, and central to her use of Derrida is his claim "that democracy has the structure of a promise, 'a promise that is kept in memory, that is handed down . . . inherited, claimed, and taken up.'"[8] In this way Norval endorses the relation of inheritance that democracy carries, claiming it crucial to theorizing a democratic ethos more satisfactory than is currently found in poststructuralist and deliberative democratic thinking. Thus, although conscious of some of the dangers that Derrida sees in democracy to come, Norval nonetheless has hope in the inheritance it entails, a hope that through its relation to the past democracy might be improved. By contrast, Ananda Abeysekara, in his *The Politics of Postsecular Religion*, uses Derrida's work to argue the opposite in the context of religious and postcolonial studies. He claims that Derrida's writings demonstrate how "the heritage of the name/identity" of democracy means that it "cannot be changed and improved"; Abeysekara advocates instead that we "un-inherit" this name, a strategy "not reducible to a ready-made binary of remembering/forgetting or embracing/abandoning."[9] He thus interprets Derrida's thinking of democracy to come as demonstrating the inevitable failure of any inheritance of the democratic tradition to improve the current state of politics.

Much more would need to be said to do justice to Norval's and Abeysekara's use of Derrida. Here I simply wish to suggest that the existence of accounts so opposed attest to the complexity of Derrida's own position and the potential richness of his work for thinking inheritance in democracy. In addition, I would note that accounts such as these are relatively uncommon among the responses to Derrida's work on democracy. Although it would be too much to say that there exists a dominant interpretation of this work—it is still too new for comprehensive interpretations to have yet emerged—it is the case that one finds a dominant tendency to privilege the future in the many scholars engaging with or referring to Derrida on this topic. Thinking that the future is the primary temporal modality of Derrida's theorization of democracy is of course understandable, given his own emphasis on it, exemplified in the very vocabulary of the "to come." But it is my contention that such a singular focus misses out on the most original and interesting aspect of this theorization, namely that there is a democratic injunction to inherit from the past in a very particular way. Without appreciating this fact, democracy to come is very quickly reduced to a simple passivity or utopianism in the face of what happens, which in turn allows for no response other than resigned acceptance or flat-out rejection. By contrast, I aim to show that recognizing democracy to come as involving inheritance not only better represents Derrida's own view but that it also opens up a space for richer responses to be pursued.

To make my argument, I first develop a general account of Derridean inheritance. Chapter 1 begins at a certain distance from the themes of inheritance and democracy by analyzing the structure of aporia. This lays the groundwork for all the claims that follow, since I will argue that for Derrida all legacies are aporetic. I pursue my analysis by focusing on the specific case of hospitality, whose structure is exemplary of aporias and central to Derrida's engagement with democracy, and show how he argues that being hospitable requires a response to two injunctions, one unconditional and the other conditional. These injunctions contradict one another at the same time as they are in an asymmetrical relation of interdependence, implying that their contradiction cannot be resolved, only negotiated. Having presented the features of this structure in detail, I then argue that, contrary to what is often assumed, unconditional hospitality does not operate as an ideal in Derrida's writings. I acknowledge that my interpretation might be seen to encourage political paralysis, but I suggest that this worry is reduced when one appreciates the relation between aporias and inheritance.

Chapter 2 examines inheritance directly and articulates Derrida's understanding of its general features. Focusing primarily on claims made in two works, *Specters of Marx* and *For What Tomorrow*, I argue that although Derrida presents inheritance as a necessary relation that one has to aporias, this relation is not fully determined.[10] For Derridean inheritance does contain a restricted sphere of choice, and I show this by examining the way that, in his readings of others, Derrida himself chooses to privilege the most living part of a legacy by aggressively raising the stakes of the aporetic tensions he receives, attempting to open them up to transformation. I then complete my general account by explaining the temporal logic of "spacing" to which Derridean inheritance adheres, and the relation between inheritance and justice that this reveals.

Chapter 3 moves to the heart of my argument by connecting the general theory of inheritance I have developed to Derrida's theorization of democracy. I begin by expanding on the link Derrida makes between democracy and the idea of a promise. This provides the characteristics that democracy ought to have, including an aporetic structure, instability in its name, an essential dimension of nonknowledge, and an undecidability between safety and danger. To show that for Derrida democracy indeed has these traits I next turn to "The Reason of the Strongest," focusing in particular on this essay's central concept, "autoimmunity." With Derrida's understanding of democracy articulated, I then examine the role that inheritance plays in his account. I first establish that democracy is inherited according to the theory developed in Chapter 2, showing that it conforms to the aporetic structure and the logic of spacing. I then argue for a second, stronger claim, that through his emphasis on the role of self-critique in democratic practice, Derrida can be read as asserting that participants in democracy must inherit if they are to pursue its promise. Democracy is thus not only inherited; it also contains the injunction to inherit, and democratic action requires an active response to this injunction. In this way Derrida's notion of democracy to come harbors an inextricable link to the past.

With my interpretation established, the second half of the book is devoted to pursuing its implications. Chapter 4 addresses the normative status of Derrida's work.

This issue has been in the background of my account, with Chapter 2 arguing that Derridean inheritance contains a certain space for choice, and Chapter 3 that Derrida values democracy despite its inevitable dangers. My interpretation thus underlines the fact that Derrida's writings contain normative claims. However, there is disagreement in the secondary literature as to whether Derrida is justified in making such claims. I analyze this issue by examining two prominent interpretations—Leonard Lawlor, who in *This Is Not Sufficient* attempts to justify Derrida's normative claims through appeals to a "lesser violence," and Martin Hägglund, who in *Radical Atheism* argues that Derrida cannot support such claims when performing a deconstructive analysis.[11] I argue that neither interpretation is satisfactory, and propose an alternative account. On my interpretation, since the structures Derrida theorizes must be linked to language that is inherited (in words such as "democracy," "hospitality," and so on), a field of normative values associated with the history of this language is opened up in his writings. I thus argue that Derrida's writings contain possibilities for making legitimate normative claims, without these claims being immune to critique or question.

Chapter 5 highlights one such normative claim by analyzing the most developed example of democratic inheritance in Derrida's writings, *Politics of Friendship*.[12] I show that in this work's engagement with discourses of friendship and political belonging in the Western tradition, Derrida inherits according to the scheme I have articulated, raising the stakes of traditional theories in order to call for a transformation in conceptions of democratic citizenship that would break with the language of fraternity. It is in this resistance to fraternity that Derrida's strategy of inheritance can be seen to be democratic, since it responds to the injunction to promote greater inclusiveness. This is not to say, however, that Derrida's inheritance of the tradition is safe from all critique, and I draw attention to two of its aspects that can be called into question. First, I argue that despite the feminist impulse in Derrida's inheritance of the tradition, he nonetheless perpetuates a certain exclusion of women in determining this tradition's makeup as being exclusively male. Second, I note that Derrida's resistance to fraternity relies on a particular understanding of birth as a past, negative necessity that is immune to all revision, and I suggest that one need not be restricted by this narrow definition.

Chapter 6 takes up this last theme, that of birth, seeking to inherit Derrida's democratic discourse so as to open it up to further transformation. I first show that in addition to the negative determination as past necessity presupposed in *Politics of Friendship*, Derrida's writings seem also to contain an alternative understanding of birth, as a positive figure for contingency that lies in the future. I argue, however, that this division is misleading and that properly understood there is only one conception of birth that can be said to operate across Derrida's writings. I make this argument in two steps. First, I show that within the Derridean framework the second understanding of birth cannot be purely positive, but it is ambivalent, and lies in a time between past and future that is one of inheritance. Second, I argue that the first understanding of birth also possesses this structure, showing how Derrida transforms this supposed figure of necessity precisely through an act of inheritance.

To conclude, I reflect on my analysis in order to outline a model for inheriting from Derrida's work as a whole. Deconstruction is an exercise in inheritance, and my reading of *Politics of Friendship* highlights the central feature of this exercise—I demonstrate how Derrida provisionally stabilizes one aspect of the tradition (the meaning of birth) in order to destabilize other aspects (the links between fraternity, friendship, and democracy). This stabilization is necessary for the success of Derrida's intervention. But at the same time it marks a point requiring further engagement, since, as I show, birth cannot be reduced once and for all to any single determination. This suggests a general strategy for future readings of Derrida: every time he inherits, which occurs every time he writes, look for those points of seeming stability and exploit their underlying instability in order to generate further possibilities for carrying his work forward.

Across his writings Derrida inherits from writers and thinkers working in a number of traditions and genres, resulting in a rich and multifaceted oeuvre that resists mastery. This complexity is one of the reasons for the impressive multidisciplinary impact of his work. It also leaves one with diverse methodological options of how to go about responding to what Derrida has written. In this book I have chosen to analyze Derrida's texts on their own terms, uncovering connections and tensions within them in order to articulate and develop further a conceptual framework that is often only implicitly or partially theorized by Derrida himself. There are thus no chapters or long sections analyzing other thinkers or issues external to Derrida scholarship. The obvious danger of this approach is that of producing an elaborate edifice, perhaps intriguing in some respects, but sealed and isolated in its own internal relations. Needless to say, I have sought to avoid such an outcome, and in any case I thought it a risk worth running in order to present the originality, sophistication, and occasional strangeness of Derrida's position on democracy in all of its complexity. I hope that the result is a clear, comprehensible, and comprehensive interpretation that I and others may take up in the future and connect more fully to related thinkers and topics. As Derrida states in *Specters of Marx*, "Inheritance is never a *given*, it is always a task. It remains before us" (*SOM*, 54/*SDM*, 94).

1 The Structure of Aporia

Aporias

Despite the many different topics on which he writes, and the large diversity of authors he reads, Derrida's texts return the reader with insistence to what seems to be the same logical structure. This structure goes by various names, including undecidable, double bind, double constraint, aporia, contradictory injunction, antinomy, and process of autoimmunity. In each case, at stake is a relation between two elements that contradict each other at the same time that they depend on each other. It is thus a necessary contradiction, which cannot be resolved by traditional means such as denying one of the elements or lifting the relation up in a dialectical movement. The power of Derrida's analyses lies in his demonstration of the ways traditional modes of thinking lead to such irresolvable contradictions, and it is impressive that he is able to show this so consistently across readings of so many different authors, texts, subjects, and traditions.

Now Derrida himself resists reducing all of these analyses to one master structure or term that would hold sway over the others, even while the similarities among them are so striking. Otherwise put, the variation in names has not occurred by chance. Each name carries different connotations and resonates in a particular way with its specific context. For example, "aporia," meaning "without passage" or having no way to move forward, receives its most extensive discussion in a text (*Aporias*) first delivered at the Cerisy-la-Salle conference titled "The Passage of Frontiers."[1] Derrida uses "antinomy" most often in discussions that approach Kant, yet precisely at the point in which he wishes to distinguish himself from Kant, examining how the law (*nomos*) seems to undo itself in a hyperbolic raising of the stakes.[2] And the originally biological term "autoimmunity" appears when Derrida examines a certain kind of life (the life of religion, the life of democracy) which partially destroys its own immune system in order to live on.[3] These names thus work because of their respective contexts, and one cannot easily transfer them across the different texts in which they appear.

But this is not to say that such a transfer is impossible. Indeed, Derrida does this all the time, speaking of the aporetic structure of an antinomy, the antinomic nature of autoimmunity, and so on. This does not contradict what I have just claimed, for these interchanges are always provisional, one might even say experimental. The text mentioned above, *Aporias*, provides a good example of this strategy. Here, as is appropriate in the context of a conference devoted to his own work, Derrida takes the time to examine what he sees as his past invocations of aporias and aporetic structures (*A*, 12–21/*AP*, 31–48). He notes that "*aporia*, this tired word of philosophy and logic, has often imposed itself upon me, and recently it has done so even more often," and then goes on to provide a kind of "aporetology or aporetography" in which he lists and cites a number of his texts (*A*, 12–13, 15/*AP*, 32, 35).[4] In these texts it is not always the case that "aporia" is the central term used to focus on the contradictory structure in question, and sometimes the word itself does not even appear. Yet Derrida is nonetheless willing in this context to group them under this name. He risks calling them all aporias, even though he may have used different names in the past.

Having provided an overview of aporias across his writings, Derrida's self-reflection in *Aporias* then focuses more narrowly on one text, *The Other Heading*, in which he discusses "nine or eleven times . . . the same aporetic duty" (*A*, 17/*AP*, 39).[5] As further evidence of a willingness to move between different names, it is worth noting that this duty is described in *The Other Heading* as an "antinomy" rather than an "aporia." But whatever name it is given, even as Derrida labels these discussions as instances of the *same* duty, he also points out that they are not themselves identical to each other. The aporias have a plurality, and can be classified into three broad groups.

A plural logic of the aporia thus takes shape. It appears to be paradoxical enough so that the partitioning [*partage*] among multiple figures of aporia does not oppose figures to each other, but instead installs the haunting of the one in the other. In one case, the nonpassage resembles an impermeability; it would stem from the opaque existence of an uncrossable border: a door that does not open or that only opens according to an unlocatable condition, according to the inaccessible secret of some shibboleth. Such is the case for all closed borders (exemplarily during war). In another case, the nonpassage, the impasse or aporia, stems from the fact that there is no limit. There is not yet or there is no longer a border to cross, no opposition between two sides: the limit is too porous, permeable, and indeterminate. There is no longer a home [*chez-soi*] and a not-home [*chez-l'autre*]. . . . Finally, the third time of aporia, the impossible, the antinomy, or the contradiction, is a nonpassage because its elementary milieu does not allow for something that could be called passage, step, walk, gait, displacement, or replacement, a kinesis in general. There is no more path (*odos, methodos, Weg,* or *Holzweg*). The impasse itself would be impossible. (*A,* 20–21/*AP,* 44–47)

The claim in this passage is that there is a plural logic of the aporia at work in *The Other Heading,* and that this plurality can be classified into three groups.[6] The lines of this classification provide a good example of the way that terms used by Derrida resonate with their context, for in choosing to classify what were formerly described as antinomies according to their relation to the concept of passage, Derrida to some extent justifies his renaming of "antinomies" as "aporias." In a conference titled "The Passage of Frontiers," "aporia" presents itself as the most appropriate word to describe the situation that was formerly called an "antinomy."

This classification is not, however, a firm one, for Derrida introduces it with the caveat that in the plural logic "the partitioning [*partage*] among multiple figures of aporia does not oppose figures to each other, but instead installs the haunting of the one in the other." This "haunting" implies that the divisions drawn are not hard and fast, and that each figure of the aporia bears the traces of the others. This is confirmed in the rest of the text. *Aporias* is devoted to exploring the sense of "my death," a phrase Derrida interprets as aporetic primarily in the third sense listed above. He thus writes that "I will say very quickly now why 'my death' will be the subject of this small aporetic oration. First, I'll address the aporia, that is, the impossible, the impossibility, as what cannot pass [*passer*] or come to pass [*se passer*]: it is not even the *non-pas,* the not-step, but rather the deprivation of the *pas* (the privative form would be a kind of *a-pas*)" (*A,* 22–23/*AP,* 50). Derrida's dizzying interrogation of the Heideggerian definition of death as "the possibility of the absolute impossibility of Dasein" confirms this understanding, seeking to show that death is an aporia that departs from the vocabulary of passage altogether, and in this way moves from the possible to the impossible. But—and this is the moment of "haunting"—part of Derrida's demonstration involves an appeal to the presence of the other senses of aporia listed above. To cite just one example, Derrida challenges Heidegger's insistence on the "mineness" of my death by locating the aporia of hospitality as a necessary element in the event that would be death (*A,* 33–35/*AP,* 65–68). Hospitality is an example of the second type of aporia, in which there is "no longer a home [*chez-soi*] and a not-home [*chez-l'autre*]." Thus the aporia of death, initially aligned with the third type in the classification above, is "haunted" by an aporia of the second type.

This contamination of the different types of aporia resonates in one of the hyperbolic conclusions that appears at the end of *Aporias.* There, after having terrorized so many frontiers—between the self and the other, the human and the animal, anthropology and philosophy, and life and death—Derrida writes:

> What we have glimpsed, I hope, and the lesson that I draw for the usage I was able or may be able from now on to make of the aporia, is that if one must endure the aporia, if such is the law of all decisions, of all responsibilities, of all duties without duty, and of all the border problems that ever can arise, *the aporia can never simply be endured*

as such. The ultimate aporia is the impossibility of the aporia *as such*. The reservoir of this statement seems to be incalculable. This statement is made with and reckons with the incalculable itself. (*A*, 78/*AP*, 136–37)

That the aporia can never be endured as such is a claim, first and foremost, that the aporia does not belong to the realm of endurance, of presence, of calculability—it is marked by an essential absence, impossible as such. In addition, this claim also attests to the contamination described earlier in the text. Again, it is unclear precisely what the referent for "the aporia" is in this citation. Strictly speaking, it should be the aporia that is "my death," since this was the explicit object of the analysis of which this claim is the result. But "the aporia" can also be here taken to refer to any and all aporias, since "my death" cannot itself be isolated from other aporias. First, because Derrida argues that other aporias are at work in "my death," and second, because through their association with an essential absence, all aporias carry the mark of "death."[7] Thus *the* aporia referred to in this passage is not one. There is no single, isolated aporia that one can qualify with the definite article. As the title of the text suggests, there are, at best, aporias.

For now I will not pursue further the intricacies of *Aporias*, although the themes of life and death will return throughout my analyses of inheritance and democracy. And it is not yet clear just what the conclusion "The ultimate aporia is the impossibility of the aporia *as such*" really means—understanding it is one of the goals of this chapter. At this point I simply want to emphasize the way in which Derrida here negotiates the difficulty of speaking about aporias in general. He starts with a general identification of multiple aporias that appear in different texts under different names, a kind of "aporetology or aporetography." He then moves to a particular text (*The Other Heading*) in which the aporetic structure appears under a particular name ("antinomy"). But this restriction to one text and one name does not reduce the multiplicity at work in "the" aporetic structure, for even in this particular instance, there is a plurality of figures of the aporia, which itself can only be provisionally classified since there is no absolutely clean division between the different types. Finally, at the end of a process that is a hyperbolic reduction—the focus is on the singularity of "my death," on this singular "moment" of this singular "experience"—the aporia still eludes presentation. Even in this singularity one cannot speak of "the" aporia.

From this movement from generality to singularity, from an aporetography to the failed writing of even just one aporia, I draw two important lessons. First, Derrida demonstrates why the plurality of the title "*Aporias*" is essential. There is no unique aporia, no unique structure that gives the form that would be applicable to all aporetic instances. It makes no sense to describe "the" structure of aporia, as if this would make sense of every instance in which Derrida invokes, implicitly or explicitly, something that seems to be aporetic.[8] But second, it is also apparent that focusing on one particular aporetic instance will not resolve the problem, since the integrity of any such instance is itself called into question. Any aporetic instance is in the first instance plural (even in one text or one passage the one aporia has multiple references), and ultimately absent (that is, one cannot in the end properly use this language of reference. There is no aporia, either presented here in a text or referred to elsewhere). The consequence of these twists and turns is that aporias cannot be presented as such, either as a general structure or as a singular instance.

What, then, am I to do if I want to speak of them? How should I proceed if "aporias" constitute my present theme?

I do not have a fully satisfactory answer to this question. But what I propose to do in response is to follow Derrida in focusing on a singular aporetic instance and context, while being aware that this singularity is not isolated from a wider generality. I will thus give a reading of one aporia that is discussed by Derrida, that of hospitality as it is theorized at a particular moment in a particular text, while informing my reading by other aporetic moments from Derrida's work. In this way I aim to demonstrate certain things about other aporias of hospitality, and other aporias more generally. As will be seen in Chapter 2, my reason for beginning with the aporetic structure is that it is an essential element in the Derridean theory of inheritance. And the choice to focus on the particular aporia of hospitality is not arbitrary, for as I will show in Chapter 3, hospitality plays an important role in Derrida's understanding of democracy.[9] Analyzing this aporia at length will thus lay the groundwork for the central claims of this book concerning inheritance and democracy.

Before turning to hospitality, I should note one final point. I have already made the decision to speak of an aporia of hospitality, in spite of the fact that in the text to which I devote the most attention, *Of Hospitality*, Derrida speaks more of an "antinomy" than an "aporia."[10] I do this partly out of convenience—even if it is ultimately unpresentable, I have to give this thing a name in order to speak of it. But in choosing this name, I want also to keep in play its connotations of immobility, of a lack of passage, of finding oneself in a situation where one can see no way out, as these capture the kind of experience the analysis of Derrida's work invokes, particularly when it is read with the kind of political issues in mind that are the focus of the following chapters.

Hospitality

Hospitality is a theme that took on increasing importance in Derrida's later work, appearing in several lectures, seminar transcripts, and interviews published in this period. Derrida pursues his analysis of this notion along two related paths. First, he examines how hospitality has been theorized in texts, implicitly and explicitly, both in works by philosophers and writers such as Plato, Sophocles, Kant, Klossowski, Massignon, Benveniste, and Levinas, and in contemporary debates concerning immigrants, refugees, and government surveillance. Second, Derrida also develops a refined understanding of hospitality's aporetic structure, articulating it in abstract, formal terms.[11] It is one such formalization (that found in *Of Hospitality* on pages 75–83 [DH 71–77]) that I analyze in what follows, with occasional reference to other texts, in order to articulate more fully the logic and consequences of Derrida's view. This is not to say that this description contains all Derrida has to say about hospitality, but it does contain the essential elements in play in all of his writings on the subject. It also provides an example of the structure Derrida sees at work in several normative concepts interrogated in his later writings, including forgiveness, giving, responsibility, and justice, and so the results of my analysis are generalizable beyond this single case.[12]

Derrida's account in these pages focuses on the relationship between two regimes of law, both of which are inherited from the Abrahamic tradition—a phrase he uses to designate Judaic, Christian, and Islamic cultures in a broad sense, including their secular derivations. The first regime is what Derrida calls "*the* law of absolute, *unconditional*, hyperbolical hospitality" (*OH*, 75/*DH*, 71). This is a law that mandates an absolute openness, a welcome that allows for the coming of any other, without question or imposed limitations. To be hospitable, according to this law, is to welcome whomever or whatever, no matter who or what they are or when or how they come. This demand entails some extreme consequences that one might not first associate with hospitality. If hospitality is to be truly unconditional, this law is not guaranteed to produce good or desirable effects. As Derrida states in conversation with Elisabeth Roudinesco, "Pure hospitality consists in leaving one's house open to the unforeseeable arrival, which can be an intrusion, even a dangerous intrusion, liable eventually to cause harm" (*FW*, 59/*DQ*, 102). Being unconditionally open means being open to what is good and bad, friend and foe. There is thus nothing to guarantee that one would remain safe in following this law.[13] Further, pushing the demand for unconditionality to its limit, there might no longer even be a home, a *chez soi* over which the self remains master and from which the welcome is made, since these would constitute conditions and thus transgress the law: "Even if the other deprives you of your mastery or your home, you have to accept this. It is terrible to accept this, but that is the condition of unconditional hospitality: that you give up the mastery of your space, your home, your nation."[14] Finally, Derrida is clear in stating that "this pure or unconditional hospitality is not a political or juridical concept" (*FW*, 59/*DQ*, 102). The unconditional law exceeds the concepts that belong to politics and law, domains Derrida sees as demanding clear distinctions and an exercise of a certain mastery or sovereignty in order to make decisions of inclusion and exclusion. Being absolutely open to all who come is thus not a principle that can be translated intact, for example, into immigration law, since it troubles the very notions of frontiers and borders on which such law is based.

In contrast to this law of unconditional hospitality, there are "the laws (in the plural) of hospitality, namely, the conditions, the norms, the rights and the duties that are imposed on hosts and hostesses, on the men or women who give a welcome as well as the men or women who receive it" (*OH*, 75–77/*DH*, 71). These laws are anything but unconditional, as they are constituted by complex systems of the norms, customs, rules, and regulations stating when hospitality is appropriate, and how to go about performing it. So while these conditional laws concern one's relation to alterity, they do not imply a relation of absolute openness. They involve, rather, choices and decisions that distinguish between others who are worthy of welcome and other others who are not. It is in engaging with these laws that one enters the political realm: "Once the field of conditional hospitality has been circumscribed, it becomes possible to discuss a policy" (*FW*, 60/*DQ*, 104).

These two regimes of law thereby contradict each other, as one demands an openness without limitation, and the other imposes limits. Yet Derrida goes on to claim that one must nonetheless follow both regimes, at once. This is because each depends on the other, and so the affirmation of one necessarily leads to the affirmation of the other. The unconditional law, on its own, is not enough to achieve hospitality, for following this law *as such* is impossible.

> It wouldn't be effectively unconditional, the law, if it didn't *have to become* effective, concrete, determined, if that were not its being as having-to-be. It would risk being abstract, utopian, illusory, and so turning over to its opposite. In order to be what it is, *the* law thus needs the laws, which, however, deny it, or at any rate threaten it, sometimes corrupt or pervert it. And must always be able to do this. (*OH*, 79/*DH*, 75)

If it is to be a law, the unconditional law must be able to be effective. Without this possibility it would lose this status and be simply a utopian ideal. This means, however, that the unconditional law requires conditions—it demands that there be rules and regulations that guide any act of hospitality. That is, the unconditional law needs the conditional laws, even as these threaten its rule precisely in their prescription of limitations on hospitality. And it is important to emphasize here that the danger posed by the unconditional law, in the absence of the conditional laws, is not just that hospitality would be simply unobtainable. The danger is more troubling, namely that the unconditional law would then risk "turning over into its opposite." This last phrase is here left unexplained, but elsewhere Derrida explores it further, tying it back to this law's "intrinsic danger of perversion."

> In effect, the one I welcome can be a thief, a murderer, he can ransack my house: so many contingencies that cannot be excluded. . . . From the very fact that it essentially and irreducibly inhabits the pure principle of hospitality, this threat gives rise to anxiety and hatred. In her examination of what happened in Europe before the Second World War II with the decline of nation-states, Hannah Arendt shows that one already here witnessed huge displacements not of people exiled, but of populations without status and without state guarantees, which constituted a sort of call for pure hospitality. She thus explains the genesis of hatred and those violent events to which one had not been accustomed outside the classical forms of exile. Situations of pure hospitality thus contain an internal tragedy. The passage to law, politics, and the third constitutes in a certain manner a kind of fall, but at the same time it is what guarantees hospitality's effectiveness.[15]

The conditional laws thus not only provide an (albeit imperfect) instantiation of the unconditional law, an instantiation without which hospitality would simply be an impotent desire. The unconditional law, precisely because it opens one up to such dangerous threats, can induce a reactive anguish and hatred, and it is in defense against such a possibility that the conditional laws are erected. The ineffectiveness of the unconditional law is thus related both to its impossibility as such and to the inhospitable possibilities that arise in the face of the dangers it invites.

For these reasons the affirmation of the unconditional law necessarily leads to the affirmation of the conditional laws. To pursue an unconditional welcome is to simultaneously call for conditions. But in addition, a relation of dependence holds in the opposite direction. In their turn, Derrida claims, the conditional laws of hospitality depend on the unconditional law in order to be laws of hospitality and not of something else: "And vice versa, conditional laws would cease to be laws of hospitality if they were not guided, given inspiration, given aspiration, required, even, by the law of unconditional hospitality" (*OH*, 79/*DH*, 75). Without the unconditional law as their guide and inspiration, the conditional laws risk losing their sense as hospitable and would simply be laws of economy. A welcome governed only by such laws would be the first move in an exchange whose completion lies in the guest's fulfillment of her reciprocal obligations, something that one would not, Derrida maintains, label a scene of hospitality. In such a situation the conditional laws would still function as laws, but not as laws of hospitality. For hospitality to have a chance, Derrida's claim is that the conditional laws need to be in relation to the law demanding an unconditional openness.

The two regimes of laws of hospitality are thus in a relation of mutual dependence. In this way they form an aporia, in Derrida's sense of the word, since there seems no way out of this contradictory bind. Affirming one arm of the aporia entails affirming the other, and so it is impossible to negate just one of the regimes of law. Of course, even accepting this, one might still wonder why one has to assert either regime of law in the first place. Why not simply abandon both regimes at once? Derrida's answer follows from the fundamental assertion that a relation to alterity is inescapable, a claim he supports in several ways. First, he argues that openness to the other is a necessary feature of any home: "In order to constitute the space of a habitable house and a home, you also need an opening, a door and windows, you have to give up a passage to the outside world [*l'étranger*]. There is no house or interior without a door or windows" (*OH*, 61/*DH*, 57–59). More broadly, Derrida claims that hospitality is also a necessary feature of culture: "Not only is there a culture of hospitality, but there is no culture that is not also a culture of hospitality."[16] Indeed, across all of his writings Derrida argues that anything that can be considered a self or an identity is constituted through a relation to alterity. This means that insofar as a relation to the other is in play, which it always is, hospitality remains an issue.[17]

But although the dependence between the two regimes of law is mutual, Derrida also claims that the relation between them is not symmetrical. "There is a strange hierarchy in this. *The* law is above the laws. It is thus illegal, transgressive, outside the law, like a lawless law, *nomos anomos*, law above the laws and law outside the law" (*OH*, 79/

DH, 73). This asymmetry follows from the fact that the aporia of hospitality does not involve two orders of injunction of the same quality, with the same internal structure. One sees this first by further articulating the nature of the dependence in each case. The unconditional law requires the conditional laws for its being effective, while the conditional laws require the unconditional law for their meaning as hospitable. In other words, one could say that the unconditional law depends on the conditional laws *in order to be a law*, whereas the conditional laws depend on the unconditional law *in order to be hospitable*. Thus even as there is a dependence in both directions between the two sets of injunction, it is a different dependence in each case.

More light is shed on these relations by taking a closer look at the nature of transgression or contradiction that operates in each case. A conditional law of hospitality contradicts the unconditional law, for in setting limits to hospitality it goes directly against the injunction of "no limits" or pure welcome. In its turn, the unconditional law of hospitality transgresses every conditional law, in that it demands the removal of any limit that could be ordained. But in addition, the unconditional law distinguishes itself in involving a certain self-transgression. As a law, it necessarily involves a relation to its being effective, and so calls for the conditional laws of hospitality. But this is just to say that the unconditional law calls for its own transgression—it requires that it give itself over to conditionality. One could say that in order to be a law, the unconditional law cannot be itself. The unconditional law is thus unstable in its status of being a law, since in commanding that one be absolutely open, it also commands the transgression of this commandment in simultaneously commanding a turn to the conditional laws. This particular kind of self-transgression does not hold for these laws. The conditional laws do call for their own transgression insofar as they rely on the unconditional law for their sense. But this is just to say that their sense as hospitable is unstable. What is not in question is their status as laws. The fact that they command is clear; what is in question is whether what they command is hospitality. There is thus a different relation of dependence in each direction between the two regimes of law, which is a reflection of the different status of law in each regime. The hierarchy here is indeed "strange." The unconditional law is "above" when viewed from the perspective of the conditional laws, since it is necessary to their sense as hospitable. But at the same time, in its height, the unconditional law is outside the law, without law, an outlaw. Not only does it transgress the individual conditional laws, it transgresses the very notion of what it is to be a law.

This brings the analysis to the very heart of the force of the unconditional law, which Derrida calls elsewhere a "weak force."[18] The force of this law is weak because without a series of clear and coherent orders placing it in the realm of politics, it does not move one to act in any particular way. Further, in commanding its own transgression, the unconditional law seems to demand its own dissolution. It is thus unclear what it would actually mean to follow such a commandment. The weakness of this law suggests therefore that "commandment" may be too strong a word to describe it. But this is not to say that this law does nothing. Derrida writes that it is a "call which mandates without commanding [*appel qui mande sans commander*]" (*DH*, 77).[19] "*Mander*" means to transmit an order, to summon, but also to write. The unconditional law thus acts by writing.

Following this lead, Derrida's reading of the aporia of hospitality can be related to another analysis he performed earlier in his career, that of iterability. This is the word that he used originally in "Signature Event Context" to describe "the logic which ties repetition to alterity."[20] I have shown that the unconditional law of hospitality is effective only in calling forth the conditional laws. And any conditional law, while being guided by the unconditional law for its sense as hospitable, nevertheless simultaneously displays itself as transgressing this law, precisely in its prescription of limits. In this transgression, each conditional law thereby gives rise to the possibility of its own reinscription into another conditional law of hospitality. One could thus say of the conditional laws, because of their relation to the unconditional law, that which Derrida claims of all marks—each "can break with every given context, and can engender infinitely new contexts in an absolutely nonsaturable fashion."[21] The conditional injunctions of hospitality form a chain of iterations, each one different from the last, at the same time as they relate to the impossible identity of the unconditional law. They are thus implicated precisely in the play between identity and difference that iterability seeks to describe.[22] Further, as any one iteration involves the imperfect instantiation of the unconditional law in a conditional law, hospitality is never present at any one moment. Its time is divided, across these iterations. Hospitality thus remains always to come as it calls forth more iterations in an endless attempt to resolve the aporia, to bring the two arms of the aporia into alignment. This force of iterability, which is the force of writing, is in this way weaker than both a causal force and the force of normativity contained in a coherent command. But in this very weakness the chains of conditional laws of hospitality—of traditions of hospitality—are produced. The unconditional law of hospitality, in its weakness, has a certain strength.

Recognizing the presence of the logic of iterability also makes sense of other remarks made in these pages from *Of Hospitality*. The plurality of the laws, Derrida writes, is a

> strange plural, [a] plural grammar of *two plurals that are different at the same time.* One of these two plurals says the laws of hospitality, conditional laws, etc. The other plural says the antinomic addition, the one that adds conditional laws to the unique and singular and absolutely only great Law of hospitality, to *the* law of hospitality, to the categorical imperative of hospitality. In this second case, the plural is made up of One + a multiplicity, whereas in the first case, it was only multiplicity, distribution, differentiation. In one case, you have One + n; in the other, n + n + n, etc. (*OH*, 81/ *DH*, 75-77)

On the one hand, the chains of iterations that constitute the traditions of conditional hospitality are multiplicities of the form n + n + n . . . , a plurality across time whose internal divisions can be demarcated with relative clarity. But on the other hand, these chains also involve a relation to the unconditional law at each moment, in order to be traditions of hospitality and not of something else. This second plurality, that of the One + n, is thus not to be understood as a linear progression, in which one would *first* have the unconditional law, which would *then* give rise to subsequent conditional laws. Not only does this assume that the unconditional law can somehow take place as pure, it would also be equivalent to doing away with the aporia, for there would be no sense in which one is subject to both regimes of law *at the same time*, and there would be no contradiction felt in the injunction to be hospitable. Rather, One + n signifies that at each iteration the unconditional law is at work together with the conditional laws. Each n is to be coupled with the One, and it is the irresolvable tension of this coupling that causes the iterations to pass over into one another. And since both pluralities are present at once, the simplicity of the sequence n + n + n . . . is troubled. As a result, it would be more appropriate to say that rather than a simple distribution of conditional laws of hospitality across time, there is here a dissemination. The individual identities of the conditional laws cannot be so easily separated, because of their relation to the unconditional law, and the productive force of this relation.

In this way the aporia cannot be understood in a temporal sequence of self-present moments, which leads Derrida to write that the "moments" here involve a "simultaneity without simultaneity, instant of impossible synchrony, moment without moment" (*OH*, 81/*DH*, 75). At any given moment in the chain of iterations, the two arms of the aporia of hospitality are not each present in the same way. The unconditional law is never present as such, because its status as a law is unstable. It is only ever present in relation to a conditional law, as a transgression of itself. A conditional law, in contrast, can be present as a law (as much as any law can be),[23] just never fully as a conditional law of hospitality, since its status as hospitable is always at risk. The co-presence in the aporia, or equivalently in any one iteration (the coupling One + n), is thus one of an impossible law of hospitality (a law impossible as a law) and a possible law (yet only ever possibly, never actually, a law of hospitality). It is a simultaneity of two different modalities of law, two laws present at the same time but in different ways. This difference is yet another way of explaining the necessity of the aporia—the contradiction cannot be resolved because it involves two modalities of law.

Returning to my preliminary discussion of *Aporias*, one can now better understand what I labeled the "essential absence" that marks an aporia, a phrase I used to articulate one of the lessons to be taken from Derrida's conclusion that "the ultimate aporia is the impossibility of the aporia *as such*" (*A*, 78/*AP*, 136–37). The two regimes of the laws of hospitality are not experienced in a moment as a simple co-presence. Rather, this moment harbors within it an irreducible absence.[24] The aporia as such thus cannot be fully present. If it were, then this disjointed temporality would be brought into alignment, dispelling the aporia altogether. Absence is thus the condition of an aporia's resistance to mastery, which in turn sustains its necessity. Now this absence does not imply that the aporia is to be found elsewhere, that it is absent from where one happens to be but present in another location. It is precisely in their absence that aporias impose themselves. To emphasize this point, Derrida regularly speaks of the "urgency" associated with aporetic negotiations, claiming that they are experienced "here and now."[25] Aporias do not wait and their tension cannot be deferred to a future date.

Against the Ideal

The aporia of hospitality thus has a rich and complex structure, and, as I stated earlier, across Derrida's later writings versions of this structure can be found in his analyses of several ethical and political concepts. But before leaving my explication and turning to inheritance, there remains a final issue to address. In a passage from *Of Hospitality* cited above, Derrida refers to the unconditional law, almost in passing, as "the categorical imperative of hospitality" (*OH*, 81/*DH*, 77). I have already noted that this law is said to guide and give inspiration to the conditional laws, as that to which the latter must refer to retain their sense as hospitable. But to call the unconditional law a categorical imperative raises the stakes considerably. Such terminology suggests that it is the ideal act, that against which all acts of hospitality are judged, and that the best action approximates this ideal to the greatest degree. That is, by invoking the categorical imperative Derrida would seem to imply that one should always strive to be as open as possible, even as he acknowledges that complete openness is impossible.

Is this the case? Does the unconditional law operate as an ideal in the aporia? Although some of Derrida's remarks suggest that it does, a closer look at the logic he has developed shows this cannot be true.

To see this, the first point to note is that in *Of Hospitality* Derrida in fact qualifies his claim, refusing a strict identification between the unconditional law and a categorical imperative. At the end of the analysis I have been examining, Derrida opens a parenthesis and states:

> (Let us note parenthetically that as a quasi-synonym for "unconditional," the Kantian expression of "categorical imperative" is not unproblematic; we will keep it with some reservations, under erasure, if you like, or under *epoche*. For to be what it "must" be, hospitality must not pay a debt, or be governed by a duty: it is gracious, and "must" not open itself to the guest [invited or visitor], either "conforming to duty" or even, to use the Kantian distinction again, "out of duty." This unconditional law of hospitality, if such a thing is thinkable, would then be a law without imperative, without order and without duty. A call which mandates without commanding. A law without law, in short. For if I practice hospitality "*out of* duty" [and not only "*in conforming with* duty"], this hospitality of paying up is no longer an absolute hospitality, it is no longer graciously offered beyond debt and economy, offered to the other, a hospitality invented for the singularity of the new arrival [*arrivant*], of the unexpected visitor.) (*OH*, 81–83/*DH*, 77)[26]

Derrida thus argues that while using the language of the categorical imperative, he conceives the unconditional law of hospitality differently than might Kant. This difference is articulated according to a certain understanding of obligation. For Kant it is not enough simply to act in conformity with one's duty to the law—one must, if one is moral, act out of duty. In response to this position, which many have thought already too severe, Derrida ups the ante, and claims that acting out of duty is inadequate in the face of the demands of unconditional hospitality. To be unconditional, the absolute law of hospitality cannot even demand that one obey it out of duty, for this, too, would be a condition.[27] And it is not by chance that it is precisely at this point that Derrida touches on the weakness of the unconditional law, for in moving beyond obligation, the law exposes itself as weak, as incapable of providing an order—it is an imperative "without imperative," a "law without law, in short." This last statement attests to the conclusion I discussed above, that in its weakness it is unclear whether the unconditional law can be properly called a law at all. What does it command? What does it oblige one to do? Nothing, is Derrida's answer. It is at this limit, beyond obligation or duty, that Derrida's unconditional law passes beyond anything that practical reason as it is understood by Kant is capable of providing.[28]

Although it thus complicates the understanding of the unconditional law, this qualification in *Of Hospitality* would nonetheless preserve Derrida's claim concerning its ideal status. It would in fact be a law higher, more worthy of being strived for, than the commands theorized by Kant—Kant is thought to have set the standard, but Derrida raises the bar even further. And this is not the only time Derrida makes such a claim. Around the same time, Derrida responds to a paper presented by Richard Kearney claiming that he provides no criteria for distinguishing a good from a bad guest with the following remarks:

> I would not recommend giving up all criteria, all knowledge and politics. I would simply say that, if I want to improve the conditions of hospitality, and I think we would agree about that, if I want to improve the conditions of hospitality, the politics of hospitality, I have to refer to pure hospitality, if only to have a criterion to distinguish between the more limited hospitality and the less limited hospitality. So I need what Kant would call the regulating idea of pure hospitality, if only to control the distance between in-hospitality, less hospitality, and more hospitality. This could also lead us beyond Kant's own concept of hospitality as a regulating idea.[29]

The terminology has shifted from the categorical imperative to a regulative idea, but the point remains the same. The unconditional law lies beyond what operates as ideal in the Kantian system, but it remains ideal nonetheless.

These passages thus suggest that the unconditional law is indeed an impossible ideal toward which one should strive, a goal all the more ethical for being more pure than anything imagined by Kant. However, I want to argue that, despite an apparent plausibility, this interpretation is incorrect. It misses the fact that the unconditional law, while labeled "pure," is fundamentally impure. This follows from its essential pervertibility. As Derrida states elsewhere: "But the problem is not limited to this sole question of a moral purity of hospitality (which would give rise to unanimous agreement) that is then to be incarnated in laborious fashion in conditions of mediation a lot less angelic. Pure hospitality, the welcome of the other without condition and without question, contains an intrinsic threat of perversion."[30] The problem with the unconditional law is not just that it is impossible to fully instantiate, but that, as I emphasized above, it mandates a welcome to all forms of alterity. It thus invites the undesirable as well as the desirable, and the greater the level of hospitality, the greater the risk: "Hospitality is thus immediately pervertible and perfectible: there is no model hospitality, but only processes always on the way to perverting themselves and improving themselves, this improvement itself containing the risks of perversion."[31] This means that unconditional hospitality cannot be inherently desirable in and of itself, for in addition to desiring improvement, this would be to simultaneously desire destruction. The essential co-implication of perfectibility and pervertibility thus complicates considerably any attempt to make the unconditional law an ideal, that is, something that would *always* be preferable. Sometimes, being more open would be to welcome what is worse.[32]

Of course, one might respond by arguing that this is a risk worth running, since it is the only way that injustice can be fought and a better state of affairs achieved. And one might go further and claim that this is precisely what Derrida is advocating in the response to Kearney cited above, since he aligns an improvement in the conditions of hospitality with a reference to pure hospitality. But consider this response more carefully. Derrida qualifies his remarks by stating "if I want to improve the conditions of hospitality, and I think we would agree about that . . . ." This points to what is really at stake, namely whether one does indeed want to improve the conditions of hospitality, whether "we would agree about that." What, precisely, is the context in which this agreement is being presupposed? It is a context similar to that in which Derrida consistently mobilizes his remarks on hospitality, namely in implicit reference to the particular constellation of political issues concerning restrictive immigration policies in France, Europe, and the United States. This is, of course, no accident, and such debates may well have been behind Derrida's turn to hospitality in the first place.[33] Now, with respect to this cluster of issues, greater openness is almost certainly to be advocated by thinkers who share Derrida's general political sensibilities, a characterization that can more or less safely be attributed to his usual audience. But this is just to say that Derrida's remarks are highly conditioned. Of concern are the policies and laws of developed nations, in particular their implicit and explicit xenophobia as expressed toward individuals and peoples from less developed regions of the world.[34] "We" no doubt would all agree that here the conditions of hospitality should be improved. But what of a different situation? Would there be unanimous agreement in calling for greater openness when considering the policies and laws of developing nations? In demanding that such nations open up to more investment from developed nations? To neocolonialism? To armies from the developed world? I do not think that Derrida and his audience would all agree to these demands, but they are precisely what the affirmation of the unconditional law of hospitality as an ideal entails. Absolute openness thus should not be approached in all situations, even as it is impossible. To acknowledge this, conceding that one must examine each case individually and weigh the pros and cons of different degrees of openness is precisely to affirm a negotiation with different conditional laws of hospitality. As Derrida claims in a different discussion: "When you oppose a restrictive policy on 'the undocumented [*les sans-papiers*],' for example, it's not a matter of demanding that the state open its frontiers to any new arrival and practice an unconditional hospitality that would risk causing perverse results (even though it conforms to the idea of pure hospitality, in other words hospitality itself). The state is simply being asked to change the laws, and especially the way the law is implemented, without yielding to fantasies of security or demagogy or vote seeking."[35] More hospitality is not desirable in and of itself. Unconditional hospitality is not an ideal.

All of this is to say, once again, that hospitality is an aporia—to engage it is to grapple with two contradictory regimes of law that nonetheless rely on each other. Viewing the unconditional law as an ideal dispels this tension, and so is not consistent with Derrida's view. Of course, this also underlines the extreme difficulties that arise in aporetic situations. One is faced with two contradictory laws, neither of which points to the choice that must be made, and yet one still must choose in acting. A decision must be taken in the absence of any clear criteria, even in the form of an impossible ideal. It might thereby seem that aporias are paralyzing, where one fails to move forward because the tension is overwhelming. Derrida acknowledges this interpretation and to a certain extent accepts it, but his unique contribution to thinking about aporias is to valorize it as a positive thing: "My hypothesis or thesis would be that this necessary aporia is not negative; and that without the repeated enduring of this paralysis in contradiction, the responsibility of hospitality, hospitality *tout court*—when we do not yet know and will never know what it is—would have no chance of coming to pass, of coming, of making or letting welcome [*d'advenir, de venir, de faire ou de laisser bienvenir*]."[36] And, when speaking of the situation of nonknowledge in hospitality: "Poetic speech arises there: it is necessary to invent a language. Hospitality should be so inventive, modeled on the other and on the welcome of the other, that each experience of hospitality must invent a new language."[37] Thus for Derrida the experience of paralysis is necessary for the responsibility of hospitality to come to pass, and the coming of this responsibility is linked to the invention of a new language.

But how is one to do this? And if invention is the task, what does one gain from having endured the aporetic experience of paralysis? For the invention of a new language would seem to imply a suspension of all that has gone before, rendering irrelevant experience one has previously undergone. To avoid this conclusion, there must be some aspect of the experience of an aporia that makes it at least helpful in the invention Derrida thinks one is thereby called to undertake. It is here that I would suggest leaving the formal account of the aporetic structure and recalling the other dimension of Derrida's analyses, for in addition to articulating hospitality's formal features, Derrida also engages this notion in a manner closer to his more dominant practice of reading, examining its manifestations and operations in texts understood in a wide sense, from written works to events in contemporary politics. These readings are not simply interesting exercises, pedagogical tools that might be helpful but add nothing essential to his engagement with the aporia of hospitality. Rather, the formal account demands them. To engage with hospitality is to find oneself confronted with conditional understandings of what it means to be hospitable, those "instances" in the iterated chains that constitute traditions of hospitality. The aporia of hospitality comes from the past, from inherited traditions. From where else does one get the idea that hospitality must be, on the one hand, unconditional? From where else, on the other hand, come the conditions? From where else does the very language of hospitality arrive? Each moment in the iterated chain is a moment of inheritance of the contradictory laws, and so each engagement with the aporia of hospitality is an act of inheritance.

Thus inheritance can be inscribed as a name for all confrontations with aporias, since the negotiation between the conditional and unconditional laws is an engagement with the past meanings and language of a practice—which is to say that it is precisely in this inheritance that invention is to take place. The invention of which Derrida speaks is not the creation of something out of nothing. Rather, as I argue in the following chapter, Derridean invention involves an inheritance of the past, where inheritance is understood in a very precise manner. It is thus through understanding inheritance that one can better understand how to move forward, to find passage in the place where no passage seems possible.

2 Derridean Inheritance

PROVIDING A GENERAL account of Derrida's understanding of inheritance is not straightforward, for although the theme appears across the entirety of Derrida's oeuvre, it does so with varying degrees of importance and weight. In the majority of Derrida's texts it operates subtly, lightly—the words "inheritance," "heritage," "heir," "legacy," and so on are found in all sorts of discussions, yet with little apparent connection to the surrounding context and little reflection on their significance and meaning. Less frequently, as in the writings on Freud or in *Specters of Marx*, "inheritance" is a term that occupies a position more central in Derrida's reading of another's work, at the same time that it also receives explicit attention. Yet even in these texts, it is far from fully or clearly theorized, often being described in dense and enigmatic terms. This diversity of contexts with the apparent differences in weight, along with the fact that Derrida never gives a complete or final word on the subject, makes giving a single account of inheritance in his writings a difficult task.

In this chapter I provide such an account by focusing primarily on remarks Derrida makes in two works. I begin with a discussion of 1993's *Specters of Marx*. Here the theme of inheritance features prominently, as Derrida questions what remains of Marx's legacy in the wake of the collapse of communism. But although Derrida's discussion of inheritance in this work is rich, going far beyond the specific case of Marxism, it does not contain all that he has to say on the matter. To articulate further features of Derridean inheritance I thus turn to *For What Tomorrow*, a long interview given to Elisabeth Roudinesco published in 2001. In contrast to those in *Specters of Marx*, the remarks here concerning inheritance appear in isolation from any particular reading of another thinker. Finally, I conclude my account by returning to *Specters of Marx* to articulate the relationship between inheritance and spacing, which will lead to a discussion of inheritance and justice, particularly as the latter is theorized in Derrida's "Force of Law." My analysis thus begins and remains in the orbit of the specific context of Derrida's reading of Marx, with the aim of constructing a general account applicable to all of Derrida's writings. In Chapter 3 I will return inheritance from this generality by relating it to the particular topic of democracy.[1]

Inheritance in *Specters of Marx*

Early in *Specters of Marx*, discussing Blanchot's "Marx's Three Voices," Derrida writes:

> Let us consider first of all, the radical and necessary *heterogeneity* of an inheritance, the difference without opposition that has to mark it, a "disparate" and a quasi-juxtaposition without dialectic (the very plural of what we will later call Marx's spirit*s*). An inheritance is never gathered together, it is never one with itself. Its presumed unity, if there is one, can consist only in the *injunction* to *reaffirm in choosing*. "One must" [*Il faut*] means *one must* filter, sift, criticize, one must sort out several different possibilities that inhabit the same injunction. And inhabit it in a contradictory fashion around a secret. If the readability of a legacy were given, natural, transparent, univocal, if it did not call for and at the same time defy interpretation, we would never have anything to inherit from it. We would be affected by it as by a cause—natural or genetic. One always inherits from a secret—which says "read me, will you ever be able to do so?" The critical choice called for by any reaffirmation of the inheritance is also, like memory itself, the condition of finitude. The infinite does not inherit, it does not inherit (from) itself. The injunction itself (it always says "choose and decide from among what you inherit") can only be one by dividing itself, tearing itself apart, differing/deferring itself, by speaking at the same time several times—and in several voices. (*SOM*, 16/*SDM*, 40)

Derrida takes from Blanchot the insight that there are multiple voices in Marx and that these cannot be combined into a single, stable, unified whole. They resist homogenization. But this is not restricted to being simply about Marx—Derrida immediately shifts the focus to speak of the inheritance of injunctions in general. An injunction must be disparate in this way, he claims, in order for the relation to it to be one of inheritance. This is not to say that all injunctions must be thus divided; only that if they are not, then one does not *inherit* them, on Derrida's understanding of the word. Such unified injunctions would be better understood as causal forces. Causal forces can be resisted, as unified injunctions can be ignored. But they demand no other response other than simple acceptance or rejection. A legacy calls for more.

Although Derrida does not use the word here, one can graft the term "aporia" onto this structure of a divided legacy. I suggested at the end of Chapter 1 that the structure of aporia is necessarily an inherited one, since the conditional laws that form one arm of the contradiction are found in chains of historical practices and norms. What I am claiming now is that the divided legacies described in the above passage can be understood as aporetic. The description of contradictions that can never be resolved, of disjunctions that are marked by the absence of a secret, of structures that "call for and at the same time defy interpretation," matches precisely the characteristics of aporias. In what follows, therefore, I will use aporias as exemplary of the structure of legacies.

Continuing, even as he insists on the necessary disunity of inherited injunctions, Derrida also suggests that there is something that could be said to hold them together. This is a second injunction to which legacies give rise, the injunction "to *reaffirm in choosing*" in one's response to them. Such a command may appear puzzling, for being ordered to reaffirm a legacy does not seem to leave room for much of a choice. Further, the aporetic structure of legacies implies that there are limits to what one can choose. Consider the case of the legacy of the injunction to be hospitable. I have shown how for Derrida this aporia is divided—there is never one law of hospitality, but a multiplicity consisting of an unconditional law and conditional laws. This multiplicity is irreducible, since each regime of law relies on the other even as they are in contradiction with each other. This being the case, what could it mean to choose among the multiple strands of this legacy? One cannot choose one arm of the aporia over the other, for that would dispel the aporia. Instead, the choice involved must in some way affirm the aporia and maintain its contradictory tension. The choice made by an heir cannot negate the necessary disunity of the injunction.

This explains Derrida's immediate qualification of this reaffirmation through choice: "'One must' [il faut] means one must filter, sift, criticize, one must sort out several different possibilities that inhabit the same injunction." The vocabulary of filtering and sorting suggests that the challenge posed by legacies is not to resolve them into a unity but somehow to deal with them while maintaining their division. And it is linked in the above citation to the condition of finitude. An infinite being has no need to sort and filter, because it is not limited in what is received. By contrast, to be finite is to have to make choices among what is given.[2] Still, just what the choice in inheritance involves is not yet clear. If the division of a legacy must be maintained, one may well ask whether there is anything that can really be done in inheriting it. Derrida wants to avoid an understanding of inheritance that is so active as to deny the inherent tensions in legacies, without at the same time reducing it to a passivity in which one does nothing. The challenge is to theorize inheritance in a way that avoids these two extremes.

One can start to meet this challenge by examining what Derrida himself does in his own inheritance of Marx. Throughout *Specters of Marx*, Derrida does not cease to remind the reader that there is no single legacy of Marx, but several. There is no single voice, no single spirit, and no single specter. They are always more than one. Derrida's task is thus to maintain this plurality in his engagement with these legacies. How does he proceed? Addressing directly his inheritance of Marxism, he writes that "one must [*il faut*] filter, select, differentiate, restructure the questions . . . one *must assume the inheritance* of Marxism, assume its most 'living' part, which is to say, paradoxically, that which continues to put back on the drawing board the question of life, spirit, or the spectral, of life-death beyond the opposition between life and death" (*SOM*, 54/*SDM*, 93–94). This suggests that for Derrida the action of sorting constituting his inheritance from Marxism centers on the question of specters, as announced in the title of the book. And it is precisely here that Derrida locates a stark division in Marx's work.[3] On the one hand, Derrida argues that Marx was obsessed by ghosts—they appear continuously across his oeuvre—and much of the analysis is concerned with examining those moments when ghosts are in play. But on the other hand, Derrida demonstrates how, in all of these instances, Marx tries to chase these ghosts away and resolve their indetermination. Marx's legacy vis-à-vis specters is thus divided, and this division is captured in the double meaning of the word "conjuration." This means both to evoke a spirit *and* to exorcise it. Marx conjures ghosts—he calls them up in order to send them away (*SOM*, 41, 48/*SDM*, 74, 84).[4]

Derrida's response to this division, his inheritance of it, is not simply to leave it as it is. He attempts to "filter, select, differentiate, restructure" it. He does this by emphasizing the maintenance of spirits over their exorcism—Derrida advocates a hauntology over the materialist ontology to which he sees Marx continually returning. He thereby privileges the dimension of "opening" and "constant transformation" over "the Marxist dogmatics linked to the apparatuses of orthodoxy," distinguishing "the *spirit* of the Marxist critique . . . from Marxism as ontology, philosophical or metaphysical system, as 'dialectical materialism,' from Marxism as historical materialism or method, and from Marxism incorporated in the apparatuses of party, State, or workers' International" (*SOM*, 64, 68/*SDM*, 109, 116–17). Thus in his inheritance Derrida makes a choice with respect to Marxism, choosing that dimension which promotes its openness to transformation and self-transformation that he sees resisting the closure of a materialist ontology.

This choice for openness does not entail, however, a negation of the other more dominant tendency in Marx's writings. That is, Derrida does not claim to choose the transformative aspect of Marx's writings so as to leave the materialist ontology behind. As he writes in the book's final pages: "If something seems not to have shifted between *The German Ideology* and *Capital*, it is two axioms whose inheritance is equally important for us. But it is the inheritance of a double bind which, moreover, signals toward the double bind of any inheritance and thus of any responsible decision. Contradiction and secret inhabit the injunction (the spirit of the father, if one prefers)." Derrida then goes on to outline the double bind here in question, one caught between a Marx who moves beyond a traditional understanding of ideality ("Marx insists on respecting the originality and the proper efficacity, the autonomization and automatization of ideality as finite-infinite processes differance"), and a Marx who returns to the tradition in seeking a materialist ontology ("Marx continues to want to ground his critique or his exorcism of the spectral simulacrum in an ontology") (*SOM*, 169–70/*SDM*, 269). So in claiming that the inheritance of this double bind points to the double bind of all inheritance, Derrida suggests that one cannot so easily resolve the contradiction and choose one spirit over another. This makes sense of why Derrida describes his inheritance of Marx as an assumption of the spectral—rather than spiritual—dimension in Marx, which involves "life-death beyond the opposition between life and death." It is not a question of simply aligning life with transformation and death with a static ontology, and choosing one over the other. The choice in inheritance can privilege one over the other, certainly, but not in a way that this other is dispelled.[5]

Returning to the injunction "to *reaffirm in choosing*," one sees that in issuing this command, legacies conjoin necessity and choice in a very precise way—the choice made to privilege different strands of a legacy, within the confines of the necessity that all the strands are maintained. To be a finite being is thus not to be able to place any parts of a legacy forever outside one's limits, beyond all possibility of recovery. All aspects of an inherited aporia remain in play, even when some are emphasized over others. However, this is not the only way that Derrida understands necessity in inheritance, for in *Specters of Marx* he also theorizes necessity as operating at a more fundamental level, namely in the necessity of inheriting itself. Throughout the book Derrida mentions several times that in the past he had discussed Marx very little. This might be taken as a sign that he had previously refused the legacies of Marx, only to be take them up now, in 1993, rather late in the game.[6] And it would also suggest that Derrida has some control over his inheritance of legacies, having a choice at the beginning whether to inherit or not. Derrida argues against this being the case, both in terms of his specific inheritance of Marx and at the level of inheritance in general. With respect to Marx, he claims that deconstruction "would have been impossible and unthinkable in a pre-Marxist space. Deconstruction has never had any sense or interest, in my view at least, except as a radicalization, which is to say also *in the tradition* of a certain Marxism, of a certain *spirit of Marxism*" (*SOM*, 92/*SDM*, 151). Derrida inscribes his own work, even where it did not directly address Marx (which is to say, almost everywhere), in the inheritance of the legacy of Marxist critique. Thus at least if one takes Derrida at his word, it is a mistake to think that he had previously refused to inherit from Marx. He was inheriting all the time.

Nonetheless, accepting Derrida's claim that he did not refuse to inherit from Marx, one can still ask whether he could have done so. Derrida's answer to this is also negative, because of the necessity of inheritance in general. He argues that one never chooses to inherit or not—inheritance is a relation within which one always find oneself, before any such choice can be made.

> This inheritance must be reaffirmed [*Cet héritage, il faut le réaffirmer*] by transforming it as radically as will be necessary. Such a reaffirmation would be both faithful to something that resonates in Marx's appeal—let us say once again in the spirit of his injunction—and in conformity with the concept of inheritance in general. Inheritance is never a *given*, it is always a task. It remains before us just as unquestionably as we are heirs of Marxism, even before wanting or refusing to be, and,

> like all inheritors, we are in mourning. In mourning in particular for what is called Marxism. *To be*, this word in which we earlier saw the word of the spirit, means, for the same reason, to inherit. All the questions on the subject of being or of what is to be (or not to be) are questions of inheritance. There is no backward-looking fervor in this reminder, no traditionalist flavor. Reaction, reactionary, or reactive are but interpretations of the structure of inheritance. That we *are* heirs does not mean that we *have* or we *receive* this or that, some inheritance that enriches us one day with this or that, but that the *being* of what we are *is* first of all inheritance, whether we like it or know it or not. (*SOM*, 54/*SDM*, 94)

Derrida's strong claim here is that inheritance lies at the very center of one's being. Legacies are received before any choice to do so is made. This reinforces the qualification of the choice in inheritance as a reaffirmation—one is always already inheriting, and one's response to this in the sorting and filtering reaffirms this fact. But again, even while acknowledging this, Derrida at the same time resists characterizing inheritance as a purely passive enterprise in which whatever comes is simply accepted, for the form of this response is left undetermined. Inheritance is thus "always a task": In the reception of a legacy there is something left to be done, and it is always so, because of the irresolvable nature of the legacies received. One will never be finished with inheriting, as the aporias that it involves will never be reconciled, always calling for more.

Inheritance in *Specters of Marx* thus emerges as a particular combination of necessity and choice. To reaffirm in choosing means to reaffirm the necessity of being an heir, and the necessity of the legacies inherited being aporetic, through choosing to privilege some elements of the aporia over others, in an action of filtering and sorting. This coexistence of necessity and choice is contained in words repeated in virtually all of Derrida's discussions of inheritance, the phrase "*il faut*." In French, and in its English translation as "one must," this is ambiguous between being, on the one hand, a statement of necessary fact, and, on the other, a recommendation advised but that need not be followed. In some of its appearances in *Specters of Marx*, "*il faut*" operates in the first sense. For example, in the citation with which I began my analysis, the statement "'*One must*' [il faut] means *one must* filter, sift, criticize . . . " speaks of the necessity of inheritance, a fact that one can do nothing about. Even ignoring a legacy or being ignorant of one's relations to it is itself a kind of filtering. By contrast, when Derrida writes that "one *must assume the inheritance* of Marxism, assume its most 'living' part," he is advocating the kind of choice he thinks one *should* make in inheriting. It is not necessary to assume the most living part of the legacy of Marx, and the implicit charge in *Specters* is that many of Marx's other heirs have precisely failed to do so. Similarly, to claim that "this inheritance must be reaffirmed [*Cet héritage, il faut le réaffirmer*] by transforming it as radically as will be necessary" is to advise one way of dealing with the legacy of Marx over others. Keeping this distinction between the different uses of "*il faut*" is crucial to understanding the normative significance of Derrida's claims, particularly when he is discussing political concepts. It is only by doing so that one can appreciate those elements that are presented as necessary to affirm as opposed to those that are offered as a choice to take up or reject. As I pursue my analysis of Derridean inheritance I will track the different senses in which Derrida uses "*il faut.*" This will provide material needed to discuss the extent to which Derrida's work can be said to be normative at all, which I address in Chapter 4.

Inheritance in *For What Tomorrow*

To further develop my account of Derridean inheritance, I now turn to a second text in which this theme is discussed, *For What Tomorrow.* Elisabeth Roudinesco opens this long interview by presenting Derrida as "the heir to the major works of the second half of the century . . . Claude Lévi-Strauss, Michel Foucault, Louis Althusser, and Jacques Lacan" (*FW*, 1/*DQ*, 11–12).[7] In response, Derrida begins by proposing "a few generalities on the notion of inheritance."[8]

> The heir must always respond to a sort of double injunction, a contradictory assig-nation: It is necessary [*il faut*] first of all to know and to know how to *reaffirm* what comes "before us" [*avant nous*], which we therefore receive before even choosing it and behaving in this respect as a free subject [*que donc nous recevons avant même de le choisir, et de nous comporter à cet égard en sujet libre*]. Yes, *it is necessary* [il faut] (and this *it is necessary* is inscribed directly on and within the received inheritance), it is necessary to do everything to appropriate a past even though we know that it remains fundamentally inappropriable, whether it is a question of philosophical memory or the precedence of a language, a culture, and a filiation in general. What does it mean to reaffirm? It means not simply accepting this heritage but relaunch-ing [*relancer*] it otherwise and keeping it alive. Not choosing it (since what charac-terizes inheritance is first of all that one does not choose it; it is what violently elects us), but choosing to keep it alive. (*FW*, 3/*DQ*, 15–16; translation slightly modified)

This passage contains all of the elements in play in *Specters of Marx*. Once again a leg-acy is presented as a double injunction that is not chosen. Once again Derrida insists that there is, nevertheless, a choice at stake, one that is linked to an act of reaffirmation at the same time that it is governed by an ambiguous necessity carried in the "*il faut*" (words here italicized and repeated, just as in *Specters*). Derrida thus reiterates, in 2001, the earlier discussion of inheritance from 1993.

However, even given the close correspondence, these remarks are not simply rep-etition of what was previously said. Here Derrida shifts the focus ever so slightly in describing the action of reaffirming a heritage as "relaunching it otherwise and keep-ing it alive." More can thus be learned by reflecting on the meaning of this phrase. Regarding its second half, Derrida's invocation of life echoes his privileging of those elements in Marx's legacy that are open to change and transformation—those labeled the most "living." But whereas in *Specters of Marx* it was a question of Derrida's specific inheritance of Marx, in *For What Tomorrow* the context is explicitly of inheritance in general. Further, reaffirmation is described more particularly in the next sentence as "choosing to keep it alive." It would thus seem that the choice in inheritance is to be located in a decision made by the heir to keep a legacy alive, a decision that need not be taken. Is this, therefore, another aspect of inheritance that lies on the side of choice rather than necessity? I will argue that this is in fact not the case, and that Derrida's invocation of choice at this precise moment is misleading. This does not mean that the vocabulary of life and the living is also inappropriate. Rather, the lack of choice here on the part of the heir illuminates Derrida's very particular understanding of life, as survival. Having argued this, I will then focus on the first half of Derrida's description of the reaffirmation of a legacy, as "relaunching it otherwise."

Taken at face value, Derrida's claim that reaffirming a legacy is "choosing to keep it alive" does appear to suggest that one could do otherwise, that one could alternatively put a legacy to death. And other moments in the exchange seems to support this interpretation. For example, Roudinesco describes Derrida's relationship to the texts he reads as making them "speak from within themselves, through their fault lines, their blanks, their margins, their contradictions, but without trying to kill them" (*FW*, 2/*DQ*, 13). In his response Derrida agrees: "I have always forbidden myself—as far as possible, of course, and however 'radical' or inflexible an act of deconstruction ought to be—to injure or to put to death. It is always by reaffirming the inheritance that one can avoid this putting to death" (*FW*, 4/*DQ*, 16). Derrida's own practice of inheritance, through reaffirmation, is thus distinguished from a different kind of act, one that would end a legacy's life.

The same contrast is also suggested in two descriptions Derrida subsequently gives that further delimit his method of analysis. The first description is of structuralism, which he claims paid a price in order to advance knowledge—"namely [the price of] a certain naïveté, the somewhat jubilatory repetition of old philosophical gestures, the rather somnambulist submission to a history of metaphysics that I was driven to decipher in terms of its program, its combinatorial procedures, all the possibilities that in my eyes had become tired and exhausted . . . the sterilizing, precipitous, even dogmatic elements of this program" (*FW*, 6–7/*DQ*, 19). Old gestures, somnambulist submission, tired, exhausted, sterilizing . . . Derrida's choice of words implies that if structuralism was not yet dead, then it was certainly very close to it. Derrida's deconstructive interventions into structuralist texts might therefore be understood in opposition to this, pulling them back from the brink of death.

Second, turning his gaze inward, Derrida also sorts between differing tendencies inhabiting his own oeuvre: "In no case do I want deconstruction to be used to denigrate, injure, or diminish the force or the necessity of a movement—and if it is necessary to do that here or there in polemical moments, I regret it in advance" (*FW*, 7/*DQ*, 21). Here Derrida confesses that on occasion he transgresses the law he gives himself, seeking instead to indeed injure another. These polemical moments Derrida earlier describes as forcing him "to speak of what [he does] not admire," moments which he "never initiate[s]" (*FW*, 5/*DQ*, 18), and they presumably include his responses to attacks on his work as found in the exchange with John Searle reprinted in *Limited Inc*, his comments on Habermas's reading of him in *Philosophical Discourse of Modernity* (in a long footnote in *Limited Inc*, and mentioned here [*FW*, 17/*DQ*, 37]), as well as remarks made in the present interview on Ferry and Renaut's *French Philosophy of the Sixties*.[9] These polemical turns in Derrida's writings would depart from the life-guarding path of deconstructive readings, since his aim is to extinguish such attacks, not to keep them alive.

There is thus a distinction drawn in this interview between actions of inheritance that would choose to keep a legacy alive and those that would put it to death. I, however, question the coherence of this distinction. I argued above in my reading of *Specters of Marx* that for Derrida there can be no clear line drawn between life, on the one hand, and death, on the other. This is confirmed in other remarks made in *For What Tomorrow*. Repeating the formula from *Specters* describing inheritance as "to select, to filter, to interpret, and therefore to transform," Derrida states that this is "not to leave intact or unharmed, not to leave *safe* the very thing one claims to respect before all else. And after all. Not to leave it safe: to save it, perhaps, yet again, for a time, but without the illusion of a final salvation" (*FW*, 4/*DQ*, 16). The keeping alive of a legacy thus cannot be isolated from all acts of injury, which are themselves associated with a putting to death. Quite the contrary, since a deconstructive reading precisely requires some kind of intervention to disrupt a text's integrity. This is given further support in Derrida's discussion of his love for the tradition he inherits. He describes this love as contradictory, since he is both "mad for the past" but also "dreads fixation on the past, nostalgia, the cult of remembrance." And while deconstruction is never "without this love," Derrida at the same time describes it as "taking on [*s'en prendre*]" the tradition (*FW*, 4–5/ *DQ*, 16–17). This phrase, as Fort explains in a translator's note, "can mean 'to attack,' 'to take it out' on someone or something, in the sense of 'to blame,' also 'to challenge' and thus 'to take on' in a contest" (*FW*, 199). The love in deconstruction, that practice of inheritance that would seek to keep a legacy alive, thus has an irreducible dimension of aggression.[10] Finally, even the polemical engagements that Derrida contrasts with his more usual "loving" relations with the texts of others cannot be placed wholly on the side of injury and death, foreign to all acts of keeping alive. This holds both for the attacks on Derrida's work and for his responses. To take one example, consider Ferry and Renaut's *French Philosophy of the Sixties*. Of this work Derrida states the following:

> Since you brought it up again, the authors of *French Philosophy of the Sixties*, who were never capable of reading all those people, wrote a book full of oafish blunders and crude gestures, a null book, but a symptomatic one. Interesting because symptomatic! By mixing everything together, they end up ignoring the critiques, directed at Nietzsche and especially at Heidegger, that were contained in this "Nietzschean-Heideggerian" filiation. They acted without looking closely, as if the choice of a heritage could be confused with a blind incorporation. They did not see the difference manifested, in each one, in relation to Nietzsche or Heidegger. (*FW*, 14/*DQ*, 31)

Derrida here opposes Ferry and Renaut's understanding of inheritance to his own. They fail to see that inheritance involves a filtering and sorting, and consequently accuse Derrida's generation of thinkers of simply blindly incorporating Nietzsche and Heidegger, an accusation that itself fails to filter and sort. In the terms of the present discussion, such a failure might be translated as a failure to keep the legacy of French philosophy in the sixties alive. Now while putting this legacy to death was very likely Ferry and Renaut's aim, one can still ask whether this result is possible. How could this legacy be extinguished, once and for all? Certainly not through writing a book on it, since the very act of speaking of it keeps the tradition in play. No matter how undifferentiated their analysis may be, Ferry and Renaut invite a response, and so manage, perhaps in spite of themselves, to keep this legacy alive. Turning now to one such response—Derrida's own in *For What Tomorrow*—the same can be said. While Derrida would seem to wish to avoid inheriting this work (he asks Roudinesco, "Must we really speak of it again? do you insist?" (*FW*, 8/*DQ*, 21)), he appears unable to put its legacy to death. This is betrayed in the exclamation that the book is "Interesting because symptomatic!" That is, also perhaps in spite of himself, Derrida finds what is in his opinion the most interesting, the most open to transformation, the most alive elements in Ferry and Renaut's work. Thus polemical exchange, which Derrida concedes involves injury and the reduction of force, cannot be opposed to a practice of life-supporting inheritance such as is found in deconstruction. It too keeps legacies alive.

In these ways there is an entanglement between a practice of inheritance that would keep a legacy alive and one that would put it to death. These two practices cannot be cleanly distinguished. As a consequence, the line cited above stating that reaffirming a legacy means "not choosing it (since what characterizes inheritance is first of all that one does not choose it; it is what violently elects us), but choosing to keep it alive" is misleading. There is no contrast here between something one cannot choose (the heritage itself) and something one can (to keep it alive). One has no option but to keep legacies alive when inheriting them. This also means that the act of reaffirmation of a legacy is not chosen. All heirs reaffirm what they inherit, for none can avoid keeping a legacy alive, even when what is strived for is to put it to death. Such an attempt will always fail. Reaffirmation is thus a necessity, in the sense of necessarily pertaining to all acts of inheritance.

This impossibility of ever putting a legacy to death, once and for all, means that another name for inheritance could be "survival," in the sense that Derrida uses the word. In his thinking, pure life and pure death, understood in opposition to or in isolation from one another, are out of the question, always, as the outcome of a subject's choice. What there is, instead, is survival, or living-on (*sur-vie*), the process of life as differentiation that thus always contains an element of death.[11] Legacies partake in this very structure. To inherit, which is never chosen, is thus automatically to keep a legacy living on, which is to say to keep it alive. Refusing this is beyond the power of the heir.

But although the fact of keeping a legacy alive is not something that can be chosen, it is not the case that choice has disappeared altogether from the scene of inheritance. Although all heirs will reaffirm the legacies they do not choose to receive, and will thus be necessarily caught up in the movement of their survival, there are different ways that this can be carried out. Indeed, this is suggested in a citation from *Specters of Marx* I made earlier, where Derrida claims that "one *must assume the inheritance* of Marxism, assume its most 'living' part . . . life-death beyond the opposition between life and death. This inheritance must be reaffirmed by transforming it as radically as will be necessary" (SOM, 54/SDM, 93–94). Derrida's use of the word "most" implies that there are different degrees of living on, to be measured, as the following sentence intimates, according to the level of transformation that occurs in each act of inheritance. Similarly, such a space of differentiation in which choices can be made is marked in my initial citation from *For What Tomorrow*. There "*il faut*" is not used to make statements of necessary fact ("It is necessary [*il faut*] first of all to know and to know how to *reaffirm* what comes 'before us.' . . . It is necessary to do everything to appropriate a past even though we know that it remains fundamentally inappropriable"). Rather, these are recommendations that can be ignored. One need not "know" and "know how to reaffirm" the legacies one inherits, nor "do everything to appropriate" the past. One could act otherwise in response to what is received. At this moment Derrida's discourse operates normatively, advising one particular way to inherit among others, and it is here that choices can be made.

This confirms that Derrida's discourse on inheritance divides into two kinds of statements, those articulating facts of every act of inheritance and those advocating one way of inheriting over others. Thus far I have concentrated on the former, showing how one has no choice but to inherit, and in doing so must keep an inheritance alive. The question now arises concerning the element of choice that an heir does have, and the particular choice that Derrida counsels. What kind of strategy in inheritance does Derrida suggest one follow? How should one appropriate what remains "fundamentally inappropriable"? Answers are found in the other half of Derrida's description of the meaning of reaffirming a legacy, which I have not yet discussed, namely as "relaunching [*relancer*] it otherwise."

The word "*relancer*" does not appear in the discussions of inheritance in *Specters of Marx*, and it has several meanings that all work here to provide further specificity to Derrida's position. First, *relancer* carries the sense of keeping the inheritance in play, of launching it in one's turn. When an inheritance is received, it is the heir's turn to do something with it. And since the command here is to do this "otherwise," what is to be done is not just a simple repetition of the past. This attests to the active dimension of inheritance, in which the heir has a role to play in making a difference to what is transmitted. At the same time, the "other" in "otherwise" also marks the fact that this first meaning of *relancer* does not imply that inheritance is left solely up to the heir. That one inherits in one's turn signals the place of this action in a historical chain of actions. Others have inherited before, and others will come to inherit after. This takes place beyond the heir's control and is an irreducible part of the inheritance relation. In this way there is an important place occupied by alterity in inheritance, and the activity of relaunching is balanced against the passivity that this entails.

The relation to alterity is both amplified and given a more specific articulation in the second meaning of *relancer*, as *renvoyer*. This term, which appears across Derrida's oeuvre, means a sending away, sending back (to the source), and/or sending on. It thus reinforces the first meaning's image of inheritance as constituted in a chain of actions, where a legacy is both acknowledged as given from a past other, and passed on to another to come to live on. But in addition, *renvoyer* also has connotations of banishment and a sending into exile. This introduces a certain aggression into the relation to alterity, resonating with Derrida's other remarks discussed above that fold an irreducible element of injury and combat into his love of the past.

Finally, two other meanings of *relancer* also evoke aggression, further drawing the inheritance relation in the direction of conflict. These are *relancer* as the action of beginning a chase or pursuit of an other anew, and *relancer* as reprimanding or admonishing an other for some failure on its part. The third meaning, that of the chase, appears throughout *Specters of Marx* in order to describe Marx's relation to specters—he calls them up to chase them away. Its presence in *For What Tomorrow* suggests that the action of chasing the other is integral to inheritance in general. The fourth meaning, to reprimand, casts inheritance in a more competitive light still. In some way others are to be judged inferior or in error in the heir's reception of a legacy.

The semantic field of *relancer* thus further clarifies what occurs in the action of inheritance. In his description of the reaffirmation of a legacy as "relaunching it otherwise," Derrida presents the heir as one who plays an active role in receiving a legacy, which is to say in transforming it, while he at the same time acknowledges the irreducible dimension of alterity involved that is distributed across time. "Relaunching it otherwise" can thus be seen as yet another attempt on Derrida's part to find the right vocabulary that would describe the point of balance between activity and passivity implied in inheritance. And this vocabulary makes more prominent another dimension of inheritance, that of competition and aggression. The relation of an heir to alterity is not necessarily peaceful or benign, for there is banishment, the chase, and admonishment in the picture.

Now some of these elements remain in the sphere of necessity. The act itself of relaunching otherwise is a necessary part of inheriting, as is the irreducible dimension of alterity. And as was shown above, aggression can never be fully separated from the reception of a legacy. Thus with respect to the presence of these aspects of inheritance, still no choice is made. Nevertheless, how one goes about these acts—which direction the heir relaunches the legacy, and what kind of aggression is expressed—contains some degree of freedom. This is demonstrated in the ways Derrida himself inherits from those who have gone before him. For example, as was seen in his inheritance of Marx, and as will be seen in the next chapter in his inheritance of democracy, Derrida consistently opts for the direction of greater openness and self-transformation. This is not a move that all heirs must make in all situations. Similarly, Derrida expresses aggression toward those he reads deconstructively in a very precise and consistent manner. This is suggested in another remark made in *For What Tomorrow*. Shortly after characterizing deconstruction as "taking on" the legacies of those to which it pays homage, Derrida states:

> Deconstruction is seen as hyperconceptual, and indeed it is; it carries out a large-scale consumption of concepts that it produces as much as it inherits—but only to the point where a certain writing, a writing that thinks, exceeds the conceptual "take" and its mastery. It therefore attempts to think the limit of the concept; it even endures the experience of this excess; it lovingly lets itself be exceeded. (*FW*, 5/*DQ*, 17)

The meaning of this passage is illuminated by returning to the structure of aporia. Derrida inherits by taking concepts at work in the writings of others, and, in his turn, exposes their aporetic structure, something not explicitly recognized in the texts themselves. What is it to expose an aporia? It is not to show it in all of its aspects, since an aporia always contains an essential absence. Aporias cannot be fully or finally presented—they elude total mastery. But what can be done is to heighten an aporia's tension, foregrounding the necessary contradiction that it contains. Although it is not used here, this heightening of tension can be described through recourse to another word that recurs frequently in Derrida's writings, "*surenchère*"— a raising of the stakes, outbidding, or upping the ante.[12] When he inherits, Derrida raises what is at stake in the concept in question, upping the ante on the tensions it contains. It is in this way that he aggressively transforms the concepts of others through pushing them to exceed their supposed limits. This describes the "hyperconceptuality" in the above citation, deconstruction's consumption of conceptual status, where the stakes of the concept are raised to the point where its very status as a concept is called into the question.

In the previous chapter I analyzed one example of *surenchère* in examining the ways Derrida distinguishes his notion of unconditional hospitality from a Kantian categorical imperative. Derrida admonishes Kant for clinging to the condition of acting out of duty in order to classify acts as moral, and he goes one step further by demanding that even this condition be dropped in response to the impossible demand of unconditional hospitality. One could thus say that in Derrida's eyes Kant fails to recognize the aporia, where a true demand for unconditionality must move beyond duty, and in doing so affirm the unconditional "law without law." This does not leave all conditionality behind—doing so is neither possible nor desirable. Rather it affirms that what is at stake in the inheritance of hospitality is the inheritance of the aporia constituted by both regimes of law. In this way Derrida inherits the structure of the categorical imperative from Kant, but, by upping the ante, exceeds Kant's conceptual limits. Derrida pushes the Kantian project to its own extremes so as to maintain the aporia rather than to avoid it. Further, this example also illustrates how the strategy of upping the ante is consistent with Derrida's choice in his inheritance of Marx—to "assume its most 'living' part"—where the use of "most" suggests degrees of life to be measured in terms of the level of change and transformation. In recalling Kant to an unconditionality beyond duty, Derrida transforms the Kantian legacy. This transformation would not necessarily occur in other strategies of inheritance, for example those that accept the Kantian limitations on duty. In this respect one can thereby claim that Derrida's inheritance of Kant chooses more life than others. There is thus a connection between the *surenchère* and Derrida's call for more life, for greater openness and transformation.

Beyond his engagement with Kant, I would contend that the *surenchère* is found in all of Derrida's inheritances of others, even those who are closest to him. To take two prominent examples, when Derrida reads Heidegger, he always returns to the interplay between presence and absence in the latter's work, and always seeks to push things one step further beyond a point where, in his view, Heidegger rests on a certain foundation of presence. With respect to Levinas, one of Derrida's constant moves is to intensify the role and position of the third in the ethical relation, opening this relation up in a contradictory manner to the issues of justice and politics. Always at stake in these readings, and this is the stake that is always raised, is the position and recognition of an aporetic structure. Derrida argues against the tendency of those he reads to deny aporias and their attempts to resolve them or ignore them. The seemingly stable concepts assumed by others are thus shaken, opened up, and transformed precisely through inheritance. Derrida receives the work of others by heightening their aporetic tensions, demonstrating the points of instability and contradiction without ever achieving a reconciliation or resolution.

This last qualification is crucial, for, to repeat, one can never finally or fully reveal an aporia. It is never the case that an aporia, *as such*, is inherited once and for all. This is equivalent to claiming that legacies cannot be put to death. Suppose that Derrida, or anyone else, fully succeeded in inheriting an aporia as such—what then would be left of this legacy for those to come? What more would there be to say? The inheritance would stop at this moment, which is to say it would be put to death, not kept alive as is stated as necessary in *For What Tomorrow*. The *surenchère* cannot therefore be taken to its limit—one cannot up the ante to a maximal degree, to the point where an other can no longer respond.

Returning now to my first citation from *For What Tomorrow*, one can now better understand the action counseled in Derrida's injunctions of inheritance—the commands that "it is necessary first of all to know and to know how to *reaffirm* what comes 'before us,'" and "it is necessary to do everything to appropriate a past even though we know that it remains fundamentally inappropriable." As aporetic, the past in question eludes all mastery, and so eludes full appropriation. Nevertheless, Derrida argues that one should attempt to appropriate it, which is to strive to reveal the aporetic structure even as this is impossible. This he accomplishes in his own work through the strategy of the *surenchère*, of increasing the tension in the aporias received. To know how to do this is thus to know how to inherit in a manner Derrida recommends. Part of this knowledge, to be sure, is a knowledge of the factual necessity in inheritance. Knowing that one has no choice but to inherit, and knowing that what one inherits is aporetic in structure, are necessary presuppositions of any attempt to expose the aporia. But this second step, that of the attempted exposure, is not necessary. Rather, it is a choice Derrida himself makes, and one he suggests that others make too.

To conclude this section, I should make explicit a point that is perhaps already apparent, since it has imposed itself in my account at various junctures. This is the fact that, given its characteristics, inheritance is more or less a synonym for Derrida's particular practice of reading, deconstruction. As I stated in my Introduction, Derrida himself claims as much, stating, "This is one of the possible definitions of deconstruction—as inheritance."[13] The danger of such pronouncements, especially given the regularity with which Derrida makes them, is that the specificity of both terms is lost. In the present instance I hope this is not the case, and that deconstruction is illuminated by considering it in terms of the very precise combination of necessity and choice that Derridean inheritance entails. Cast in this light, deconstruction is one way of responding to legacies, a way that responds to the necessity of inheritance by choosing to heighten the aporetic tension in the concepts of the past through a competitive movement of raising the stakes.

Inheritance, Spacing, and Justice

In my discussion of the meanings of *relancer*, I emphasized the fact that every act of inheritance takes place within a historical chain of actions. This suggests the obvious point that inheritance is related to a past, present, and future—to time. The most straightforward way to understand this relation would be to see a legacy as something first of all present in the past, which is then made present again when inherited in the here and now. Future generations would in their turn inherit from the present (then rendered past) in much the same way. Assumed in this view is a conception of time as linear—"the *successive* linking of presents identical to themselves and contemporary with themselves" (*SOM*, 70/*SDM*, 119)—which provides a frame or container within which inheritance takes place. Inheritance would fit neatly into this order of successive presents.

Not surprisingly, given the centrality of the challenge to presence in Derrida's work, Derridean inheritance breaks with this model of time. This is confirmed in *Specters of Marx* in the descriptions of inheritance that invoke temporal terms such as the past and the future. For example, with reference to Blanchot's "Marx's Three Voices," shortly after the passage I cited at the beginning of this chapter, Derrida writes:

> "Since Marx" continues to designate the place of assignation from which we are *pledged*. But if there is pledge or assignation, injunction or promise, if there has been this appeal beginning with a word that resounds before us, the "since" marks a place and a time that doubtless precedes us, but so as to be as much *in front of*

us as *before us* [devant nous *qu'*avant nous]. Since the future [*l'avenir*], then, since the past as absolute future. . . . If "since Marx" names a future-to-come [*à-venir*] as much as a past, the past of a proper name, it is because the proper of a proper name will always remain to come [*à venir*]. And secret. It will remain to come not like the future now [*maintenant futur*] of that which "holds together" the "disparate." . . . What has been uttered "since Marx" can only promise or remind one to maintain together, in a speech that defers, deferring not what it affirms but deferring just *so as to* affirm, to affirm *justly*, so as to have the power (a power without power) to affirm the coming of the event, its future-to-come itself [*son à-venir même*]. (SOM, 17/SDM, 41)

This passage alludes to the complex temporal structure by which the inheritance of all that lies under the name "Marx" is to be understood. It is a structure that cannot be reduced to a linear temporality because of the seeming interchangeability of the past and the future. In writing "Since the future, then, since the past as absolute future," Derrida implies that the inheritance from Marx has as much to do with the future as with the past. A similar temporal pattern appeared in an earlier citation I made where Derrida claims that "inheritance is never a *given*, it is always a task. It remains before [*devant*] us" (SOM, 54/SDM, 94). Again the suggestion is that inheritance can be located just as much in what is to come as in what has already been. Further, in labeling the future as "absolute," Derrida distinguishes it from a future "now" that is understood as a future present. An absolute future, marked here as a "future to come [*à-venir*]," is suggested to be irreducible to any present.[14]

The time of inheritance is thus one of a disrupted linearity. The present does not follow from the past, nor is it to be followed by the future. Rather, what comes in the present comes from both past and future, which themselves cannot be reduced to presence. As Derrida repeats across *Specters of Marx*, citing *Hamlet*, "The time is out of joint." This last phrase, however, itself has multiple meanings, which Derrida highlights by discussing its translations in four different French editions of Shakespeare's text. The first two of these ("'Le temps est hors de ses gonds,' time is off its hinges. . . . 'Le temps est détraqué,' time is broken down, unhinged, out of sorts" [SOM, 19/SDM, 43–44]) translate the English more literally in naming "time" as their subject. These translations thus suggest that it is time itself—the very structure of temporality—that is out of joint, supporting the view that the time of inheritance is one of a disrupted linearity.[15] How, then, to justify this claim? One can answer this question in multiple ways, since, as I have mentioned, the disruption of the present is the most insistent theme recurring across Derrida's writings.[16] In terms of the analysis I have performed, the disjuncture of time can first of all be seen to follow from the logic of the aporetic structure embedded in inheritance. Because one inherits irresolvable aporias that ultimately resist appropriation, the work of inheritance can never be completed. Any legacy that is thought to lie in the past contains a remainder that eludes mastery in the present, a remainder that therefore awaits the heir in the future. It is in this sense that Derrida can interchange the past and the future in the above citations—a legacy is always both behind and in front of the heir, since, as aporetic, it can never be located fully in a present (a present past, present, or future).

Thus the time is out of joint in the first instance because inherited legacies are aporetic. Aporias disjoin linear time, disrupting its order and resisting its limits. At the same time, there is another layer in Derrida's account that further complicates the temporal picture. Although the disjuncture of time involves a splitting of the present, Derrida also insists that this does not result in a complete delay of the injunction being inherited. That is, Derrida argues that in the interruption of the present the injunction is not displaced to another time in the past or the future, nor is its force reduced. Rather, even as an inherited injunction is split, and time rendered, it is nonetheless experienced here and now, urgently.

> What also resonates in "Marx's three voices" is the *appeal* or the political injunction, the pledge or the promise . . . whose force of *rupture* produces the institution or the constitution, the law itself. . . . *Violence* of the law before [*avant*] the law and before meaning, violence that interrupts time, disarticulates it, dislodges it, displaces it out of its natural lodging: "out of joint." It is there that differ*a*nce, if it remains irreducible, irreducibly required by the spacing [*espacement*] of any promise and by the future-to-come [*l'à-venir*] that comes to open it, does not mean only (as some people have too often believed and so naively) deferral, lateness, delay, postponement. In the incoercible differ*a*nce the here-now [*l'ici-maintenant*] unfurls. Without lateness, without delay, but without presence, it is the precipitation of an absolute singularity, singular because differing, precisely [*justement*], and always other, binding itself necessarily to the form of the instant, in *imminence and in urgency.* . . . No differ*a*nce without alterity, no alterity without singularity, no singularity without here-now. (*SOM*, 30–31/*SDM*, 59–60)

Thus even while Derrida distances the temporality of the inherited injunction from a linear succession of instants, he claims that it remains bound "necessarily to the form of the instant, in *imminence and in urgency*." The necessity appealed to here is a necessity of fact—an injunction in its very structure arrives here and now. This too is traceable to its aporetic nature, for, as I discussed in Chapter 1, it is precisely the necessity of the contradiction in an aporia that makes it so urgent. To see an injunction as delayed, deferred, or arriving later is to say that at this instant, here and now, it is not contradictory—some kind of resolution would at this instant have been reached.

Further, the use of the words "here-now [*ici-maintenant*]" mark another disjunction in the temporality of inheritance, namely the interruption of time by space. "Here-now" evokes neither pure space (here) nor pure time (now), but a combination of the two. A similar occurrence takes place in the citations I have made from *Specters of Marx* where Derrida relies on the words "*devant*" and "*avenir.*" "*Devant*" can have a temporal meaning, but its primary sense is spatial—it designates the place "before" or "in front of" an object.[17] Similarly, "*avenir*" ordinarily means "future," but in breaking this word apart, either through the use of a hyphen (*à-venir*) or splitting it into the preposition and infinitive (*à venir*), Derrida transforms its meaning. "*A(-)venir*" now no longer strictly refers to the future, but also alludes to a "coming," or "that which is to come," to an event that is in some sense already happening and which perhaps can be located in space.

I will have more to say on the meaning and role of the "*à(-)venir*" in Chapter 3 where the focus will be on democracy to come. For now I simply wish to highlight the work done by this vocabulary with respect to temporality. Words such as "*ici-maintenant*," "*devant*," and "*à(-)venir*" point to a further disjuncture in the time of inheritance, such that it is no longer just a question of time, but of space as well. This evokes the notion of "spacing [*espacement*]," itself named in the last passage cited, and a very old theme in Derrida's writings. Derrida used this term in his early work to designate the "temporality" of the trace in his early readings of Husserl, Heidegger, and Freud. Spacing designates not a structure of pure time, but the "the becoming-space of time and the becoming-time of space"[18]—a structure in which space and time are irreducibly entwined. Now as a result of this co-implication the very status of this structure as "temporal" is questionable. At certain moments Derrida suggests that what is here at stake is an alternative structure of time; at others he implies that the properly temporal has been left behind.[19] But for my present point what is important is that spacing underlines another aspect of the disjuncture of time in inheritance. The time is out of joint not just because the aporetic structure entails a coming in the here and now from both the past and the future, but also because this structure entails spatial dimensions as much as temporal ones. The "place," therefore, of a legacy—for example, that which is left under the name "Marx," but this would hold for everything inherited on Derrida's understanding of the word—is not localizable in space or in time. It lies "before [*devant*] us," which is to say, as Derrida remarks in another context with respect to this "before," "outside," beyond one's reach, always eluding appropriation and mastery.[20]

Read thus, "the time is out of joint" is a statement about the temporality of inheritance, signaling a time disrupted to the point that it starts to depart from a temporal structure altogether. But this is to focus on just one possible meaning of the phrase. As I stated above, it can be interpreted in several ways. An alternative possibility is to read it with an ethical or political inflection. Derrida highlights this by citing another of its French translations, "'Cette époque est déshonorée,' this age is dishonored. . . . 'Out of joint' would qualify the moral decadence or corruption of the city, the dissolution or perversion of customs. It is easy to go from disadjusted to unjust" (*SOM*, 19/*SDM*, 44). This interpretation is supported by Hamlet's subsequent words—"Oh cursed spight, that ever was I borne to set it right"—suggesting that at stake is a corruption in the moral order of things, which the heir to the situation must address. Hamlet inherits the duty to redress the crime of his father's murder. Or, in other words, inheritance calls for justice.

Now to claim that particular legacies call for such responses might appear uncontroversial. Like Hamlet, heirs often find themselves inheriting a past in which wrongs have been committed, and thus it would seem obvious that they are called upon to respond with justice. However, from a Derridean perspective, this is not a given, because the aporetic nature of legacies ensures that such a "setting right" is inherently impossible. An aporia can never be "set right"—it is always out of joint. What kind of response is thus called for in the face of the wrongs of the past? What is justice in situations of necessary disjuncture? Derrida's answer in *Specters of Marx* is to propose an understanding of justice "as incalculability of the gift and singularity of the an-eco-nomic ex-position to others. 'The relation to others—that is to say, justice,' writes Lévi-nas" (*SOM*, 23/*SDM*, 48–49).²¹ Justice here is understood as an excess or overflowing of all calculation, something rendered to an other beyond the limitations and mastery of the self. And Derrida claims that this conception of justice presupposes the disjunc-ture of time, for this is the only condition on which a relation to the other is possible. That the time is out of joint thus provides a chance for justice in a Levinasian sense.

In this way in *Specters of Marx* Derrida opposes justice as the relation to alterity to justice understood in terms of calculation and restitution, the "setting right" of which Hamlet speaks. However, even while Derrida here seems to embrace a Levinasian defi-nition of justice, and to demarcate it clearly from an economic conception, what he has written elsewhere, particularly in "Force of Law" (footnoted in this discussion in *Spec-ters of Marx*) complicates the picture considerably. There Derrida also cites Levinas's concept of justice as one that has some proximity to his own understanding. But he immediately backs away from embracing it, because of "other difficult questions about Levinas' difficult discourse" (*FOL*, 250/*FDL*, 49). More importantly, Derrida's theori-zation of justice in this text shows precisely why Levinas's definition is inadequate, and Derrida argues against what one might take to be implied in the remarks in *Specters of Marx* concerning the opposition between justice as a relation to alterity and justice as calculation and restitution. In "Force of Law" Derrida does distinguish between these two conceptions. Associating the second conception with the law, he argues that "law is not justice. Law is the element of calculation, and it is just that there be law, but jus-tice is incalculable, it demands that one calculate with the incalculable," and he speaks of "a difficult and unstable distinction between justice and law, between justice (infi-nite, incalculable, rebellious to rule and foreign to symmetry, heterogeneous and het-erotropic) on the one hand, and, on the other, the exercise of justice as law, legitimacy or legality, a stabilizable, statutory and calculable apparatus [*dispositif*], a system of coded prescriptions" (*FOL*, 244, 250/*FDL*, 38, 48). However, at the same time, Derrida asserts that this "difficult and unstable distinction" is not based on an opposition, for the couple justice/law forms an aporia. Much like the unconditional law of hospitality, justice lies outside the sphere of calculation, yet it also "demands for itself that it be established in the name of a law that must be put to work [*mis en oeuvre*] (constituted and applied) by force 'enforced'" (*FOL*, 251/*FDL*, 49–50). Similarly, if law is to aspire to something beyond a simple calculation or transaction (something not necessary for law as such, but necessary for lawful decisions that are to be deemed responsible, which Derrida assumes systems of law generally require), then it requires an appeal to the excessive movement Derrida identifies with justice. Derrida argues that this relationship between justice and law is irreducible, and that "there is no justice without this experience, however impossible it may be, of aporia" (FOL, 244/FDL, 38).

The justice that is conditioned by the disjoining of time is thus neither a setting right of this fault, nor the negation of all such rectitude. It takes place in the aporetic relation between an incalculable alterity and the calculation of law. As an aporia, this configuration of justice and law thus has an important relation to inheritance—following the interpretation of inheritance I have developed, this will mean that it is experienced in the reception of inherited understandings of both justice and the law. But in "Force of Law" Derrida goes beyond this claim to make a stronger one, arguing that the task of inheriting this aporia is something to be undertaken in response to the demand of justice itself. That is, he suggests that one must inherit this aporia if one wishes to be just.

> As to the legacy we have received under the name of justice, and in more than one language, the *task* of a historical and interpretative memory is at the heart of deconstruction. This is not only a philologico-etymological task or the historian's task but the responsibility in face of a heritage that is at the same time the heritage of an imperative or of a sheaf of injunctions. Deconstruction is already pledged, engaged [*gagée, engagée*] by this demand for infinite justice, which can take the aspect of this "mystique" I spoke of earlier. One must [*Il faut*] be *juste* with justice, and the first justice to be done is to hear it, to try to understand where it comes from, what it wants from us, knowing that it does so through singular idioms (*Dikē, Jus, justitia, justice, Gerechtigkeit,* to limit ourselves to European idioms that it may also be necessary to delimit, in relation to others—we shall come back to this later). One must [*il faut*] know that this justice always addresses itself to singularity, to the singularity of the other, despite or even because it pretends to universality. (FOL, 248/FDL, 44)

The repeated "One must's" here do not name strict necessities, but rather necessities that follow from the decision to respond positively to the call of justice. If one wants justice to be done, Derrida claims, one must inherit what is bequeathed from the tradition under its name. And Derrida places this legacy "at the heart of deconstruction," suggesting that the latter follows from the demand for infinite justice. As the passage continues, this link is confirmed, and intensified, through the figure of the *surenchère*.

> Consequently, never to yield on this point, constantly to maintain a questioning of the origin, grounds and limits of our conceptual, theoretical or normative apparatus surrounding justice—this is, from the point of view of a rigorous deconstruction, anything but a neutralization of the interest in justice, an insensitivity towards injustice. On the contrary, it hyperbolically raises the stakes [*C'est au contraire une surenchère hyperbolique*] in the demand for justice, the sensitivity to a kind of essential disproportion that must inscribe excess and inadequation to itself. It compels to denounce not only theoretical limits but also concrete injustices, with the most palpable effects, in the good conscience that dogmatically stops before any inherited determination of justice. (FOL, 248/FDL, 44–45)

Derrida here ties the hyperbolic raising of the stakes that I have argued character-izes his own particular strategy of inheriting in deconstructive reading with a positive response to the call for justice. To interrogate the inadequacies of received conceptions of justice is not the sign of a disregard or indifference for justice, but a heightened (and heightening) sensitivity to it. The inheritance of justice thus not only follows necessar-ily from its aporetic structure. In addition, Derrida is suggesting that to inherit in the particular manner he counsels and raise the stakes of the aporia is itself an attempt to do what justice demands.

Now this association between justice, inheritance, and deconstruction could be seen to make sense of Derrida's famous claim, made earlier in "Force of Law," that *"Deconstruction is justice"* (FOL, 243/FDL, 35). Deconstruction would be justice because deconstruction responds to justice by intensifying the aporia in which the latter is necessarily entwined. Nonetheless, as attractive as it is, I hesitate in yielding too quickly to this interpretation, for two reasons. First, it is unclear whether the state-ment *"Deconstruction is justice"* can ever be fully comprehended, given the difficulty in defining the two nouns involved. Derrida questions whether "deconstruction" and "justice" can be said to exist, even as ideals, and so much of "Force of Law" is aimed at troubling settled understandings of both terms, so it would be hasty to assume that one knows what the phrase *"Deconstruction is justice"* actually means. Further, as I have already noted, Derrida makes this kind of identity statement regularly, linking deconstruction to all sorts of terms. *"Deconstruction is justice"* thus functions more as a provocative call to further thinking than as a statement of established fact.

Second, in this passage Derrida presents one configuration of justice, deconstruc-tion, and inheritance, but it is not the only one possible. Although deconstruction, understood through the particular operation of the *surenchère*, is here placed on the side of justice, it could just as easily be aligned with injustice, for as I argued in the last chapter, there is nothing inherently good in an increasing openness or increasing intensification of an aporia. It is always the case, from the Derridean point of view, that improvement or progress cannot be protected against what is bad. This is acknowl-edged in "Force of Law" in the necessity that justice engage law, together with the irreducibility of violence in all law. And this necessity is both conceptual and norma-tive. Justice is aporetic, so necessarily tied to the law, and justice ought to be tied to the law, since, as Derrida notes, "abandoned to itself, the incalculable and giving [*dona-trice*] idea of justice is always very close to the bad, even to the worst, for it can always be reappropriated by the most perverse calculation. It is always possible, and this is part of the madness of which we were speaking. An absolute assurance against this risk can only saturate or suture the opening of the call to justice, a call that is always wounded" (FOL, 257/FDL, 61). Thus what seems to be a positive response to the call of justice, through a deconstructive inheritance of its names, could always turn out to promote injustice, and such a possibility can never be foreclosed. Now even as he notes this, Derrida does not promote injustice in "Force of Law"; he spends much more time showing that deconstruction can be placed on the side of justice. That he does so is understandable, given the context of the essay's first delivery. Derrida is responding to a dominant stream of interpretation that at best would see deconstruction as having nothing to do with ethico-political questions, and at worst accuse it of unbridled depravity and nihilism.[22] In the face of such a general agreement, Derrida characteristically emphasizes the contrary. But one should be cautious in following him too far in this direction and simply affirm deconstruction as just. By Derrida's own account, the aporia of justice does not admit of any such resolution.

As a consequence, all one should assert is that while inheritance is a necessary element in any relation to justice, inheriting in the manner that Derrida counsels (or indeed in any particular manner) does not thereby ensure that one will do better justice to what justice demands. A call for justice may well resound from the disjuncture of time, and one can indeed move in this aporia, sorting through the legacies that are bequeathed from the past. But this movement will never be made with the assurance of its being just.

It is here that I conclude my general account of Derridean inheritance. I hope to have shown that there is much that is necessary in inheritance for Derrida, but at the same time choices can be made in how one receives legacies from the past. Derrida himself advocates some choices over others, both explicitly in his discussions of inheritance and implicitly in the ways he inherits from the traditions with which he engages. With this established, I am now in a position to turn to the central concern of this book, democracy.

3 Inheriting Democracy to Come

ALTHOUGH IT IS plausible to read an implicit negotiation of political themes across Derrida's oeuvre, as he and many commentators have claimed, this is harder to maintain for the specific case of democracy.[1] For democracy was absent in name from Derrida's writings for a long time. It only started appearing regularly in his work in the early 1990s, and the majority of these appearances involve a fleeting reference to the term "democracy" in a variety of discussions, some closely related to it, others more distant. Indeed, it is only in two texts, *Politics of Friendship* and "The Reason of the Strongest (Are There Rogue States?)," that democracy is subject to a sustained analysis. In the former, which arose out of his 1988–89 seminar and was published 1994, Derrida interrogates the relationships among fraternity, friendship, and political belonging in a wide range of thinkers, including Plato, Aristotle, Cicero, Montaigne, Kant, Nietzsche, Schmitt, and Blanchot. It is a long and complex work, with the focus more on "the political" than specifically on "democracy." "The Reason of the Strongest," first delivered at Cerisy in 2002 and subsequently published in *Rogues*, is a more comprehensive and detailed reflection on democracy, following a pattern very much like that of *Aporias* (a text, as I noted in Chapter 1, that was also presented at a Cerisy conference devoted to Derrida's work), where Derrida returns to a term present but more or less unexamined in his previous writings. In this reinterpretation of "democracy to come," Derrida draws out its implicit meanings, analyzes its operation, and redeploys it anew.

It is thus the case that although Derrida does explicitly focus on democracy in some of his writings, there remain many aspects of his analysis that call for further articulation. In this chapter I pursue one theme raised but undeveloped by Derrida:

the role played by inheritance. I argue that for Derrida not only is democracy inherited, a claim he explicitly makes, but also that implicit in his position is the claim that inheritance itself can be a democratic action.

I will proceed by first expanding on one of Derrida's earliest descriptions of democracy, where he links it to the idea of a promise, before turning to the more complete account found in "The Reason of the Strongest" (I examine *Politics of Friendship* at length in Chapter 5, reading it as a particular example of democratic inheritance). But before continuing, I should make one point regarding terminology. When "democracy" appears in Derrida's writings, it rarely does so alone. More often than not, what is named is not just of "democracy," but "democracy to come." In Chapter 2 I touched on some of the connotations of the qualifier "to come" in Derrida's work, and another aim of this chapter is to explore these more fully. A complete appreciation of this term's implications will thus have to wait. But I can say in advance that "democracy" and "democracy to come" are not two competing concepts or two opposed political structures in Derrida's writings. "Democracy to come" is not a blueprint of what democracy ought to be, an updated or improved version of what is usually called "democracy." Rather, Derrida argues that because of its particular characteristics democracy has always been "to come." He writes "democracy to come" when he wants to emphasize this fact. But when he speaks only of "democracy," one should also hear the trace of the "to come" resonating with it. Following Derrida in this respect, throughout this chapter I will thus speak both of democracy and democracy to come, interchanging the terms freely.

The Inheritance of a Promise

One of the earliest appearances of democracy to come in Derrida's work is in 1991's *The Other Heading*. This text is devoted to the question of how one might inherit the legacy of Europe in the light of the radical changes that took place with the fall of the Soviet Union. I argued in the previous chapter that for Derrida legacies are always divided and contradictory, and the legacy of Europe is no exception. At the heart of its contradiction is a law that Derrida takes to be axiomatic: "*What is proper to a culture is to not be identical to itself.*"[2] According to this axiom, a culture is always different from itself and thus different from the very idea of "being with itself"—a culture is never one, resisting unification, involving difference and an unassumable remainder. In the particular culture of Europe, Derrida locates this difference in an aporia of universalization. He argues that modern philosophical discourse (in particular the work of Husserl, Heidegger, and Valéry) holds that Europe carries the universal spirit of humanity, while this spirit is at the same time inscribed in a particular culture, heritage, and idiom. Europe is thus presented as both universal and particular. It has its own identity, but this identity lies in its universalizing tendency, in which it surpasses its own identity. This contradiction is equally in play within Europe in a different sense, as it moves toward an increasing unification that would both represent a single spirit while respecting national differences.

As always for Derrida, the question is how one is to respond to this contradiction. This is a question of inheritance, posed in a vocabulary that should be now quite familiar.

> We must ourselves be responsible for this discourse of the modern tradition. We bear the responsibility for this heritage, right along with the capitalizing memory that we have of it. We did not choose this responsibility; it imposes itself upon us, and in an even more imperative way, in that it is, as other, and from the other, the language of our language. How then does one assume this responsibility, this capital duty [*devoir*]? How does one respond? And above all, how does one assume a responsibility that announces itself as contradictory because it inscribes us from the very beginning of the game into a kind of necessarily double obligation, a *double bind*? The injunction in effect divides us; it puts us always at fault or in default since it doubles the *il faut*, the *it is necessary*: it is necessary to make ourselves the guardians of an idea of Europe, of a difference of Europe, *but* of a Europe that consists precisely in not closing itself off in its own identity and in advancing itself in an exemplary way toward what it is not, toward the other heading or the heading of the other, indeed—and this is perhaps something else altogether—toward the other *of* the heading, which would be the beyond of this modern tradition, another border structure, another shore.³

The legacy of Europe is here presented as a contradictory injunction that imposes itself necessarily, without consent. And its division is also necessary, harboring within it an alterity that offers the chance of something altogether other, beyond the economy of the modern tradition that is received. This legacy is thus exemplary of the structure of Derridean inheritance I developed in Chapter 2.

For my present purpose, what is most interesting in *The Other Heading* is the position occupied by democracy. The essay ends with a list of several duties that arise from this tension between the universal and the particular in the identity and heritage of Europe. I have in fact already mentioned these duties—they were the subject of Derrida's self-reflection in *Aporias* that I discussed at the beginning of Chapter 1. One of them runs as follows:

> The *same duty* dictates assuming the European, and *uniquely* European, heritage of an idea of democracy, while also recognizing that this idea, like that of international law, is never simply given, that its status is not even that of a regulative idea in the Kantian sense, but rather something that remains to be thought and *to come* [*à venir*]: not something that is certain to happen tomorrow, not the democracy (national or international, state or trans-state) of the *future*, but a democracy that must have the structure of a promise—*and thus the memory of that which carries the future, the to-come, here and now.*⁴

Here Derrida repeats another aspect of legacies that I have analyzed, namely their adherence to the logic of spacing. The heritage of democracy involves all three tenses of time, and a dimension of space, in the specific configuration that presents the past as carrying the future in the here and now. However, what is new here is a further claim linking democracy to the structure of a promise. This is why it can be said to be "to come." Democracy is thus presented here not as a political system with clearly defined rules or criteria (and Derrida distances democracy from this more and more as time goes on), nor is it necessarily an idea, Kantian or otherwise. It is a promise. A similar claim is made in the dialogue "Sauf le nom," dating from the same period, where, at the end of a long discussion of negative theology, Derrida again turns to questions of European inheritance and raises "the example of democracy, of the idea of democracy, of democracy to come (neither the Idea in the Kantian sense, nor the current, limited, and determined concept of democracy, but democracy as the inheritance of a promise)."[5]

Thus in two of its earliest appearances in Derrida's texts, "democracy to come" is affirmed as inherited and is identified with the structure of a promise.[6] At this point inheritance needs no further explanation, but I have not yet discussed the nature of a promise. Derrida analyzes this notion extensively in his writings, and one of its later appearances is in "Avances," the preface to Serge Margel's *Le tombeau du dieu artisan*.[7] Margel's book focuses on Plato's *Timaeus*, a text Derrida also discussed on a number of occasions, most notably for its invocation of khōra. Khōra will reappear later in my analysis of democracy, but for now I want to examine what Derrida says in this text about the promise. Extending Margel's work, Derrida writes that "there is here an intrinsic aporia of the concept of the promise" (AV, 26). Once again, an aporia is named. However, it is never enough to simply accept Derrida's ascription of an aporia—one must ask each time precisely how the particular notion in question indeed is aporetic. In this case Derrida argues that the aporia is constituted by a necessary contradiction between the need for a promise to be both infinite and finite, which is quickly assimilated to a distinction between the calculable and the incalculable. The promise

> must always be, *at once, at the same time, infinite and finite* in its principle: It is *infinite* because it must be able to be carried beyond any possible program, and because to promise only the calculable and the certain is no longer to promise; it is *finite* because to promise the infinite to the infinite is no longer to promise anything presentable, and hence no longer to promise. To be a promise, a promise *must be able to* be untenable [*intenable*] and so be able *not to be* a promise (for an untenable promise is not a promise). Conclusion: one will never *state*, no more than for the gift, *that there is or there has been* a promise. (AV, 26)

If a promise promises only the calculable, Derrida claims, then it is no longer a promise. Hence the need to promise what is beyond the calculable. But at the same time, Derrida also maintains that if a promise promises beyond the calculable, it promises the unpresentable, which entails also that it no longer be a promise. Thus a promise is required to be both calculable and incalculable. It is aporetic.

There are a number of statements here that need justification. To consider the second claim first, one may well question why the unpresentable is unacceptable as the content of a promise. Here Derrida relies on what he presents as a classical definition of the promise, in which the intentionality and sovereignty of the speaker must be assumed in order for the promise to be counted as such. "No doubt, in order to promise, it is necessary *to know seriously*, before all, what is promised. By whom and to whom—and what we mean and know when we say *we promise to each other* [nous nous promettons]. Knowledge and seriousness, the self-presence of intentional consciousness as such belong without doubt to the essence of promising" (AV, 41). For a promise to be a promise, according to this view, one must know what is promised, by whom and to whom. However, if one promises the unpresentable, then this knowledge is what is lacking. Thus one of the traditionally essential attributes of the promise is missing if one promises something beyond the calculable.

This accounts for one arm of the aporia—to contain an element of the incalculable is enough to threaten the integrity of the promise. But what of the other arm? Why is a calculable promise no longer a promise? Derrida gives an answer to this question when he writes:

> But if the promised of the promise (including the meaning, the subject and the object of the act of promising that are part of the promised content) is absolutely known, determined, pre-sensed or presentable, if it even already has an adequate name, there is no more promise, there is only calculation, program, anticipation, providence, prevision, prognostic: everything will have already happened, *everything is beforehand* [tout est auparavant], repeated in advance. As that which it is, indeed (perhaps a certain Aristotle would have said) as that which it will have been or will have been destined to be: *To ti ēn einai.* We conjugate here only in the future anterior. Ruining the placement [*la mise*], this antecedence of the *before* [avant] puts the pro-position of the promise in danger—that it nonetheless opens and puts to work. (AV, 41)

One must proceed slowly here because Derrida is advancing a complicated claim. He states that if one promises only the calculable, the absolutely known or determined, then when what is promised arrives, it arrives as *having already* arrived. Derrida is right to highlight the future anterior, for its use here is essential. The claim is not that to promise what is already known is to make it happen in the instant that it is promised—by promising what is known one does not bring it about in the very same moment. Rather, Derrida's claim is that in promising the certain, one makes it happen, when it happens, as having already happened. It is thus to have a specific effect on the nature of the promise's arrival, ensuring that it arrives as the return of what has already taken place.

This, however, raises a further question, namely of what justifies the move from this claim to the conclusion that promising the calculable is not to promise at all. To answer this, another assumption is needed, which is that a promise must promise the new. This assumption is revealed as Derrida continues, writing that the dimension of incalculability he acknowledges in the promise "is not an empirical blindness or imprudence. Heterogeneous to calculation, it *lets come* or it *makes come* on the condition, and this is the condition of the event, of no longer seeing come, on the condition of overflowing sight or knowledge, of gaining speed over them even when they remain needed" (AV, 41–42). For Derrida, a promise must be an event, and by this he means that it must contain an element of surprise, something unforeseen, not programmed, and beyond control. Given this requirement, what is promised cannot arrive as the return of what has already happened, and so it cannot involve the calculable alone.

The final question to ask thus concerns this requirement of the new. Why must a promise be an event? Why can one not promise only what is certain to happen, or what happens as having already happened? While Derrida does not here make this connection, this assumption can be explained by recalling his analysis of iterability, which I discussed in Chapter 1. As a mark, a promise is iterable, which means that its perfect repetition is strictly impossible. There is always the possibility that it will be repeated differently, and so one can never be certain that what is promised to happen will actually come to pass. Promising thus retains an element of the new, a dimension of incalculability, and so is aporetic in its structure.

Derrida is thus justified in labeling the promise as aporetic, divided between the dual demands of calculability and incalculability, and so remains beyond all mastery and knowledge. One would thereby expect democracy to come to have this characteristic, given the description of it as "the inheritance of a promise." In addition, Derrida proposes in "Avances" two consequences of his analysis that will also be relevant to democracy.[8] First, he argues that the essential dimension of nonknowledge in the promise results in an instability around the status of names. This is touched on in one of the previous citations, when Derrida refuses the promise "an adequate name," and is developed later in the text when he writes, "For all to depend on it and be inscribed there *without knowing it*, it is necessary that the names are lacking to 'us.' *The names are necessary*, it is necessary that the names be in default, but this default ought not be the negativity of a lack. . . . We do not know if these names that we lack are absent because buried far below a given memory or more distant than any given future" (AV, 42). Taken out of context, these words are enigmatic. They allude, in part, to the difficulty in naming what is given the name "khōra," which I will return to later in this chapter. But for now note the instability here described, for Derrida claims both that names are necessary and that it is necessary that these names are in default. Further, the logic of spacing is evoked in his remark that one does not know whether these names lie buried below the past or remain beyond any future.

The second consequence relevant to democracy is Derrida's claim that the promise cannot remain immune to all threat. "For a promise to *remain* a promise, must it not then *risk*, this is its obsessive fear [*c'est sa hantise*], must it not risk continuously, incessantly, in an endless imminence, to pervert itself into a threat? Not only that it threatens to remain untenable but threatens to become threatening?" (AV, 42–43). The threat here is not just that the promise will undermine itself, or fail to come to pass, but that what is promised will be threatening. For Derrida, promises promise both the good and the bad, the safe and the dangerous, and the possibility of danger can never be erased.

This detour through Derrida's analysis of the promise thus suggests several of the characteristics that democracy—"the inheritance of a promise"—should possess. Democracy should be aporetic with respect to calculability and incalculability, its affirmation will involve an essential dimension of nonknowledge, there will be an instability around the status of its name, and it promises both safety and danger. As I will now show, these features, and more, are indeed found in Derrida's more direct engagements with democracy.

Democracy in "The Reason of the Strongest"

One feature of Derrida's analysis of the promise is its generality. Derrida does not write about this or that promise, outlining any one promise's particular content, but discusses "the promise" in the abstract. Because of this, there is a danger that when Derrida identifies democracy with a promise, the specificity of the former is lost in the generality of the latter. This danger is only amplified by Derrida's insistence on the nonknowledge that a promise entails. If all promises involve nonknowledge and a degree of indeterminacy, if they are all aporetic on the question of calculability, and if they are all unstable with respect to their name, then it is unclear what distinguishes the promise that is democracy. One thus must say more in order to determine what is special about this particular promise such that it merits the name democracy, despite its instability, and not another.

To do so I turn to Derrida's "The Reason of the Strongest." As I stated above, this text contains Derrida's most detailed and sustained discussion of democracy. This is not surprising given its initial context—the Cerisy conference at which it was first delivered in July 2002 was devoted to the theme of "democracy to come" in Derrida's work. In addition, the wider context of world politics at that time also encouraged an exploration of this theme. The events of September 11, 2001, had placed the issue of security in democracy center stage, and the commencement of the war in Afghanistan together with the beginnings of the Bush Administration's rumblings against Iraq made real the idea of invasion and occupation in the name of democracy. Closer to Derrida's home, in April 2002 Le Pen passed to the second round of the French presidential elections, giving rise to the possibility of a government that is openly racist and xenophobic coming to power in France with democratic legitimacy. Questions of democracy's future were thus being raised on a grand scale.[9]

Derrida approaches his topic by privileging the theme of freedom. This theme is somewhat of a novelty in his writings, since it is not a term to which he had elsewhere devoted much attention, but its presence here follows from its importance in any discussion of democracy. As Derrida states, "It is on the basis of freedom that we will have conceived of the concept of democracy. This will be true throughout the entire history of this concept, from Plato's Greece onwards" (*R*, 22/*V*, 45). Democracy presupposes that the people are free to govern themselves. But this freedom is never unbounded. For one thing, as Derrida notes, there is a fine line between liberty and license (*eleutheria* and *exousia* in Plato's Greece). Most democrats are in favor of liberty over license, and so restrictions on liberty are needed in democracy to prevent it passing over into its less desirable double. Further, even while freedom remains an irreducible element of democracy—a system of governing that has no place for freedom would hardly be called democratic—it is not its only trait. Most notably, democracy also essentially requires reference to equality. As there is always a plurality in democracy, one is never alone in self-government, and so the freedom that democracy demands must be an equal one. This is not to say that all those ruled in a democracy must have an equal share of freedom. Democracies have always excluded some from citizenship at the same time as it governs their lives, a feature that Derrida will examine at length. But among those who do qualify as citizens, the expectation is that they will share equally in the freedom that democracy promises.

Given this dual commitment, democrats are thus faced with the task of balancing freedom against equality. How might equal freedom be achieved such that all citizens remain equally free to govern themselves? Derrida highlights an answer discussed by Aristotle which proposes that each citizen governs in turn. Under this system of taking turns (*tour à tour*) citizens are sometimes rulers and sometimes ruled.[10] It is a compromise solution, since no citizen is free to govern himself all of the time. Freedom is thus curtailed in the name of democratic equality. Yet it is one way of attempting to share freedom equally—everyone has some time governing and some time being governed, in equal measure. Of course, today a strict application of taking turns is not taken seriously as a viable option for democracy, since there is no question of letting everyone govern in his or her turn, regardless of personal qualities. Yet the general idea of taking turns is still the cornerstone of modern democracy with its system of elections. In theory, a modern democracy gives all citizens an equal share not in governing, but in electing their government at regular intervals.

Ultimately Derrida is not concerned with the details of the notion of taking turns. Rather, what interests him most is the significance of this particular response to the challenge of reconciling equality and freedom. The circular motion of the alternation of government (itself a response to the circular motion of the autodetermination demanded by the democratic ideal), together with the inability to cleanly distinguish liberty from license, are emblematic of what Derrida sees as democracy's essential indeterminacy. "This freedom . . . presupposes, more radically still, more originally, a freedom of play, an opening of indetermination and indecidability *in the very concept* of democracy, in the interpretation of the democratic" (*R*, 25/*V*, 47). Democracy operates through the possibility of continual change, and so there is no single form that stands for it. All types of government are possible. This was, on Derrida's reading, Plato's main complaint against democracy as a system of government.

Insofar as each person in this democracy can lead the life (*bion*) he chooses, we find in this regime, this *politeia*—which, as we will see, is not quite a regime, neither a constitution nor an authentic *politeia*—all sorts of people, a greater variety than anywhere else. Whence the multicolored beauty of democracy. . . . Because of the freedom and the multicoloredness of a democracy peopled by such a diversity of men, one would seek in vain a single constitution or *politeia* within it. Given over to freedom, to *exousia* this time, democracy contains all the different kinds of constitutions, of regimes or states. . . . Plato already announces that "democracy" is, in the end, neither the name of a regime nor the name of a constitution. It is not a constitutional form among others. (*R*, 26/*V*, 48–49)

In its emphasis on freedom, democracy has a structure that is opened up to constant transformation. It thus designates neither a single constitution nor a single regime— the name does not refer to any single form of government. This is one reason Plato has such distaste for democracy, for in its mutability it can have no single, eternal Form. It is also why, Derrida suggests, "there have in fact been, in addition to the monarchic, plutocratic, and tyrannical democracies of antiquity, so many so-called modern democratic regimes" (*R*, 26–27/*V*, 49). Almost every government in today's world calls itself a democracy, regardless of its internal structure. Derrida proposes that this is not just hypocrisy on the part of most (or even all) of these governments, but rather a consequence of the structure of democracy itself. It has no one model, no one form, for it makes possible many.[11]

Focusing on freedom and the taking turns thus leads Derrida to emphasize an indeterminacy in the concept of democracy. This is, of course, not a new point to make, as is evident in the reference to Plato. Later in "The Reason of the Strongest" Derrida cites similar remarks from Rousseau, who in *On the Social Contract* writes that no other government "tends so forcefully and continuously to change its form."[12] Rousseau thus also picks out democracy's mutability as one of its central features. However, where Plato took this to be a sign of weakness, Rousseau, at least as he is read by Derrida, associates it with a strength: "In this revival [*relance*] of the Platonic philosopheme concerning the plasticity of democracy, Rousseau names (and in two different places) force, the force that forces the form, the force that forces a change in form, and then, right after, the force required of the citizen to remain a democrat despite this unpresentability" (*R*, 74/*V*, 108). Derrida's claim is that for Rousseau the fact that democracy cannot be presented is not a failing on democracy's part. Rather, it is a sign of the great strength needed by the democrat. Now this is not to say that Rousseau thereby embraces democracy, for he sees the strength needed for democracy to work to be so great that he famously claims, as Derrida highlights, "Were there a people of gods, it would govern itself democratically. So perfect a government is not suited to men."[13] But even if Rousseau shares with Plato an opposition to democracy, a shift has nonetheless taken place in his "revival [*relance*] of the Platonic philosopheme."

That this shift takes place should not be all that surprising, for as is signaled by the presence of the word "*relance*," Derrida is here describing an act of inheritance of democracy. Like all such acts, it is not a simple repetition, but contains, as I demonstrated in Chapter 2, a degree of freedom where that which is "relaunched [*relancé*]" may be relaunched otherwise. In this instance what is perceived by Plato to be a weakness comes to be associated in Rousseau with a strength. Further, the inheritance here taking place involves not only Rousseau and Plato. There is at least one other heir on the scene, namely Derrida himself. In examining the movement of this idea from Plato to Rousseau, Derrida is inheriting from both of them, relaunching it in his turn. The question, therefore, is how Derrida's understanding of the essential indeterminacy of democracy differs from that of those who have come before him. If Plato sees weakness in democracy's lack of form, where Rousseau finds strength, what does Derrida perceive?

The answer is that Derrida sees both weakness and strength, for he argues that democracy harbors both a danger and a chance. That is, Derrida inherits according to the scheme I developed in Chapter 2, where he chooses to raise the stakes of what he reveals as aporetic, heightening the tension between the opposing poles of strength and weakness, chance and threat. This strategy of inheritance is revealed most clearly in Derrida's recourse to the term "autoimmunity," which occupies a central position in "The Reason of the Strongest." Derrida uses this notion here and elsewhere to describe democracy's particular instability, an instability that turns on its lack of form. Autoimmunity is thus key to understanding Derrida's inheritance of democracy. In order to best articulate what it means, I will first analyze this term's earlier deployment in Derrida's writings. Another detour, but one that will return to the heart of Derrida's understanding of democracy.

"Autoimmunity" makes its first substantial appearance in the 1996 essay "Faith and Knowledge: The Two Sources of 'Religion' at the Limits of Reason Alone," a text examining religion's relationship with technology.[14] There, Derrida argues that this relationship is divided between contradictory yet equally necessary tendencies. On the one hand, he claims that religion is committed to distancing itself from technology, because one of the two sources of religion is the notion of "the unscathed [*l'indemne*] (the safe and sound, the immune, the holy, the sacred, *heilig*)" (the other is "faith") (FK, 93/FS, 88). Religions aim for a purity that is protected from the corrupting influence of the mechanical reproduction of the technical. On the other hand, Derrida also claims that this contamination is at the same time precisely what religions cannot avoid. In their attempt to secure the sacred as sacred (and to establish security in faith), religions must iterate themselves, give themselves over to a repetitive duplicity that further divides their already doubled self at the source. "Why should there always have to be *more than one* source? . . . *there are at least two.* Because there are, for the best and for the worst, division and iterability of the source" (FK, 100/FS, 99). That is, religions must use technology to stay alive, as is evident in "the multiplicity, the unprecedented speed and scope of the moves of a Pope versed in televisual rhetoric . . . airborne pilgrimages to Mecca . . . the international and televisual diplomacy of the Dalai Lama, etc." (FK, 62/FS, 40). In order to survive, religions must therefore act against their own tendency to protect their sacredness. They attack their own protection so as to live on, and it is this action that Derrida labels autoimmune.

> The same movement that renders indissociable religion and tele-technoscientific reason in its most critical aspect reacts inevitably *to itself*. It secretes its own antidote but also its own power of auto-immunity. We are here in a space where all self-protection of the unscathed, of the safe and sound, of the sacred (*heilig*, holy) must protect itself against its own protection, its own police, its own power of rejection, in short against its own, which is to say, against its own immunity. It is this terrifying but fatal logic of the *auto-immunity of the unscathed* that will always associate Science and Religion. (FK, 79–80/FS, 67)

Autoimmunity is a paradoxical process whereby an entity attacks its own defenses in order to defend itself. Autoimmunity thus never involves an attack by a self against all of itself, but only against a part of itself. Further, it does not describe an attack against any part of the self, but that particular part that is part of its own protection. This specificity is reinforced by what Derrida cites as the biological sources of the term, where "the process of auto-immunization . . . consists for a living organism, as is well known and in short, of protecting itself against its self-protection by destroying its own immune system" (FK, 80/FS, 67). If, therefore, parts of the self other than its defenses or immune system are attacked (if there are any), then one is no longer talking about a process of autoimmunity, but of something else.

There are two important consequences that follow from the operation of autoimmunity, consequences that evoke old themes in Derrida's writings. First, it is difficult to maintain any clear distinction between the inside and the outside of an autoimmune entity, between a self and its others. Speaking of the reaction of religion against modern technology, Derrida writes:

> This internal and immediate reactivity, at once immunitary and auto-immune, can alone account for what will be called the religious resurgence in its double and contradictory phenomenon. The word *resurgence <déferlement>* imposes itself upon us to suggest the redoubling of a wave that appropriates even that to which, enfolding itself, it seems to be opposed—and simultaneously gets carried away itself, sometimes in terror and terrorism, taking with it precisely that which protects it, its own "antibodies." Allying itself with the enemy, hospitable to the antigens, bearing away the other with itself, this resurgence grows and *swells* with the power of the adversary. (FK, 81–82/FS, 70)

This highlights the instability between the inside and outside that autoimmunity implies. An attack can no longer be taken on its own as a sign of an external threat. It can just as easily come from within as from without, as one can never know whether that which seems to come from the outside has not been in fact enlisted from within, appropriated as a means for a self to attack itself. Through an autoimmune process a self thus grows and extends itself to incorporate its enemies, precisely through self-attack.

Derrida will follow through these implications right up to the point where it becomes difficult to speak of any coherent "self" here at all.[15]

Second, the claim that autoimmunity is at work in religion reconfigures the relationship between life and death in this domain. That the term originates in biology means that life is already on the table. And it is the same kind of life that was at work in my discussion of Derrida's inheritance of Marx—a life intimately tied to death. According to Derrida, religion operates according to a "mechanical principle [that] is apparently very simple: life has *absolute* value only if it is worth *more than life*" (FK, 87/ FS, 78).[16] Religion thus cannot be seen on the side of life against death (as a principle of absolute respect for life, something readily associated with the religious, might imply), but rather, as that which incorporates "the dead in the living." At stake is not simply life, but an "excess above and beyond the living," for autoimmunity always involves a measure of death "in view of some sort of invisible and spectral sur-vival" (FK, 86–87/ FS, 78–79). Autoimmunity involves a self putting a part of itself to death in order not to live, but to live-on, and is thus another expression of Derrida's challenge to accepted understandings of life, death, and survival.

This analysis of autoimmunity at work in religion forms the basis of Derrida's use of the term in his discussion of democracy. In "The Reason of the Strongest," as well as in its companion piece, the interview "Autoimmunity: Real and Symbolic Suicides," Derrida argues that democracy is best understood according to processes of autoimmunity, and he does so by focusing on two examples from recent democratic history. The first is the case of Algeria in 1992, where elections were interrupted in the face of the perceived threat that they would result in the formation of a fundamentalist Islamic government. If this result had come to pass, and the subsequent government in fact introduced antidemocratic laws as imagined (something that, as Derrida notes, will never be known), then it would have been the case that democracy democratically passed over into an antidemocratic regime.[17] This possibility, Derrida argues, is present for all democracies, for it follows from the fundamental structure of the taking turns. It is always possible that a nondemocratic regime will result from a normal and well-functioning democratic electoral process, since if a party or candidate with an antidemocratic agenda receives enough votes, then it/he/she will arrive to power with democratic legitimacy. "The great question of modern parliamentary and representative democracy, perhaps of all democracy, in this logic of the turn or round, of the other turn or round, of the other time and thus of the other, of the *alter* in general, is that the *alternative to* democracy can always be *represented* as a democratic *alternation*" (R, 30–31/V, 54).[18]

Derrida labels this situation autoimmune, for the possibility of this attack against democracy comes from itself. The threat of an antidemocratic government is produced from the internal workings of democracy. It is thus unclear to what extent those others who would want to pass antidemocratic laws are indeed "other"—one cannot so easily distinguish democracy from its enemies, since the latter here arrive with some democratic legitimacy. And importantly, they did not come out of nowhere. Derrida inscribes this example of an autoimmune "moment" into a history of similar actions; he argues that it is a part of "a whole series of examples of an autoimmune pervertibility of democracy," in which the imposition of a colonizing power identifying itself as a democracy produces "exactly the opposite of democracy (French Algeria)," which itself produces a civil war, later named a war of independence seen to be fought in the name of the very democratic principles that the colonizing power first proclaimed (*R*, 34–35/*V*, 59). This example is thus situated in a long historical chain.

Equally important is the fact that this chain also extends into the future. Confronting the projected threat of Islamic fundamentalism, democracy attacked itself though the suspension of elections: "The Algerian government and a large part, although not a majority, of the Algerian people (as well as people outside Algeria) . . . thus preferred to put an end to [democracy] themselves. They decided in a sovereign fashion to suspend, at least provisionally, democracy *for its own good*, so as to take care of it, so as to immunize it against a much worse and very likely assault" (*R*, 33/*V*, 57). Here too autoimmunity is at work—democracy attacks a part of itself (in this case elections) in order to allow itself as a whole to live on. So the response that was made to the perceived threat to democracy coming from Islamic fundamentalism may have averted this particular danger (at least in the short term), but it did not prevent democracy from being attacked. An attack still took place, one seen to be a form of defense against what was seen to be an even greater threat.

Derrida thus uses the case of Algeria to demonstrate one of the ways that autoimmunity operates in democracy. A democracy makes possible the threat of an attack against itself from certain "others," and its response to this threat is to attack itself. A second example that Derrida invokes are the attacks of September 11.

> It is perhaps because the United States has a culture and a system of law that are largely democratic that it was able to open itself up and expose its greatest vulnerability to immigrants, to, for example, pilots in training, experienced and suicidal "terrorists" who, before turning against others but also against themselves the aerial bombs that they had become, and before hurling them by hurling themselves into the two World Trade Towers, were trained on the sovereign soil of the United States, under the nose of the CIA and the FBI, perhaps not without some autoimmune consent on the part of an administration with at once more and less foresight than one tends to think when it is faced with what is claimed to be a major, unforeseeable event. (*R*, 40/*V*, 65)[19]

This example differs from that of the Algerian elections, since it is not a question here of democracy's openness to a plurality of forms of government. Rather, the root of the problem lies in democracy's openness to others. Derrida's claim is that the United States was being democratic in exposing itself to the threat that became September 11 through its relatively open borders and support of those who were to turn against it. But despite the difference in the kind of openness involved, what is common to both

September 11 and the Algerian elections is the fact that the threat can be seen as a possibility internal to democracy.

Further, there are strong parallels between these two cases regarding the location of the threat in a historical chain. In the case of September 11 there is a long history that could also be described as "a whole series of examples of an autoimmune pervertibility of democracy," in which the troops trained by the United States to fight against what is seen to be the antidemocratic threat of the Soviet Union in Afghanistan return to attack these same United States.[20] So again the threat did not suddenly appear, but emerged over a long period more or less internal to democracy. And here too this history of autoimmunity also extends into the future. After September 11 "we see an American administration, potentially followed by others in Europe and in the rest of the world, claiming that in the war it is waging against the 'axis of evil,' against the enemies of freedom and the assassins of democracy throughout the world, it must restrict within its own country certain so-called democratic freedoms and the exercise of certain rights by, for example, increasing the powers of police investigations and interrogations, without anyone, any democrat, being really able to oppose such measures" (R, 40/V, 64–65). Thus again there is a perceived threat to a democracy (this time in the form of the threat of future attacks against the United States) that leads this democracy to attack a part of itself (the suspension of certain democratic rights and freedoms) in order to ensure its survival. The United States attacks a part of itself in order to defend itself against attacks that are imagined to come in the future from a source other and more dangerous than itself.

Derrida thus claims that autoimmunity is at work in both the Algerian elections of 1992 and in the attacks of September 11. In both cases Derrida interprets the perceived danger, and the response to this danger, as part of a process of autoimmunity. Importantly, Derrida argues that these examples do not describe external accidents that befall these particular democracies, events that could be avoided if only Algeria or the United States were a bit more democratic. Democracy contains within it the possibility of welcoming an undemocratic regime, and of inviting terrorist attacks, as well as the possibility of producing another attack against itself in an attempt to divert these threats. For Derrida this process of autoimmunity is thus an essential aspect at work in the very notion of democracy.

This view receives further justification when Derrida moves the discussion to a more theoretical level and reinvigorates a term long at work in his oeuvre, "*renvoyer*"— resending: a sending away, sending back (to the source), and/or sending on. *Renvoyer* appeared in Chapter 2 when I discussed Derrida's description of inheritance as a "relaunching otherwise." Here Derrida emphasizes how the renvoi follows the logic of spacing—the "becoming-space of time or the becoming-time of space" (R, 35/V, 60)—which I showed also to be at work in inheritance. First, "in space, the autoimmune topology always dictates that democracy be *sent off* [*renvoyer*] elsewhere, that it be excluded or rejected, expelled under the pretext of protecting it on the inside by expelling, rejecting, or sending off [*renvoyant*] to the outside the domestic enemies of democracy" (*R*, 35–36/*V*, 60). Democracy thus protects itself by sending its domestic enemies into exile, reinforcing the point that these enemies are internal to democracy itself. This reflex is a reaction against democracy's openness to others, and is illustrated in the modifications to immigration and naturalization policies made by governments around the world after September 11. Second, "since the renvoi operates in time as well, autoimmunity also calls for *putting off* [renvoyer] until later the elections and the advent of democracy" (*R*, 36/*V*, 61). Here, the sending operates temporally through delaying democratic reforms and elections until the time is "safer" for democracy. This was the case in Algeria in 1992, and continues in many places in the world today, where elections are deferred in the name of protecting democracy in the long term.

It is this action of resending that Derrida uses to formulate in his own manner the Platonic insight with which this analysis began, namely that there is no essence to democracy, no self that democracy can properly be.

> This double renvoi (sending off—or to—the other and putting off, adjournment) is an autoimmune necessity inscribed *right onto* [*à même*] democracy, right onto the concept of a democracy without concept, a democracy devoid of sameness and ipseity, a democracy whose concept remains free, like a disengaged clutch, *free-wheeling*, in the free play of its indetermination; it is inscribed right onto this thing or this cause that, precisely under the name of democracy, is never properly what it is, never *itself*. For what is lacking in democracy is proper meaning, the very [*même*] meaning of the selfsame [*même*] (*ipse, metipse, metipsissimus, meisme*), the it-self [*soi-même*], the selfsame, the properly selfsame of the it-self. Democracy is defined, as is the very ideal of democracy, by this lack of the proper and the selfsame. (*R*, 36–37/*V*, 61)

One can thus see how autoimmunity underlies Derrida's inheritance of the Platonic conception of democracy. As autoimmune, there is no coherent idea of democracy, since it is always in a process of attacking itself—incorporating what is outside or turning parts of itself against itself. But this does not lead to the total destruction of democracy, its annihilation or suicide. Rather, it is through this process that democracy remains alive, living on. There is, therefore, a fundamental ambivalence in democracy. One cannot straightforwardly denounce these violent self-attacks, these seemingly undemocratic moments in democratic history, for Derrida's claim is that they are essential to democracy's survival. Without them, Derrida suggests, what might be seen as good in democracy could never be.

But what of this good? So far I have only discussed events taking place that many democrats would see as negative. And while part of the force of Derrida's analysis lies in the implication that these events are not wholly negative, since they are implicated in democracy's survival, if this is all it can produce one might wonder what value there is in keeping it alive in the first place. The next question to ask is therefore whether Derrida's understanding of democracy also accounts for those possibilities and events that are usually seen as more desirable. It does, and the particular positive character-istic that Derrida underlines is what he calls democracy's perfectibility. Democracy, Derrida argues, is not only autoimmune in that it turns against itself through being open to others, both in its government and at its borders, and sometimes brings to pass the very threats these others pose. Democracy also turns against itself through calling itself into question, critiquing itself and perfecting itself. This is a central part of what Derrida means by democracy to come.

> The expression "democracy to come" takes into account the absolute and intrinsic historicity of the only system that welcomes in itself, in its very concept, that expres-sion of autoimmunity called the right to self-critique and perfectibility. Democracy is the only system, the only constitutional paradigm, in which, in principle, one has or assumes the right to criticize everything publicly, including the idea of democ-racy, its concept, its history, and its name. Including the idea of the constitutional paradigm and the absolute authority of law. It is thus the only paradigm that is uni-versalizable, whence its chance and its fragility. (*R*, 86–87/*V*, 126–27)[21]

In this passage Derrida again links democracy's lack of stability, its ever-changing and fluid form, to the process of autoimmunity. But in contrast to what I have discussed above, this is here cast in terms that many would see as a positive thing, where democ-racy can improve precisely by attacking parts of itself through self-critique. One exam-ple of such a movement is the expansion of democratic rights. As Derrida states ear-lier in "The Reason of the Strongest," democracy "is interminable in its incompletion beyond all the limitations in areas as different as the right to vote (for example in its extension to women—but starting when?—to minors—but starting at what age?—or to foreigners—but which ones and on what lands?—to cite at random just a few exem-plary problems from among so many other similar ones), the freedom of the press, the end of social inequalities throughout the world, the right to work, or any number of other rights" (*R*, 38–39/*V*, 63).[22] The exclusion of different groups from the right to vote follows precisely a logic that aims to defend democracy from what are seen to be dangerous elements. Overcoming such exclusions therefore would be instances in which democracy attacks its own defenses. This example also makes sense of Derrida's invocation above of democracy's universalizability. The universalizing movement of expanding democratic inclusiveness is accounted for by the autoimmune process—democracy attacks itself by suspending some of its limitations in order to keep itself alive.

Autoimmunity thus involves not only the occurrence of what are traditionally seen as antidemocratic measures. It also accounts for what many would regard as prodemo-cratic, such as the expansion of democratic rights in an ever-increasing inclusiveness. However, it is at this point that the radicality of Derrida's position emerges, since it is precisely such ascriptions of anti- and pro- that his analysis starts to trouble. I stated above that the so-called negative aspects of autoimmunity in fact have an ambivalent value, insofar as they name an essential possibility of democracy's keeping itself alive.

Similarly, the solely positive value of prodemocratic actions is also challenged, for to say that democracy welcomes self-critique, and to see this in the opening of boundaries to include those formerly excluded, is to underline the hospitality in democracy.[23] But as was shown in Chapter 1 and in the above analysis of autoimmunity, such openness to an outside is simultaneously an openness to danger—it is both democracy's chance *and* its fragility. This is an unavoidable possibility inhabiting every relation to alterity. Thus the fact of democracy's openness to self-critique and improvement is at the same time a fact of its openness to what might harm and damage it. Of course, as I also argued in Chapter 1, a complete openness is impossible, meaning that hospitality is always conditional. But this just means that exclusions are an inevitable part of every inclusion, which is why Derrida states that democracy "is interminable in its incompletion." Every decision to include will itself have to draw boundaries ("starting when? . . . starting at what age? . . . which ones and on what lands?"), and so no movement of the extension of rights is itself free from exclusion. And one cannot succeed in profiting from the inevitability of exclusion by sorting between the good and bad others, admitting the first and excluding the second, since certainty in any such classification is denied by the logic of autoimmunity. Attacks may come equally from within as from without, and so the ability to distinguish friend from enemy is always in question. All of which is to say that the perfectibility of democracy cannot be affirmed as wholly positive. With its source in the autoimmune, this ability of democracy to improve itself through self-critique is at the same time an ability to undermine itself as well. The chance in democracy is inseparable from the risk.

Further perspective on this ambivalence is gained by reflecting on Derrida's occasional invocations in this context of a word mentioned above in my discussion of the promise, khōra. Khōra is used by Plato in *Timaeus* for the "matrix" or "womb" in which the Forms are given their shape. It is thus beyond the Forms, a figure beyond being, and for this reason any translation of this word is inadequate. Derrida's own interpretation—his own inheritance—of *Timaeus* "had named *khōra* (which means *locality* in general, spacing, interval) another place without age, another 'taking place,'" and he suggests that "democracy to come would be like the khōra of the political" (*R*, xiv, 82/*V*, 14, 120).

What are the consequences of this connection? One can better see its implications by looking at the role that khōra plays in Derrida's other writings. Predominantly, Derrida uses khōra as an alternative to the Platonic Good. The latter too is beyond being (*epekeina tēs ousias*) as Plato famously states in *Republic*, but it lies above, at the summit, as the highest unity in relation to which all of the Forms take their orientation. Further, the Good provides the guiding principle for the construction of Plato's ideal political community. Politics in the Platonic tradition is thus founded on the Good, and it is the model for most subsequent political theologies. This also explains why Plato condemns democracy, since this is a type of government that is foreign to the Forms and the Good. Derrida's reading of khōra is notable as an attempt to uncover an alternative way of thinking politics at the origin of the Platonic tradition. It is an inheritance, otherwise, of this tradition. In contrast to the unity provided by the Good, a unity that passes to the political community, "khōra *never presents itself as such. It is neither Being, nor the Good, nor God, nor Man, nor History. It will always resist them, will always have been . . . the very place of an infinite resistance, of an infinitely impassible persistence <restance>: an utterly faceless other*" (FK, 58–59/FS, 35). Khōra is yet another figure in the Derridean lexicon for a resistance to presence.

Derrida thus proposes putting khōra in the place of the Good, but he does not thereby wish to *found* a new politics on this base. In khōra's emptiness the logic of founding is contested—"no ethics, no politics, and no law can be, as it were, deduced from this thought. To be sure, nothing can be *done [faire]* with it. And so one would have nothing to do with it." No rules or guidelines for action follow from a thinking of khōra. However, continuing, Derrida asks, "But should we then conclude that this thought leaves no trace on what is to be done—for example in the politics, the ethics, or the law to come?" (*R*, xv/*V*, 14–15) With this he suggests that there is a trace here to be thought, an effect that is not a relation of founding and founded, but an effect nonetheless. This is precisely the kind of effect he sees occurring with the invocation of democracy to come. As "the khōra of the political" democracy to come is not a model for a regime, a structure from which one can deduce an ethics, politics, and law. Rather, it is an unstable site that resists mastery, both in its meaning and in any attempt to assign it absolute value. Democracy remains both a chance and a threat, offering no assurance that what comes from it will be good.

The fundamental ambivalence in democracy's perfectibility raises questions about the normative status of Derrida's claims, something I explore in the following chapter. But for now I wish to stay on the path I have been following concerning Derrida's understanding of democracy to come. At the beginning of this chapter I argued that Derrida's description of democracy to come as the inheritance of a promise suggests that it is aporetic, involves an essential dimension of nonknowledge, is unstable in its name, and promises both a chance and a threat. The dimension of nonknowledge in democracy follows from its absence of fixed form, and autoimmunity implies the coexistence of both chance and threat. Two of the characteristics of a promise have thus been demonstrated. What of the other two? As might be expected, democracy on Derrida's understanding can indeed be called aporetic in a number of ways. First, autoimmunity can be articulated in terms of aporetic structures. This is evident in my discussion above of the role played by hospitality in the examples of Algeria and September 11, as well as in democracy's openness to self-critique and its universalizability. Autoimmunity is aporetic because it is precisely engaged in the tension between conditional limits and the unconditional, between the need to calculate those who belong within and the incalculability of an openness to all. Further, throughout "The Reason of the Strongest" Derrida speaks just as much of aporias as of the autoimmune process, and he notes that he could inscribe the category of the autoimmune into the series of both older and more recent discourses on the *double bind* and the aporia. Although *aporia*, *double bind*, and *autoimmune process* are not exactly synonyms, what they have in common, what they are all, precisely, charged with, is, more than an internal contradiction, an indecidability, that is, an internal-external, nondialectizable antinomy that risks paralyzing and thus calls for the event of the interruptive decision. (*R*, 35/*V*, 59–60)

Although he does not make a strict identification, and cannot because of the difficulties I discussed in Chapter 1 of naming such structures, Derrida does here acknowledge the close relationship between autoimmunity and aporias.

The substitutability of these terms is in play in a second aporia at work in Derrida's analysis of democracy, that found in his treatment of the tension between freedom and equality. Reading Jean-Luc Nancy's *The Experience of Freedom*, Derrida evokes one of the central problems of political philosophy, namely

the persistence, the ineluctable return, in truth, of a sort of aporia or, if you prefer, of an antinomy at the heart of every -nomy, that is, at the source of every autoimmune process. This antinomy at the heart of the democratic has long been recognized. It is classical and canonical; it is the one between freedom and equality—that constitutive and diabolical couple of democracy. I would translate this into my own language by saying that equality tends to introduce measure and calculation (and thus conditionality) whereas freedom is by essence unconditional, indivisible, heterogeneous to calculation and measure. (*R*, 47–48/*V*, 74)

Freedom and equality are here transposed into the familiar Derridean language of conditionality and unconditionality (which, just as with the promise, he aligns with the couple calculable/incalculable), suggesting that this classic problem of democratic theory arises in the attempt to reconcile these two heterogeneous demands. Equality is thus presented as the measure or leveling down of an immeasurable freedom. Now Derrida, through his reading of Nancy, immediately complicates this schema, arguing that the same aporia is in fact at work within equality. I will leave aside the details of this argument, since it is not my direct concern. What is important to note is that Derrida argues for the aporetic status of democracy via a claim of the aporetic status of freedom and equality.[24]

In addition to the autoimmune and the relation between freedom and equality, "The Reason of the Strongest" contains a third ascription of aporia to democracy, one that occurs in a characteristic moment of Derridean hyperbole. Speaking of his use of "to come" in conjunction with democracy, Derrida writes:

The "to come" not only points to the promise but suggests that democracy will never exist, in the sense of a present existence: not because it will be deferred but because it will always remain aporetic in its structure (force *without* force, incalculable singularity *and* calculable equality, commensurability *and* incommensurability, heteronomy *and* autonomy, indivisible sovereignty *and* divisible or shared sovereignty,

an empty name, a despairing messianicity or a messianicity in despair, and so on).
(*R*, 86/*V*, 126)

The couples mentioned here in parentheses mark some, but not even all, of the aporias that Derrida claims can be found in democracy.

Thus on Derrida's understanding democracy is aporetic, and in this respect it conforms to his characterization of a promise. There is now one final point to examine on the list of traits carried by promises as articulated in "Avances," namely the instability of the name. This last feature follows rather straightforwardly from the instability in the concept of democracy, something I have already investigated at some length. As aporetic and autoimmune, the concept of democracy remains unmasterable, resistant to any attempt to fully determine its meaning. Indeed, part of the movement of auto-immunity is directed against this meaning itself, hollowing it out to the point where there seems very little content left except for a hospitality to others and to its own transformation. This then raises the question of what justifies labeling this structure "democracy" at all. Why give it this name and not another? There is no fully satisfactory answer to this question, for Derrida could have called it something else, as he acknowledged in an interview in 1989.

> Perhaps the term *democracy* is not a good term. For now it's the best term I've found. But, for example, one day I gave a lecture at Johns Hopkins on these things and a student said to me, "What you call democracy is what Hannah Arendt calls republic in order to place it in opposition to democracy." Why not? I am only employing the term *democracy* in a sentence or a discourse that determines certain things. I think that in the discursive context that dominates politics today, the choice of the term that appears in the majority of sentences in this discourse is a good choice—it's the least lousy possible. As a term, however, that's not sacred. I can, some day or another, say, "No, it's not the right term. The situation allows or demands that we use another term in other sentences." For now, it's the best term for me. And choosing this term is obviously a political choice. It's a political action.[25]

Derrida states that there is nothing necessary about the invocation of democracy in his work, which is to say that he chooses to use this name, a choice justified through appeal to strategic political value. Thus, even while he concedes that perhaps "republic" might be a better name in another context, as well as reserving the right to leave "democracy" behind, he believes that the name "democracy" resonates in a particularly useful way with the dominant political discourse of his day.[26] As mentioned above, democracy is the name to which virtually every existing political regime appeals. Carrying such force in present discourse, Derrida's attempt to transform what is heard in the word (the resonance of "to come") is an intervention into the heart of politics today.

The justification for choosing democracy thus lies in a diagnosis of the present state of political affairs and in the judgment that this name remains of strategic use for an intervention into this state. In this way Derrida's appeal to the name of democracy evokes both the present and the future—the present of today, and the future of tomorrow toward that which his intervention would bring about. This particular temporal emphasis is reinforced in remarks immediately following those cited above. Responding to Michael Sprinker's question, "Would you object to calling what you have been referring to as *democracy to come* what in the Marxist lexicon would be called *the classless society*?" Derrida states, "Why not, if the concept of class is totally reconstituted, noting the reservations I formulated a while ago with regard to the concept of class? What's important in 'democracy to come' is not 'democracy,' but 'to come.' That is, a thinking of the event, of what comes."[27] In discounting the term "democracy" Derrida discounts the dimension of the past, for it is the past that is evoked in the invocation of this name. "To come" stands open in the present toward an unknown future, while "democracy" brings with it a whole history of meaning. Saying that the former is what matters is thus to elide the force of this history.

However, to my mind Derrida's response to this question is incorrect, for in it he denies the strategic importance of "democracy" that he had just affirmed. The substitution of "the classless society" for "democracy to come" would be a different intervention into the politics of today, for these terms resonate in different ways. In other words, it is not only the present and the future that are in play in Derrida's appeal to "democracy to come," but equally the past—more precisely the past containing the many connotations of "democracy," the multiple, contradictory, indeed aporetic meanings that echo from the past into the present when this term is invoked. Which is to say that "democracy" is not just a name, but an inherited name. It is not a simply a promise, but, as I have discussed, "the inheritance of a promise." Thus the strategic value of speaking of a "democracy to come" lies not just in the future of the "to come," that promise of an open future that is evoked in democracy's hospitality. Equally, "democracy" offers resources for strategic interventions in the present because of what lies in its past, and in the relation to this past which is a relation of inheritance. It is to this relation that I now turn.

Democracy as Inheritance

Much of what I want to say concerning the relation between democracy and inheritance has been asserted implicitly throughout this chapter. First, it should be apparent that democracy qualifies as a legacy on Derrida's understanding of inheritance. Recall that in *Specters of Marx* Derrida speaks of "the radical and necessary *heterogeneity* of an inheritance, the difference without opposition that has to mark it" (*SOM*, 16/ *SDM*, 40). I interpreted this statement to mean that for Derrida legacies are always aporetic, and I have just shown at some length how democracy is aporetic in its structure. Democracy is thus a legacy in this respect. Relatedly, another characteristic of legacies is their spatiotemporal structure, which conformed to the logic of spacing. Here, too, democracy qualifies. This can be seen first in the link noted above between democracy and the action of the renvoi, via Derrida's theorization of autoimmunity: "The figure of the renvoi belongs to the schema of space and time, to what I had thematized with such insistence long ago under the name *spacing* as the becoming-space of time and the becoming-time of space" (*R*, 35/*V*, 60). That is, the resending operating in democracy's autoimmunity follows a logic of spacing, and it is this logic that Derrida ultimately inscribes on democracy in order to mark its fundamental lack of identity and self-coincidence. Second, spacing can also be found at work in democracy in the particular pattern of alternation between past and future that I highlighted in the last chapter under the description of a "time out of joint." Thus Derrida writes that democracy "is what it is only by spacing itself beyond being and even beyond ontological differ-ence; it is (without being) equal and proper to itself only insofar as it is inadequate and improper, at the same time behind and ahead of itself" (*R*, 38/*V*, 63).[28] Here again is the intertwining of space and time which results in a certain disorientation whereby democracy cannot be seen to lie fully behind or fully ahead of any present moment.

Thus according to Derrida's analysis, democracy exhibits two of the central char-acteristics of a legacy—it has an aporetic structure and follows the spatiotemporal logic of spacing. As a consequence, democracy is able to be inherited, on Derrida's under-standing of the word. Now this is perhaps an uninteresting claim to make, even given the particular characteristics Derrida theorizes inheritance to have. I argued in the last chapter that every aporetic concept is inherited, and "democracy" would thus just be one more name in the long list of aporias that Derrida has examined across his career. However, this is not all that can be said on the matter, and a stronger claim concerning democracy and inheritance can be uncovered in Derrida's work. It is implicit in a pas-sage cited above from "The Reason of the Strongest" concerning democracy's perfect-ibility, which I here repeat.

> The expression "democracy to come" takes into account the absolute and intrinsic historicity of the only system that welcomes in itself, in its very concept, that expres-sion of autoimmunity called the right to self-critique and perfectibility. Democracy is the only system, the only constitutional paradigm, in which, in principle, one has or assumes the right to criticize everything publicly, including the idea of democ-racy, its concept, its history, and its name. Including the idea of the constitutional paradigm and the absolute authority of law. It is thus the only paradigm that is uni-versalizable, whence its chance and its fragility. (*R*, 86–87/*V*, 126–27)

I have already discussed the link made in this passage between autoimmunity and the right to self-critique and perfectibility. Self-critique can be viewed as part of the autoimmune process, as democracy attacking a part of itself in order to live on, which tempers the positive value evoked by the ascription of perfectibility. Here I want to focus on the implications of Derrida's claim that democracy is the *only* system or con-stitutional paradigm to act in this way. In asserting this, Derrida is identifying the right to self-critique as a characteristic essential to democracy, and to nothing else. But what is it for democracy to critique itself? In linking it to democracy's "intrinsic his-toricity," the right to criticize "its concept, its history, and its name," Derrida suggests that self-critique lies in democracy's relation to its past. It is thus a very short step to identify this relation as a relation of inheritance. The action of self-critique in democracy would thereby be an action of inheritance, that sorting through the multiple and contradictory strands of past meaning that inhabit any present understanding. And insofar as self-critique is identified as essential to democracy, the same must be said of inheritance. Inheritance is thus required by democracy, and by no other political system. In this way Derrida not only theorizes the inheritance of democracy, something shared with so many other words and concepts. His writings also contain the seeds of an account of *democracy as inheritance*.

What does this mean, to see democracy as inheritance? It first of all grants inheritance the status of being a democratic action. Inheriting is presented as something essential to democracy; indeed, given the poverty of the meaning of democracy on Derrida's understanding, it may be one of the only such things. According to Derrida's analysis, democracy possesses very few characteristics other than an openness to critique and transformation through an engagement with its past. Every negotiation with the aporias mentioned above that constitute the meaning of democracy can be inscribed within this scheme. To engage with the dual imperatives of freedom and equality, for example, is to do so with the inherited practices and meanings associated with these concepts.

However, given what I argued in Chapter 2, this identification of inheritance with democratic action may well give one pause. Recall that for Derrida inheritance is necessary. He states in *Specters of Marx* that "the *being* of what we are *is* first of all inheritance, whether we like it or know it or not" (*SOM*, 54/*SDM*, 94), and in *For What Tomorrow* that "what characterizes inheritance is first of all that one does not choose it; it is what violently elects us" (*FW*, 3/*DQ*, 15–16). Having no choice but to inherit, where inheritance is a democratic action, one would thus seem to be automatically democratic in one's very being—a claim that cannot be correct, or, if it were, is too strong to be of any use. But I also argued in Chapter 2 that not every aspect of inheritance is a necessity. There is a space for choice, namely in the way an heir chooses to respond to the necessity of inheritance, in the particular sorting and filtering one undertakes when elected by a legacy. In this space emerged Derrida's own suggestion for how to inherit, which was the promotion of the most living aspect of a legacy, that part of it most open to change and transformation. Further, examining Derrida's own practice of inheritance, I argued that this involved a raising of the stakes (*surenchère*) of the irresolvable tensions in a legacy, an exposure of its aporetic structure. In this way Derrida's writings on inheritance articulate not just the necessary aspects of this unavoidable situation, but a normative schema outlining how he thinks an heir should act in the face of such necessity.

Including this normative dimension allows one to better understand what might be meant by democracy as inheritance. It legitimates the "short step" mentioned above needed to identify inheritance with the right to self-critique, for although Derrida sees a central feature of democracy in this right, it is not the case that every self-critique automatically qualifies as democratic. In other words, not every act of inheritance will be a democratic act. But among those acts that do qualify would be ones following the normative dimension of Derridean inheritance. This would be to up the ante on the aporetic tensions in the legacies of democracy, thereby opening them up to further change and transformation. And this is precisely what Derrida does in his own inheritance of democracy. This has already been shown in my reading of "The Reason of the Strongest," where Derrida strives to expose the aporetic structures of what had been previously covered over. But it is also apparent in the processes of filtering and selection that Derrida applies more generally to the history of democratic thought. As Matthias Fritsch notes, Derrida does not simply embrace any and all aspects of the democratic tradition but remains selective in what he chooses to promote. "It seems undeniable that Derrida's reformulation of democracy does not affirm just any form of political organization, and not even just any strains and interpretations of democratic heritage. For example, Derrida's democracy to come appears much less defined by popular sovereignty, equality, and majority rule—although Derrida recognizes their importance—than by free speech, openness to criticism and otherness, and hospitality to singularity."[29] Each of the elements that Fritsch rightly identifies as being central to Derrida's understanding of democracy involves an opening up to further change through the identification of an aporia. Free speech involves a right to say anything at all, which is at the same time impossible, since there are always limitations on what can be said in any given context. If one holds oneself open to criticizing everything, even the possibility of criticism itself, this also means that not everything can be criticized at once. And hospitality to singularity is always caught between a responsibility to the unique and to the general. The themes that Derrida consistently chooses from the democratic tradition are thus implicated in the structure of aporia I have emphasized throughout. In his negotiations with these aporias, Derrida always aims to maintain their tension, in contrast to the responses of those he reads who aim to resolve the tension in favor of one arm or the other.

The identification of democracy with inheritance is thus not as broad as it might first seem, since not all actions of inheritance would qualify as democratic. But I am suggesting that the more specific sense of inheritance that Derrida endorses—covering not just its necessary elements, but those he counsels that an heir should choose—does fit the bill, since it involves an increase in the openness to transformation that he sees as central to democracy. This being the case, one can make sense of one of Derrida's more extravagant claims concerning democracy. As I noted in the last chapter, this expanded sense of inheritance can be taken as a definition of deconstruction, as suggested by Derrida himself when he states, "This is one of the possible definitions of deconstruction—as inheritance."[30] Coupling this statement with my claim of reading democracy as inheritance, one can thus justify Derrida's statement in *Politics of Friendship* that "one keeps this indefinite right to the question, to criticism, to deconstruction (guaranteed rights, in principle, in any democracy: no deconstruction without democracy, no democracy without deconstruction)" (*PF*, 105/*PA*, 128). Democracy and deconstruction are brought together precisely through their common link to inheritance.[31]

My description of democracy as inheritance is thus restricted by the specific understanding of the latter here in play. Nonetheless, it is still the case that this formulation remains open to expansion because of the indetermination in Derrida's understanding of democracy. In the key passage from "The Reason of the Strongest" cited above Derrida maintains his avoidance of identifying democracy as a particular "regime," speaking instead of its being a "system" and a "paradigm." This is a part of his inheritance of the Platonic view that democracy has no single Form, such that it is seen to be able to give rise to many political configurations. As a consequence, the exclusivity to democracy of the action of inheritance does not rule out the possibility that political regimes that are not thus named might also share in this trait. Rather, insofar as they do inherit, then they can be labeled "democratic" in this respect. In other words, a regime would be democratic to the extent that it inherits from its past, critiquing and transforming itself through a certain engagement with its own history. This would allow the use of alternative terms, as is suggested in my earlier citation of the 1989 interview "Politics and Friendship" where Derrida acknowledges the possibility of speaking not of democracy but of "republic" or "classless society," provided they conform to this requirement and are seen to be strategically superior.

At the same time, however, this possibility of describing as democratic those regimes not initially sharing in this name is not without limit. In particular, there are certain other political systems or ideologies against which Derrida consistently opposes "democracy to come." For example, in "Politics and Friendship," immediately after the remarks I cited, Derrida claims that

> nondemocratic systems are above all systems that *close* and *close themselves off* from this coming of the other. They are systems of homogenization and of integral calculation. In the end and beyond all the classical critique of fascist, Nazi, and totalitarian violence in general, one can say that these are systems that close the "to come" and that close themselves into the presentation of the presentable.[32]

Similarly, in the later interview "Autoimmunity: Real and Symbolic Suicides," Derrida opposes a certain kind of fundamentalist Islamic terrorism by stating:

> What appears to me unacceptable in the "strategy" . . . of the "bin Laden effect" is not only the cruelty, the disregard for human life, the disrespect for law, for women, the use of what is worst in technocapitalist modernity for the purposes of religious fanaticism. No, it is, above all, the fact that such actions and such discourse *open onto no future and, in my view, have no future.* . . . Nothing of what has been so laboriously secularized in the forms of the "political," of "democracy," of "international law," and even in the nontheological form of sovereignty . . . none of this seems to have any place whatsoever in the discourse "bin Laden." That is why, in this

unleashing of violence without name, if I had to take one of the two sides and choose in a binary situation, well, I would.[33]

Both of these passages suggest a separation of terms, between a democracy that would open out onto some kind of future, and a totalitarianism and fundamentalism that cannot be thus characterized.

Now the justification that Derrida gives in these passages for his siding with democracy against certain other regimes is on the face of it inadequate. This is because it is incorrect, for reasons that Derrida himself provides, to claim that the latter "close the 'to come,'" "open onto no future," or "have no future," understood literally. At the most general level, Derrida's entire oeuvre is dedicated to demonstrating the inability of any conceptual construct to instantiate full closure in the face of alterity—*différance* is at work at the heart of all concepts, undermining their own ability to be fully self-present and so closed into "the presentation of the presentable." This is a theoretical impossibility in the strictest sense. More specifically, Derrida's own analysis in "The Reason of the Strongest" and in "Autoimmunity" shows why one cannot so easily distinguish democracy or democracy to come, on the one hand, from fascism, totalitarianism, or religious fundamentalism, on the other. As highlighted in my account of the logic of autoimmunity, Derrida focuses on two distinct phenomena, the coming into power of nondemocratic governments through democratic elections and the attacks of September 11. Derrida writes that the first is a possibility always present in democracy: "The *alternative to* democracy can always be *represented* as a democratic *alternation*" (*R*, 31/*V*, 54), and appeals to the coming into power precisely of Islamic fundamentalist, fascist, and totalitarian regimes as examples of this. This inscribes these supposed "others" as possibilities arising out of democracy, owing to the work of the autoimmune. Similarly, Derrida points out that those who attacked the World Trade Center were in many ways the products of U.S. training and support. Again, this is to argue that democracy's supposed opposite, here those who would be grouped under the "bin Laden effect," arise as a possibility from within democracy itself.

These analyses undermine the distinction Derrida makes between democracy and its others according to a simple opposition of openness or closure to the future. All regimes and political systems are necessarily open, and Derrida's own work shows how such clean lines of separation cannot be maintained. Derrida is thus wrong to claim that these other positions—those of totalitarianism and fundamentalism—have no future. In their very constitution, and in their relationship to democracy or democracy to come, these supposed others share in the future. And how could it be otherwise? How could one be so sure of the future, understood as openness itself, to know that certain ideologies have no part of it? If democracy can give rise to these undesirable regimes, how can one know that the reverse cannot take place?

However, one can retain something of the distinction Derrida here desires by reading these statements with the interpretation of the "to come" that I have proposed. To do so one would have to show that within these other regimes there is an absence of a deconstructive engagement with the past, where aporetic tensions are denied or covered over. Demonstrating this is not my present concern, although I think it would not be too difficult to do. For example, in his famous essay "The Question of Democracy," which perhaps had no small influence on Derrida's own views, Claude Lefort writes:

> We must recognize that, so long as the democratic adventure continues, so long as the terms of the contradiction continue to be displaced, the meaning of what is coming into being remains in suspense. Democracy thus proves to be the historical society *par excellence*, a society which, in its very form, welcomes and preserves indeterminacy and which provides a remarkable contrast with totalitarianism which, because it is constructed under the slogan of creating a new man, claims to understand the law of its organization and development, and which, in the modern world, secretly designates itself as *a society without history*.[34]

Lefort here contrasts democracy with totalitarianism precisely in terms of each society's relation to its own history, and it is in this relation that the indeterminacy of democracy is to be understood. My suggestion is that something similar can be read in Derrida's contrast between democracy to come and totalitarianism (and Islamic fundamentalism), provided the "to come" is understood not as a simple openness to the future, but as a stance generated by a practice of inheritance as endorsed by Derrida beyond its necessity. Following this claim one can thus maintain an indeterminacy in the scope of what can be called democracy on Derrida's understanding, such that it could be applied to regimes traditionally called other names, with certain totalitarian and fundamentalist regimes still remaining beyond its bounds. This exclusion would not be absolute, for it could be the case that such regimes come to inherit from their past, and so take on this specific democratic characteristic. It would thus still be incorrect to say that they "have no future," if what is meant by this that they contain no possibility of opening up a "to come" in the future through an act of inheritance.

Thus politics under the sign of democracy to come is not left devoid of content, a completely open space within which anything goes. Rather, democracy to come names a kind of political action involving a very specific engagement with the past, in which the aporias of past democratic thinking are inherited through an intensification of their tensions. This shows that democracy to come is marked by the resources lying already within the democratic tradition, resources that both enable and constrain the shape that democracy might take at any given time. In this way, emphasizing inheritance counterbalances the emptiness that an obsession with the future might thereby privilege, an obsession the "to come" could be well seen to encourage. Derrida himself tends to privilege the futurity in democracy, most often through emphasizing its passive dimension, a waiting without anticipation, horizon, or projection. He does this because he wants to underline the incalculability in democracy, and so must argue against any kind of decision taken in advance that would reduce democracy to a calculation, program, or rule. And as I noted in my Introduction, while there is some acknowledgment in the secondary literature that the past has a role to play in the notion of democracy to come, it is almost always left to one side as the analysis unfolds. I hope now it is clear in what way the past is central to Derrida's theorization of democracy. In addition to invoking an openness to the future, Derrida's writings on democracy also contain the injunction to inherit, and so one is reminded that the passive dimension in democracy to come does not entail doing nothing at all. There is a lot to do, for there is a call to examine democracy's history, its historicity, to negotiate this history and all that it produces. In doing this one will not fall into the trap of denying responsibility and following a calculation or a rule, precisely because the history of democracy is a history of aporias, which can never be resolved once and for all. Clearly defined rules for action, for better or worse, are not there to be found. Democracy to come is not only to come, it is inherited to come; indeed, it is only through inheritance that it can be to come at all. As Derrida states in another context, "Axiom: no to-come without inheritance [*héritage*] and the possibility of *repeating*" (FK, 83/FS, 72).

Even with this established, however, there still remain questions concerning the Derridean position I have developed. First, one might wonder just what the status is of Derrida's normative claims, those elements of his theorization of inheritance that I have argued are not necessary, but chosen, and are at the heart of the link between inheritance and democracy. I have emphasized throughout that in promoting a vision of democracy that embraces change and transformation, Derrida at the same time must divorce it from conceptions of the good. Democracy, thus understood, remains fundamentally ambivalent in its value. This being the case, do the normative claims in Derrida's account have any legitimate support? Why should one promote democracy above anything else, given that there is no assurance that it will promote what is good? Second, even having asserted the link between democracy and inheritance, the details of how this inheritance might take place, which would justify describing it as democratic, still remain to be determined. What would an example of democratic inheritance look like, one that illustrates the position I ascribe to Derrida? It is these questions that I address in the following two chapters.

4 Questioning Normativity

I HAVE ADVANCED AN interpretation of Derrida's writings arguing that inheritance can be understood as a democratic action. Inheritance here is taken not to mean just any reception of the past, but a particular strategy of engagement in which the aporias in traditional democratic thought are exposed and amplified. This strategy is what Derrida himself promotes through the specific choices he advocates in inheritance, choices that coincide with his own practice of reading, deconstruction. One can thus see that Derrida's work contains a normative dimension—he values one way of inheriting over others, and this valuation is not necessary. Given the link I have established between inheritance and democracy, one can also make sense of Derrida's siding with democracy, as opposed to totalitarianism and Islamic fundamentalism, discussed at the end of the last chapter. Derrida can promote democracy for the reason that it is the only system that inscribes, in its concept, the particular kind of self-critique that is deconstruction.

My interpretation, however, raises a fundamental question concerning the desirability of this reason, for it is also the case that Derrida's analysis uncovers a profound ambivalence at the heart of democracy. To promote openness to change and transformation is to promote openness to the chance and the threat, the good and the bad, and these dual possibilities are irreducible. I have highlighted this ambivalence in a number of concepts: in the danger inhabiting all calls for hospitality, in the uncertainty of the link between deconstruction and justice, and in democracy's autoimmunity. These are related, since the ambivalence of the relation between inheritance and justice, and that of autoimmunity, can be understood as manifestations of the fundamental duality of hospitality. The central point is that all attest to the detachment of inheritance and democracy from any stable conception of the good. But this being the case, why should Derrida (or anyone) value inheritance or democracy, or more precisely the inheritance *in* democracy that I have argued provides content to the phrase "democracy to come"? In its most basic understanding, to value something is to see it as desirable, as good in some measure. Necessarily divorced from the good, democracy to come would seem to have nothing to motivate its positive valuation.

Another way to frame this question is to contrast what is going on in Derrida's writings on democracy, all of which take place in the last fifteen or so years of his life, with work early in his career. One of the dominant themes in Derrida's early work is the demonstration of a fundamental ambivalence in binary valuation as opposed to the philosophical tradition's assertion of its coherence. The difference from the later work, however, is that Derrida never at the same time places himself on the side of one term in a binary rather than another. For example, in "Plato's Pharmacy" Derrida famously discusses Plato's distribution of values in *Phaedrus*, where Socrates elevates speech as good and denigrates writing as bad. Socrates' judgment is based on a whole system of related values privileging a number of terms, including the father, the origin, truth, life, and philosophy over their opposites the son, the copy, falsehood, death, and sophistry. Plato places speech in the first list, and writing in the second. Derrida's deconstruction of the Platonic text does not proceed by arguing that writing is good and speech bad. Rather, he first seizes on and amplifies the fundamental ambivalence carried by "*pharmakon*," a term meaning both poison and cure that Plato uses to describe writing. Underlining this ambivalence shifts the value of writing from being bad to being both good and bad. Then, showing how speech also exhibits the characteristics of the *pharmakon*, Derrida shows how it too shares in this ambivalence. So by the end of Derrida's text both speech and writing are *pharmaka*, each governed by a generalized structure of writing. In all of this, at no time does Derrida side with the *pharmakon* against the Platonic Good, in the way he endorses democracy to come.[1] At best the *pharmakon* is valued as having descriptive merit—it better describes what is really at work in speech and writing than does the traditional Platonic theory of the Forms.

From my analysis in the last chapter, one sees that Derrida does not make such a claim concerning democracy to come. He could have done so by arguing that democracy has the merit of highlighting an openness to the future that all political structures share, and so value it as descriptively superior. But instead Derrida goes further by choosing to promote a particular kind of inheritance of aporias, raising the stakes of their tension in an effort to open them up to greater change and transformation, and he suggests that this action is democratic. In this way Derrida implies that democracy is desirable for reasons more than mere descriptive accuracy. But can such a move be justified? What supports Derrida's taking such a step beyond the point of neutrality with respect to this particular normative dimension? In this chapter I aim to provide an answer to this question. I will do so by examining the opposing answers given to it that emerge out of the recent work of two commentators, Martin Hägglund and Leonard Lawlor. Through arguing that neither Hägglund's nor Lawlor's account is satisfactory, I will advance my own proposal for dealing with this issue, which lies in a space between these two positions.

The Challenge to Value

In *Radical Atheism: Derrida and the Time of Life*, Martin Hägglund provides a comprehensive interpretation of Derrida's work that challenges any attempt to justify normative claims on its basis. Hägglund's analysis is wide-ranging, examining a host of different concepts through in-depth engagements with thinkers whom Derrida reads (primarily Kant, Husserl, and Levinas) and who read him in turn (including Simon Critchley, John Caputo, and Ernesto Laclau). Since my own concerns do not coincide with the broad scope of Hägglund work, I will focus on the central theoretical structure underlying his argument and its application to the concept most relevant to my analysis, democracy to come.

Hägglund's argument against deriving normative claims from deconstructive analysis is rooted in a distinction he draws between one set of terms I have been using, "the chance and the threat," from another that also appears in Derrida's writings, "the best and the worst." Hägglund defines these terms through a reference to spacing—the fundamental structure naming the essential relation of spatial and temporal presence to alterity which I invoked in Chapters 2 and 3. Time, Hägglund asserts, is conditioned by spacing, which means that everything in time finds itself in an essential relation to alterity. Further, Hägglund argues that it is only because of this fact that anything can happen at all, since all events are constituted by the coming of something other to an entity. Without alterity, things simply remain the same, and nothing happens.

The focus of *Radical Atheism* is on life, and one of Hägglund's core claims is that all life is mortal. Being temporal, life is conditioned by spacing, and so living necessarily entails an openness to alterity. This openness to alterity is in turn an openness to a future that is essentially unpredictable, meaning that everything that is living is open to the possibility that its life will come to an end. It is here that Hägglund inscribes the chance and the threat. The openness to alterity that constitutes mortal life can be said to offer a chance for entities—they are given the chance to survive, to live on. But at the very same time there is here a threat, namely the threat that entities will not live on, but end, since this is always one of the possibilities that may come in an open future. The chance of survival and the threat of its end are thus necessary possibilities that arise in mortal life. Or, in Hägglund's words, "*The chance is the threat* since the chance is always a chance of mortal life that is intrinsically threatened by death."[2] For further precision, it is worth clarifying the meaning of the "*is*" in this claim. I would suggest that it should not be taken to refer to an identity in which these terms are asserted to be exactly the same thing. Rather, they are two different possibilities—the chance of living on, and the threat of dying—that necessarily arise together because of their source in spacing.[3] An alternative expression of this could thus be "the chance carries the threat" (or equally, "the threat carries the chance").

Turning now to the other couple, "the best and the worst," one sees a different relation. Hägglund's definition of the worst is to be understood with reference to the previous distinction, for he states that the argument concerning the chance and the threat "presupposes that being is essentially temporal (to be = to happen) and that it is inherently valuable that something happens (the worst = that nothing happens)."[4] Now I do not endorse the assertion here that it is *inherently* valuable that something happens, for, as I will argue later in this chapter, all values are contestable. Indeed, Hägglund would seem to agree with this, claiming later in the text that it is "a part of deconstructive reason to recognize that no value has an inherent value, and that any value can be used for better or for worse."[5] In any case, if "to be = to happen" then it is plausible to assert that to have nothing happen and so an absence of being is the worst of all possible states. The worst is thus the realization of the threat of the end carried in the structure of mortal life, where this end is understood as the cessation of an entity's being. What then of "the best"? This refers to what is traditionally seen as the most desirable thing, namely an existence free from all threat. Such an existence is placed in "the ideal realm of eternity . . . explicitly posited as the immutable and the inviolable."[6] If mortal life necessarily carries the threat of the worst, then it is only beyond mortality, beyond time as spacing, that the threat could be annulled. Traditionally, therefore, the best *is opposed to* the worst, since it is that which keeps the worst at bay. However, Hägglund highlights Derrida's crucial move, which is to argue that thus conceived, far from preventing it from happening, the best *is identical to* the worst. In an immutable eternity nothing happens, which is precisely the definition of the worst. Ending all possibility of threat, eternity simultaneously ends all possibility of chance and thus ends all possibility of life. As Hägglund writes, "*The best is the worst* since the best can never become better or worse and thus abolishes the chance and threat of mortal life."[7] In contrast to Hägglund's similar statement on the chance and the threat cited above, here the "*is*" should be understood as marking an identity. Hägglund claims that for Derrida the best and the worst are exactly the same state.

One result of Hägglund's interpretation is that the four initial terms—chance, threat, best, and worst—now reduce to three. The chance and the threat remain distinct, even as they necessarily arise together, but the best is nothing other than the worst. These definitions ground Hägglund's diagnosis of the challenge Derrida's work poses to the justification of normative claims. The positive ideal of the best, that which stands at the summit of what is desired, has been shown to be the most undesirable thing, the worst. This is not for merely empirical or contingent reasons, but because the supposed ideal is identical to that which it is assumed to oppose. The best thus cannot operate as an ideal toward which one ought to strive, since this would be precisely to strive for the worst. In addition, since the structure of spacing demonstrates that every chance is necessarily accompanied by a threat, deconstructive analysis (which for Hägglund is focused on articulating the structure of spacing) cannot give any reasons for privileging certain actions over others. The chance and the threat are always co-implicated, with spacing entailing that the one never comes without the possibility of the other. Thus, against those who would appeal to openness to inscribe a normative dimension into deconstruction, Hägglund asserts:

> The openness to the future is unconditional in the sense that *everything* (including every system and action) necessarily is open to the future, but it is not unconditional in the sense of a normative ideal. The mistake is thus to assume that one can derive a normative affirmation of the future from the unconditional "yes" to the coming of the future. . . . My argument is, on the contrary, that there is no such intrinsic normativity in deconstruction. Despite occasional inconsistencies, Derrida himself underscores that no norms or rules can be derived from the constitutive condition of undecidablility. In every system there is openness to the future, but there is no guarantee that it is better to be *more* open rather than *less* open to the future.[8]

Thus on Hägglund's reading, deconstruction undermines any determined normativity that might be given on its basis. The logic of deconstruction is undecidable with respect to value, and one cannot derive any particular course of action or structure from this logic.

Of direct relevance to my concerns, Hägglund carries this undecidability in value over to his reading of Derrida on democracy.

> There is no given concept, constitution, or regime of democracy, which means that a commitment to "democracy" cannot be justified in itself. To look for such justification in Derrida's work is to misunderstand the level on which his analyses operate. Derrida does not offer solutions to political problems or normative guidelines for how to approach them. On the contrary, he argues that solutions and norms cannot be justified once and for all, since they are instituted in relation to the undecidable coming of time that precedes and exceeds them.[9]

Although the focus of this passage is restricted to democracy, its claim is in one sense stronger than that made in the last passage that I cited. Here Hägglund asserts that Derrida demonstrates how democracy is subject to the undecidability contained in the structure of spacing, and this deprives democracy from operating as a positive ideal whose realization would bring about good results. On Hägglund's reading, Derrida thus shows why there can be no final justification given for an endorsement of democracy, whether the logic one uses to do so is deconstructive or not. Further, Hägglund asserts that to think Derrida does offer a justification "in itself" for democracy is to "misunderstand the level on which his analyses operate." Presumably this means that insofar as Derrida is committed to uncovering and highlighting the structure of spacing, he is not interested in the project of finding a final justification for endorsing democracy as desirable.

This is not to say, however, that Hägglund thinks there can be no justification whatsoever for democracy. Immediately following the passage just cited he lets justification back in, stating: "Far from absolving use from politics, it is the undecidable coming of time that makes politics necessary in the first place, since it precipitates the negotiation of unpredictable events. The undecidable coming of time makes it *possible* to justify decisions but at the same time makes it *impossible* for any justification to be final or sheltered from critique."[10] In speaking thus, Hägglund suggests that justification in the realm of politics is possible, if only ever provisionally. But it is unclear in Hägglund's account in what such justification would consist. Further, Hägglund goes on to specify one such way in which he thinks Derrida legitimately endorses democracy, a way that presumably can be given provisional justification.

> If Derrida privileges the concept of democracy, it is not because he thinks it can guarantee a good or just society but because the concept of democracy more evidently than other concepts takes into account the undecidable future. Strictly speaking, one cannot posit an absolute democracy even as a theoretical fiction. The very concept of democracy inscribes the relentless coming of other circumstances that one will have to negotiate.[11]

Hägglund here describes Derrida's privileging of democracy on the basis of what I called at the beginning of this chapter "descriptive merit"—democracy is to be preferred because it makes explicit the undecidability that inhabits all political concepts. It is not that democracy is more desirable as an idea with which one could order society, it is just that it does a better job of describing the alterity to which all political systems are subject. And it is worth noting that when Hägglund reiterates this claim of descriptive merit, he references the very same passage I cited in Chapter 3 to support my interpretation of the role of inheritance in democracy. This is the passage from "The Reason of the Strongest" concerning democracy's uniqueness with respect to its "absolute and intrinsic historicity . . . the right to self-critique and perfectibility" (*R*, 86–87/ *V*, 126–27). Hägglund takes this characterization of democracy to mean that "more forcefully than any other political concept, democracy brings out the autoimmunity that is the condition for life in general. . . . The concept of democracy testifies to an 'absolute and intrinsic historicity' where nothing is immune from its own destructibility."[12] Again the claim is only that democracy does a better job of illustrating what is the case for everything, democratic or not.

Piecing all of this together, a partial view of the position of normativity in Derrida's writings emerges. Hägglund is clear that no determinate norms or rules can be grounded in openness, since this is inherently undecidable when it comes to value. He also argues that Derrida's work shows why any final justification for political solutions and norms is impossible, whether grounded in deconstructive thinking or not. Finally, he highlights one way in which he thinks Derrida can legitimately endorse democracy, which is based on its superiority in terms of describing the constitutive exposure to the future that underlies all political systems.

However, I describe this view as "partial" since certain questions remain unanswered. First, it is unclear in what provisional justification would consist, such that it is not similarly subject to deconstruction's critique. Addressing this question is especially pressing since Hägglund claims that "the spacing of time is the condition not only for everything that can be cognized and experienced, but also for everything that can be thought and desired."[13] If this is the case, why doesn't the undecidability entailed by spacing automatically undermine all justifications for norms that can be thought, whether final or provisional? Second, Hägglund does not discuss whether such provisional justification can legitimately occur within a deconstructive analysis. In emphasizing undecidability as the central focus of deconstruction, he would seem to imply it cannot, even if it is the case that provisional justification is possible in some other discourse. But this issue remains open in Hägglund's account. Third, Hägglund does not state whether descriptive merit is the only justification possible for democracy. Can other justifications be given, if only ever provisionally? And combining this with the second question, can any of these justifications be considered properly a part of Derrida's deconstructive analyses?

My interpretation gives answers to some of these questions, precisely through my focus on inheritance. On my reading, in contrast to Hägglund's cited above, Derrida's remarks in "The Reason of the Strongest" on democracy's intrinsic historicity testify to the central role played by inheritance in his understanding of democracy, and it is in the relation of inheritance that I have located a normative dimension. As I argued in Chapter 2, Derrida does not inherit from others by merely describing the aporias that inhabit their work. Rather, he goes beyond description to actively amplify the tension in these aporias through the movement of *surenchère*, or upping the ante. This step beyond is a choice on Derrida's part, so it is not necessary, but I have argued that it is to be properly understood as a part of his deconstructive analysis. Further, as was seen in Chapter 3, it is in this choice that Derrida's practice of inheritance—that is to say, deconstruction—can be seen to be democratic, for it is the way that Derrida carries out the democratic injunction to self-critique. Thus, on my interpretation, deconstruction as Derrida performs it contains a normative dimension that is governed by more than an endorsement of descriptive merit, and this carries with it a particular endorsement of democracy.

The question that remains, therefore, is what legitimates this endorsement, if only ever provisionally. Why doesn't the undecidability in democracy automatically disqualify such a move? Before addressing this question directly, I will first examine an alternative interpretation justifying the presence of normativity in Derrida's work. This will allow me to analyze further the precise role played by particular normative terms in Derrida's writings. I will then return to examine Hägglund's view, in order to more fully develop and justify my own interpretation.

Against the Worst and a Lesser Violence

Across *Radical Atheism*, Hägglund uses the logic articulated above to argue against a number of influential interpretations that see an intrinsic normativity in deconstruction. In particular, he targets the Levinasian readings of Simon Critchley and Drucilla Cornell that assume Derrida's work is oriented toward an ideal of peace, and the theological interpretation of John Caputo that aligns deconstruction with a religious passion for a God who is good. These interpretations attribute the normativity in Derrida's work with reference to a positive ideal, against which Hägglund deploys the force of his argument equating the best and the worst. In this section I examine an alternative approach found in the secondary literature. This approach seeks to justify the presence of normativity in Derrida's work not through an appeal to a positive ideal that one should try to approximate—it is acknowledged that the best is necessarily compromised—but through invoking a negative ideal, the worst, that one should try to avoid, by promoting a "lesser" or "least" violence. In his *This Is Not Sufficient: An Essay on Animality and Human Nature in Derrida*, Leonard Lawlor makes such an argument.[14] As the title suggests, Lawlor's central aim in this work is to interpret and extend Derrida's reflections on animality, and is thus not directly concerned with democracy. However, in the course of his interpretation he articulates a general approach to questions of normativity and value in Derrida's writings. This, together with the role that animality plays in Derrida's political work, and the fact that many of Lawlor's claims concerning the worst are applied more broadly in his entry on Derrida in the *Stanford Encyclopedia of Philosophy*, makes it relevant to my concerns.[15] In what follows I will thus examine the general scheme Lawlor lays out, leaving aside his specific engagement with questions of the animal.

On the face of it, Lawlor would seem to agree with the statements concerning life and the worst made by Hägglund, discussed above. He speaks, for example, of a "mortalism" in Derrida's thinking, arguing that "death is in life." Further, in maintaining that the worst is to be understood as the eradication of all difference, "when the other to which one is related is completely appropriated to or completely in one's self," Lawlor claims that "in its most paradoxical formula, the worst violence would be a violence that produced something absolutely alive and absolutely dead."[16] This is to say that pure life conceived in the absence of death is in fact identical to it, and this is associated with the violence of the worst. In this way Lawlor steers clear of any appeal to a positive ideal that can be conceived free from corruption. However, unlike Hägglund, Lawlor does not argue on this basis that deconstructive analysis is normatively undecidable. Rather he maintains that the worst violence operates in *This Is Not Sufficient* as something to be avoided, something from which Derrida counsels one should do all one can to distance oneself. How is this to be done? By embracing not an ideal pure in any traditional sense, but one that is purely impure. Summing up his view in the very last lines of the book, Lawlor writes:

What is most pure in a language, in the *logos*, the pharmakon, for Derrida, is the very possibility of impurity. . . . We must be corruptible in countless ways, in all the ways possible. Being infinitely corruptible limits the worst violence with the least violence: every single other is wholly other *and* every single other corrupts us without being rejected. Every single other is received without being captured. This least violence is what is required for our today so that there might be a tomorrow.[17]

Lawlor here calls for an active amplification of impurity, linking this to "the least violence" that would act as a limitation to "the worst violence." In *This Is Not Sufficient* the way one is to do this is through pursuing a strategy of openness to alterity, as seen when Lawlor issues an invitation to "try to reverse unconditional inhospitality, the worst, into unconditional hospitality."[18] In addition, the unconditional hospitality that is here opposed to the worst is one of several terms (the others being friendship, saving, and unconditional forgiveness) which are similarly pitted against the worst through being tied to the least violence and through an association of the worst with their opposites (enmity and sacrifice).[19] Lawlor thus writes that "we can say that the least violent response is the most amiable response," that we should "not think in terms of the enemy. . . . Friendship suspends the killing, even if this suspension is violently instituted, even if the condition of friendship and peace consists in the ability to kill or be killed," and that the relation he advocates "is not a structure of sacrifice but a structure of saving by means of replacement."[20]

Considering all of these citations together, one sees that there are two logics at work in Lawlor's text. At a general level, he argues that what is required is an embrace of a logic of contamination or corruptibility. But at those precise moments in which he articulates his normative stance, he relies on a logic of opposition—unconditional inhospitality is to be reversed into unconditional hospitality, one should think the friend rather than the enemy, what is needed is saving rather than sacrifice. This second logic is at odds with the first, and, I would suggest, cannot be sustained within the Derridean framework. In the terms of Hägglund's analysis, in his normative claims Lawlor separates the chance from the threat. It is only if the least violence is free from all threat of the worst that it could be said to limit the worst violence. Similarly, it is only if unconditional hospitality carries a chance and not a threat that it could be the reverse of unconditional inhospitality or the worst. However, as I argued in Chapter 1 and as Lawlor seems also to acknowledge, unconditional hospitality, for example, cannot be thus conceived. It carries both the chance and the threat—it welcomes friend and foe—and this cannot be avoided. As a consequence, the ground for distinguishing these terms from their opposites (which is the ground of Lawlor's normative schema) falls away.[21]

Now I should note that Lawlor himself is cautious when describing the force of his normative claims. For example, one of the statements cited above is immediately qualified, with the full passage reading as follows: "Let us try to reverse unconditional inhospitality, the worst, into unconditional hospitality. Unconditional hospitality is not the best but only the less bad. Indeed, it is a kind of mirror image of the worst. By being vulnerable in the way I have described, there is no guarantee that the worst will be avoided. The recipe describes a dangerous experiment; prudence is required." Further, Lawlor continues by arguing that the terms he uses fall short of being values. "Yet hospitality and equality here do not really function as values; they are instead what I would call 'prevalues,' valuationally indeterminate."[22] But these qualifications serve only to confuse Lawlor's claims, for if they are "valuationally indeterminate," how can terms like hospitality and equality do any work at all in Lawlor's articulation of a recipe for desired action? In addition, to describe unconditional hospitality as only "less bad" than the worst is to say that it is not its "mirror image," which could be achieved through a reversal. And if it is only *less* bad, then it falls short of being the *least* violent. Not all of these statements can be true together.

This confusion in Lawlor's text can be traced to ambiguities at both ends of the value scale to which he appeals, the negative and the positive, which can in turn be seen to rest on ambiguities in Derrida's writings themselves. At the negative end, Lawlor in fact relies on two competing definitions of the worst, claiming that it is both the *actual* eradication of all difference and a *tendency* in this direction. He thus writes, on the one hand:

> The worst violence occurs—we have to wonder here if the worst is really possible or is it the impossible itself—when the other to which one is related is completely appropriated to or completely in one's self, when an address reaches its proper destination, when it reaches only its proper destination. Reaching only its proper destination, the address will exclude more, many more, and that "many more," at the limit, amounts to all. It is this complete exclusion or this extermination of the most—there is no limit to this violence—that makes this violence the worst violence. The worst is a relation that makes of more than one simply one, that makes, out of a division, an indivisible sovereignty. The worst is not the opposite of Leibniz's best possible world; it is the end of the world, no world, no future, total apocalypse.[23]

Leaving aside the question of its possibility for a moment, Lawlor here defines the worst as the state of absolute unity, where all difference disappears. The worst is thus located at the extreme end of any violence or action one might imagine, to the point where the world as such ends.

On the other hand, throughout his text Lawlor identifies the worst with a number of phenomena that fall short of this extreme state of apocalypse, even if many would agree that they are undesirable. One thus reads that "the idea of rights in general does not avoid the worst," that "the worst is, as Deleuze and Guattari say in *A Thousand Plateaus*, 'the suicidal state,' 'realized nihilism,' in a word, fascism," that "Heidegger's strategy results in the worst . . . it ends up sanctioning Nazism, or, more generally, racism," that the worst violence "consists in the attempt to eliminate the evil of the pharmakon once and for all," that "this tendency defines the worst, a tendency toward the complete appropriation of all others," and that the risks of "biological continuism and metaphysical separation . . . amount to the worst."[24] In all of these cases the worst is identified with positions that are seen to attempt to eradicate all difference, without actually achieving this goal. One may well claim that fascism, racism, and Nazism all seek to totalize and so aim for the worst (and perhaps even the ideas of rights, biological continuism, and metaphysical separation, although here I would hesitate), but none ever finally realizes this absolute state. At these moments Lawlor thus confuses the threat of the worst with the worst itself.[25] And the threat of the worst alone is not enough to establish the distinctions required, for reasons internal to his interpretation. Insofar as Lawlor maintains that the threat of the worst inhabits all positions, being a necessary possibility that always accompanies any chance, one cannot justify opposition to certain positions simply on this basis. The threat of the worst arises everywhere. These positions must be opposed, if one wishes to oppose them, for other reasons.

Acknowledging this would nonetheless seem to leave the worst intact as something to be avoided, remaining an anchor for normative injunctions. The mere threat of the worst might not be reason to avoid some positions over others, but one could still insist on avoiding the worst itself. However, here Lawlor's question of whether the worst is in fact possible becomes relevant. Is the complete eradication of all difference, the absolute end to alterity that defines the worst in Derridean thinking, an actual possibility? To answer this, I will examine what Derrida says about the worst, focusing on four of its "appearances" in his texts. I place "appearances" in scare quotes, for the worst is named as such in only two of the four texts that I discuss. But in all four cases Derrida describes a structure that conforms to what both Hägglund and Lawlor have labeled the worst, namely the complete eradication of the trace structure, without remainder. This will be somewhat of a detour from my interrogation of Lawlor's arguments, but one important in order to comprehend just what is at stake in the invocation of the worst in his interpretation of Derrida's work.

The first text to consider is Derrida's 1984 essay "No Apocalypse, Not Now: Full Speed Ahead, Seven Missiles, Seven Missives."[26] Speaking of the possibility of total nuclear war, Derrida states the following:

> Now, what the uniqueness of nuclear war, its being-for-the-first-time-and-perhaps-for-the-last-time, its absolute inventiveness gives us to think, even if it remains a decoy, a belief, a phantasmatic projection, is obviously the possibility of an irreversible destruction, leaving no traces, of the juridico-literary archive and therefore of the basis of literature and criticism. Not necessarily the destruction of humanity, of the human habitat, or even of other discourses (arts and sciences), or even indeed of poetry or the epic; these latter might reconstitute their living process and their archive, at least to the extent that the structure of this archive (that of a nonliterary memory) structurally implies reference to a real referent external to the archive itself.[27]

Derrida claims just before this passage that the singularity of literature is found in its essential constitution in a link to an objective archive. This distinguishes it from the other discourses mentioned, which can be conceived as having references other than their own material support alone. Science, for example, refers to objects in the world beyond its own record, and so as long as these objects exist, so does the possibility of its return after the eradication of this record. Now I am not so concerned with the particulars of this distinction—Derrida himself admits that what he has provisionally distinguished from literature (such as science) may in fact not have a reference beyond its own archive, and so to that extent could be said to "participate in literature." What is important is that in this discussion he speaks an event of "total and remainderless destruction of the archive," "the absolute effacement of any possible trace."[28] Understood in these terms, the worst would be the erasure of any future, achieved through the total eradication of any past archive that is in principle open to recall through the persistence of a trace. In other words, in being a destruction of the past that annuls the future, the worst would be the destruction of all possibility of inheritance. It is for this reason that Derrida argues that total nuclear war "would be waged in the name of something whose name, in this logic of total destruction, could no longer be borne, transmitted, inherited by anything living."[29]

It is also worth noting that in this context Derrida contrasts such absolute destruction, on the one hand, with the death of any single individual, on the other.

> An individual death, a destruction affecting only a part of society, tradition, or culture can always give rise to a symbolic work of mourning, with memory, compensation, internalization, idealization, displacement, and so on. In that case there is monumentalization, archivization and *work on the remainder, work of the remainder.* Similarly, my own death, so to speak, as an individual can always be anticipated phantasmatically, symbolically too, as a negativity at work—a dialectic of the work, of signature, name, heritage. Images, grief, all the resources of memory and tradition, can cushion the reality of that death, whose anticipation remains therefore interwoven with fictionality, symbolicity, or, if you prefer, literature; and this is so even if I live this anticipation in anguish, terror, despair, as a catastrophe that I have no reason not to equate with the annihilation of humanity as a whole. . . . The only absolutely real referent is thus of the scope of an absolute nuclear catastrophe that would irreversibly destroy the entire archive and all symbolic capacity, the very *survivance,* as I call it, at the heart of life.[30]

This passage claims that the death of an individual is different from the worst, for in the former a trace lives on, supported in the memories of those left behind, and in the external memory that is the material archive of that person's life. And Derrida maintains that this is the case even if it is not experienced by the individual in this way. The worst, by contrast, requires the absolute destruction of all such support, of all that surrounds life enabling it to live on.

One consequence of this qualification is that the description that one finds in Derrida's late work of each person's death as "the end of the world" should not be taken as a description of the worst.[31] Such an end to the world is not the eradication of every trace, but rather a description of the structure of interruption that constitutes the very trace structure of survival itself. I mention this because both Lawlor and Hägglund seem to ignore this distinction. Lawlor does not address it explicitly, but he could be read to suggest it in a passage cited above when he claims that "the worst is not the opposite of Leibniz's best possible world; it is the end of the world, no world, no future, total apocalypse."[32] Hägglund is more direct, for in discussing these passages from "No Apocalypse," he writes that "the hypothesis of a total nuclear holocaust reinforces the radical finitude that deconstruction articulates as the condition for life in general. As a finite being I am always living in relation to the threat of absolute destruction, since with my death the entire world that opens through me and that lives in me will be extinguished."[33] I will have more to say about Derrida's description of individual death as "the end of the world" in Chapter 6. For now, I wish simply to note that, contrary to what Lawlor and Hägglund suggest, it should not be understood as a synonym for the worst. These name different structures.

Moving on, Derrida reiterates this distinction between individual death and the worst, and develops his thinking of the worst further, a few years later in "Force of Law." At the very end of this essay Derrida speaks of "the possible complicity among these [Heideggerian and Benjaminian] discourses and the worst (here the 'final solution')" (FOL, 298/FDL, 146).[34] More thus can be learned by examining the discussion of the final solution that appears just a couple of pages earlier.

> One must try to think [the final solution] starting from the possibility of singularity, the singularity of the signature and of the name, because what the order of representation tried to exterminate was not only human lives by the millions—natural lives—but also a demand for justice, and also names: and first of all the possibility of giving, inscribing, calling, and recalling the name. Not only because there was a destruction or project of destruction of the name and the very memory of the name, of the name as memory, but also because the system of mythical violence . . . went all the way to its own limit, in a demonic fashion, on the two sides of the limit: at the same time, it kept the archive of its destruction, produced a simulacra of justificatory arguments, with a terrifying legal, bureaucratic, statist objectivity and (at the same time, therefore) it produced a system in which its logic, the logic of objectivity, made possible the invalidation and therefore effacement of testimony and responsibilities, the neutralization of the singularity of the final solution. (FOL, 296/FDL, 141–42)

Echoing the claims of "No Apocalypse," Derrida here argues that the worst goes beyond the extermination of human lives, even by the millions. Rather, what is decisive in the attribution of this description is the attempt to eradicate the trace structure of the name, preventing its giving, inscription, calling, and recollection—in other words, destroying everything that would enable a certain kind of living on through inheritance. But its means of doing so differs from the sheer or purely destructive force of a total nuclear war. The latter would simply and directly eradicate all material support that could ever carry a trace. By contrast, Derrida describes in "Force of Law" the eradication of one archive by means of the construction of another. The meticulous documenting of the process of erasure perversely serves to realize this process itself, for it replaces the traces left by those murdered with an alternative account. It is the erection of a memory that serves to radically forget, and in this way puts an end to all inheriting.

In "No Apocalypse" and "Force of Law" the worst is thus associated with two particular threats, of total nuclear war and of the final solution. However, in the third text from which I wish to cite, 1994's *Archive Fever*, the worst is taken far outside the confines of these two events, with the destruction via construction diagnosed in "Force of Law" seen to be a process at work in every archive. As with "No Apocalypse," here Derrida does not literally name the worst, speaking instead of the death drive, but what he describes mirrors its structure.

> [The death drive] is at work, but since it always operates in silence, it never leaves any archives of its own. It destroys in advance its own archive, as if that were in truth the very motivation of its most proper movement. . . .
> . . . There would indeed be no archive desire without the radical finitude, without the possibility of a forgetfulness which does not limit itself to repression. Above all, and this is the most serious, beyond or within this simple limit called finiteness or finitude, there is no archive fever without the threat of this death drive, this aggression and destruction drive. This threat is *in-finite*, it sweeps away the logic of finitude and the simple factual limits, the transcendental aesthetics, one might say, the spatio-temporal conditions of conservation.[35]

In contrast to the analyses of total nuclear war and the final solution, where the worst is presented as something caused by a force external to an archive, here Derrida describes a force of destruction at work within all archives. This force is the condition of possibility of there being a movement toward archiving in the first place, and so the "archive fever" is irreducibly dual, a desire for the archive that at the same time burns. Every archive, Derrida argues, contains both the chance of the archive's conservation and the threat of its absolute demise, at once.

This understanding of the worst is transferred to Derrida's discussion of the event in the fourth text I will mention, the second essay of *Rogues*, "The 'World' of the Enlightenment to Come," first delivered as a talk in 2002.

> For as soon as reason does not close itself off from the event that comes, the event of what or who comes, assuming it is not irrational to think that the worst can always happen, and well beyond what Kant thinks under the name "radical evil," then only the infinite possibility of the worst and of perjury can grant the possibility of the Good, of veracity and of sworn faith. This possibility remains infinite but as the very possibility of an autoimmune finitude. (*R*, 153/*V*, 211)

Derrida again describes the worst as a necessary, internal possibility, this time inhabiting autoimmune finitude, which in this text is coextensive with finitude itself.

The worst has thus moved, in this brief genealogy spanning two decades, from specific, external possibilities of the absolute destruction of the trace structure in the ideas of total nuclear war and the final solution to a necessary possibility of all finite entities conditioned by the structure of the trace, which for Derrida are all finite entities as such. Returning thus to the question with which I began, that of the worst's possibility, the answer would thus seem affirmative. Derrida explicitly claims it to be a possibility of finitude. However, I question whether Derrida is right to claim this, for beyond simply asserting it, he gives us no reason to think that the worst is indeed an internal possibility of all finite entities. To repeat, at issue is not the exposure to individual destruction that is a characteristic of every finite entity. For Derrida this is a necessary characteristic, as it follows from the necessity of the exposure to alterity that finitude entails. To be finite is to be open to an outside that is both good and bad, to that which can sustain existence as well as that which can destroy it. But in the event of this kind of destruction, a trace will always remain. Rather, what the worst names is the total eradication of all traces of an entity, without remainder. The strict elimination of every kind of living on. Could such an event take place? Is the complete and utter eradication of the trace possible? The complete eradication of *all* material support for an archive? Physical and mental, understood in the widest possible sense? The fictive example of total nuclear war comes closest to describing such a situation. But even here, assuming that this fiction is possible, one can question whether, say, the eradication of the entirety of humanity would leave *no* trace of the human past behind. One might still ask whether such a trace might be left "to the dead, to animals, to trees and rocks," as Derrida asks of democracy (*R*, 54/*V*, 82). And in the case of the final solution, it would seem that what did actually occur was not the worst in the Derridean sense. The complete replacement of the archive failed to take hold, and traces of those millions murdered continue to survive. Further, one could question whether the goal of the final solution, as an ideal, coincides with the Derridean worst, for how could traces of the destruction of the entirety of Jewish culture fail to remain in the very minds of their murderers? Even in their unconscious? Of course, much here hangs on the coherence and unity of notions such as "Jewish culture," in its entirety, but this is what the worst seems to presuppose.[36]

In suggesting that the final solution is not the worst, I am not claiming it is not as bad as one might have thought. Similarly with total nuclear war (which, bad as it is, feels to me to be less worse than the final solution). Rather, I am claiming that *there are worse things than the worst*. In other words, in the end "the worst" fails to function as a comparative term at all. Despite carrying a comparison (the "worse") in its name, it is unclear by what measure it could be compared to anything else. Its extremity is thus better understood as marking a point of absolute difference. What it names—the total eradication of the future through the complete destruction of the archive that would produce a trace—is an event altogether different from all others, from finite events that leave a trace. Events within finite limits can perhaps be judged good or bad, better or worse, although as I will argue shortly, just how we are to do this within a Derridean perspective is far from clear. But the end of finitude itself seems beyond any such scale, beyond good and evil altogether.

Now, everything I have said up to this point does not necessarily mean that the worst is not possible. This is because even if it should not be identified with total nuclear war or the final solution, the total eradication of the trace, without remainder, remains *thinkable*. But within the Derridean framework there is a difference between what is thinkable and what is possible. I propose that what is being thought under the sign of the worst would is described as an "im-possibility," in Derrida's sense. This would mean that the worst is not something governed by a notion of capability, by an "I can," or able to be brought about by a subject through her actions. An explication of im-possibility is found in "The Reason of the Strongest." Distinguishing democracy to come from a Kantian ideal, Derrida claims that the latter "remains in the order of the *possible* . . . of what is virtual or potential, of what is within the power of someone, some 'I can,' to reach." To this he opposes "the *im-possible*, of what must remain (in a nonnegative fashion) foreign to the order of my possibilities, to the order of the 'I can.' . . . It is a question here, as with the coming of any event worthy of this name, or an unforeseeable coming of the other, of a heteronomy" (*R*, 83–84/*V*, 122–23). These words are equally applicable to the worst.[37] One cannot, through one's actions, eradicate the trace altogether, put an end to repetition, or arrest the play of difference. There is always a trace, repetition, and difference. Which is not to say that the worst cannot happen. Perhaps it can. But if it happens, it could only come from elsewhere, happening to subjects from an unforeseeable other. At work here is thus a structure akin to what I described in Chapter 2 when confronting the question of whether a legacy can be put to death. There, against Derrida's suggestion to the contrary, I argued that an inheritance cannot be erased once and for all through one's actions. All attempts to kill an inheritance produce a trace as their necessary consequence, remains that live on. The same argument would here apply.

Returning now to *This Is Not Sufficient*, recall my claim that Lawlor relies on two competing definitions of the worst in his analysis—the actual eradication of all difference, and the tendency toward realizing such a thing. I argued that the latter is not enough to ground Lawlor's normative claims, for insofar as this threat of the worst is a feature of all positions that one might take, it fails to distinguish those he favors from those he opposes. One can now see that the first definition is also inadequate to ground a normative position, for given that the worst is not possible, in the sense of being the possible outcome of the actions of a sovereign I, then it has no role to play in an account of how one should act. There is nothing to be done to avoid the worst—it will happen, if it happens, due to forces beyond a subject's control. Arresting Lawlor's slide between the worst and its threat by choosing one or the other will thus fail to provide the force needed to motivate a normative stance. Neither the worst nor its threat can be used as a negative ideal, the avoidance of which should guide our actions. This may indeed explain why Lawlor oscillates between the two—appeals to the threat of the worst would be an implicit acknowledgment of its im-possibility, while appeals to the worst itself may seek to make up for the weakness of the mere threat. But this oscillation cannot cover up the lack of normative force in the worst or its threat.[38]

Now as I stated above, "the worst" is not the only notion at work in Lawlor's scheme. There is the other, more positive end of the scale, namely the "least violence" that he argues limits the worst. The next question to ask is therefore whether this can do the job required. Can the "least violence" provide a ground for claims of what one ought to do? Again the answer is no, for here too there is a related confusion. Consider the following set of statements from *This Is Not Sufficient*:

> What is required, here and now, in the age of so-called globalization, is a lesser violence, "violence against violence": as Derrida says as early as "Violence and Metaphysics," "the least possible violence." . . .
> . . . Derrida claims, in *Of Spirit*, that it is urgent to find the least bad (less worse) form of complicity with the biologistic and the metaphysical risks. The new logic of the limit is supposed to be a response to this urgency of the least bad or the less worse. . . .
> . . . What we are seeking here is a lesser violence, even the least violence.[39]

In each case Lawlor attempts to articulate that which should be sought in resistance to the worst, and in doing so equivocates between the "lesser" (or "less"), on the one hand, and the "least," on the other. There is, however, a marked difference between the two. A lesser violence names all of the positions on Lawlor's scale of values that fall short of the worst, while the least violence names the extreme position that would be opposite to the worst. Just as with the worst and its threat, I would suggest that here too neither term taken individually will do the work that Lawlor needs. Consider first "the least violence," which plays the dominant role in Lawlor's argument. Against its use one can make an argument similar to, indeed stronger than the one I advanced above concerning the possibility of the worst. Not only does "the least violent" name a strictly impossible position—any position labeled "least" in an absolute sense is subject to further division, producing another that is just a little less violent—I would maintain that it does not belong in the Derridean lexicon at all. This might be a surprising claim, since the phrases "the least violence" and "the least possible violence" come from Derrida's "Violence and Metaphysics," as Lawlor signals in one of the citations above. But the first is found only in the English version of this text, being a translation of "*la moindre violence*," a phrase translated in its other appearance in the same essay as "the lesser violence." I propose that the "the lesser violence" is the appropriate translation of "*la moindre violence*" in both cases. To see this, consider the original contexts of Derrida's use of this phrase. "*La moindre violence*" first appears in "Violence and Metaphysics" in a footnote to a description of Levinas's ambivalent view of technology.

> Levinas never simply condemns technology. It can rescue from a worse violence [*une violence pire*], the "reactionary" violence of sacred ravishment, of taking root, of the natural proximity of landscape. "Technology takes us out of the Heideggerean world and the superstitions of Place." It offers the chance "to let the human face

shine in its nudity" [*Difficult Freedom*]. We will return to this. Here, we only wish to foreshadow that *within history*—but is it meaningful elsewhere?—every philosophy of non-violence can only choose the lesser violence [*la moindre violence*] within an *economy of violence*.[40]

Derrida claims that while he is opposed to technology in some respects, Levinas also recognizes that it can be mobilized against communal and nationalistic tendencies. Both technology and these latter tendencies are violent, and Levinas supports the former in this context as the less violent of two options. In question is a comparative judgment of degree within a system in which violence is inevitable, and so translating "*la moindre violence*" as "the lesser violence" is appropriate.

Later in the essay, when Derrida articulates more fully the kind of strategic engagement with violence that he argues is necessary, "*la moindre violence*" reappears.

If light is the element of violence, one must combat light with a certain other light, in order to avoid the worst violence [*la pire violence*], that of silence and the night preceding or repressing discourse. This *vigilance* is a violence chosen as the least violence [*la moindre violence*] by a philosophy which takes history, that is finitude, seriously; a philosophy which knows itself as *historical* in each of its aspects (in a sense which tolerates neither finite totality, nor positive infinity), and knows itself, as Levinas says in another sense, as *economy*. . . . The philosopher (man) *must* speak and write within this war of light, a war in which he always already knows himself to be engaged; a war which he knows is inescapable, except by denying discourse, by risking the worst violence.[41]

In contrast to the last citation, in this passage Alan Bass translates "*la moindre violence*" as "the least violence." One can understand his reason for doing so, since here there is an implicit contrast drawn between "*la moindre violence*" and "*la pire violence*," (translated as "the worst violence"), while in the earlier passage "*la moindre violence*" ("the lesser violence") was opposed to "*une violence pire*" ("a worse violence"). I would argue, however, that in this second passage "*la moindre violence*" is also better translated as "the lesser violence," for two reasons. First, again at issue is a comparative judgment between two positions, one that is outside of or opposed to discourse, and another affirming discourse, taking finitude seriously. Derrida labels the former "the worst violence," and so the choice made here is one of a lesser violence in comparison to it. Second, it is hard to make any sense of the phrase "the least violence," understood not as a synonym for "the lesser violence," but as marking some absolute, noncomparative position. If it is a question of a scale of measurement that stretched from the most violent to the least, then the only position properly labeled "least" would be that of pure nonviolence, of peace. For, as I claimed above, any position labeled "least" and still "violent" would be exposed to further division, in which less violence could be imagined. The possibility of peace, however, is ruled out in Derrida's interpretation in this essay—it is one of the precise points on which he opposes Levinas, arguing that there is always an "economy of violence," and so no pure peace.[42]

Thus it would be better to remove "the least violence" from the translation "Violence and Metaphysics," since it implies an absoluteness that is out of place in Derrida's thinking. This is not to say that the third phrase from this essay mentioned above, "the least possible violence," should be altered, since the original "*la moindre violence possible*" would admit only this translation. But here too it is a question of a comparative judgment of the violence of a "secondary war" that would "make war upon the war" that is the worst violence. This secondary war is less violent than that of the worst, but not the "least" in any absolute sense.[43]

As a result, the only term available for use in "Violence and Metaphysics" is "the lesser violence." This, then, raises the question of whether the lesser violence can do the work Lawlor requires, with the added bonus of its having the legitimacy of Derrida's own recourse to the term. But here again the answer is no. To see why, it is first worth noting that, as far as I am aware, apart from its appearance in "Violence and Metaphysics" the phrase "the lesser violence" is not found anywhere else in Derrida's writings. Considering the constancy with which Derrida engaged the theme of violence across more than forty years of publishing, this omission is striking. Derrida is deeply concerned about violence and clearly desires its reduction in the world. Why, then, does he never again speak of the lesser violence? I would suggest that it is because this notion too is inconsistent with his views. This can be seen by examining the above citations from "Violence and Metaphysics." In the second, more developed passage, there are three distinctions at work. The first two go together, consisting of the couples discourse/silence and light/night. Derrida contrasts the worst violence, associated with silence and the night, with the lesser violence, on the side of discourse and light. A philosophy that chooses to stay inside language is thus choosing the lesser violence. But one might well wonder just what could it mean to make such a "choice." For if there is one thing Derrida's writings teach, reiterated above in my discussion of the worst, it is that one cannot actually inhabit a place completely beyond language. As I have stressed, in the Derridean framework one can never fully choose to leave the economy; one is always implicated in the structures of language, difference, the trace, and iterability. This is one of the dominant themes of "Violence and Metaphysics," and Derrida states on the same page as this citation that silence itself cannot be thought as wholly outside of language. Silence is only ever provisional, remaining a part of discourse, for it is "the strange vocation of a language called outside of itself by itself."[44] This vocation is "strange" because silence cannot be said to lie wholly within language, but neither is it wholly outside. So regarding the choice for the lesser violence, when tied to the couples discourse/silence and light/night, there is in fact no choice here to be made.

The only choice that could be meaningful is that signaled in the third distinction drawn in this passage, suggested in Derrida's talk of "a philosophy which takes history, that is finitude, seriously; a philosophy which knows itself as *historical* . . . [and] as *economy*." In raising the possibility of such a philosophy, Derrida implies that there are other philosophies, ones that would not take finitude seriously and exhibit this kind of self-knowledge. This distinction also receives further support in the first citation from "Violence and Metaphysics" speaking of a lesser violence, where it is a question of choosing between the violence of technology and "the 'reactionary' violence of sacred ravishment, of taking root, of the natural proximity of landscape."[45] Levinas chooses technology over the sacred, thus acknowledging the necessity of finitude (since technology is placed firmly within the sphere of the finite) against positions that would presumably be ignorant of this necessity (insofar as the sacred aims for the infinite). Unlike the first two distinctions, at stake here is not a choice between the economy and its outside, since both options lie within the economy. Rather, it is a question of knowing this is the case, as opposed to believing that one's finitude can be overcome. Derrida's claim is that the choice of self-knowledge is the choice for the lesser violence.

The distinction between knowledge and ignorance is thus a choice that can be made, and so it provides substantial content to the idea of choosing a lesser violence. But the question is whether the connection Derrida makes between self-knowledge and a lesser violence is in fact correct. Will being aware of one's finitude, and accepting the necessity of the economy of violence, result in the lesser violence? Does knowledge here make a difference in the amount of violence produced? Here the Derridean logic co-implicating the chance and the threat rears its head. Knowledge of one's finitude is precisely knowledge that the chance always carries the threat, and there is nothing in this knowledge that enables the threat to be diminished. This kind of knowledge will not make a difference. Thus, the choice of a philosophy that takes finitude seriously, that knows itself to be historical and as lying within an economy, is not a choice for a lesser violence. It is perhaps for this reason that along with that of a lesser violence, the talk of self-knowledge also disappears from Derrida's writings. Never again does he counsel such a strategy in his many writings on violence. My claim is that Derrida is right to leave this vocabulary behind.

Returning once again to *This Is Not Sufficient*, I would thus maintain that talk of the "lesser violence" is out of place in the Derridean framework, and so again fails to do the work required. A lesser violence may be preferable to the worst, but it also coincides with those positions that Lawlor claims tend toward the worst (fascism, biological continuism, and so on). Insofar as these positions fail to fully realize the worst, they themselves are rightly named "less violent" and so cannot be opposed to "a lesser violence." Now one might think one can accept this, and then argue that it is precisely why a lesser violence is sought—a violence less than the violence performed by these positions that explicitly attempt to realize the worst. But here again the difficulty arises of how to distinguish between these different positions. In emphasizing an essential nonknowledge of the future, in which the chance and the threat are necessary co-possibilities, the Derridean framework calls into question all such judgments. Who is to say that taking certain actions will have less violent results than others? The chance and the threat are at work in all, and one is given no way of determining that any individual position will carry a greater threat than another.[46]

Language Remains

My critique of Lawlor might reinforce the suspicion that Derrida cannot make legitimate normative claims after all, for deprived of normative force are the positive ideals of the best, the lesser violence and the least violent, and the negative ideal of the worst. I have argued that none of these terms can do the work they are sometimes asked to do in grounding norms or rules in a deconstructive analysis. Does this therefore mean that the norms endorsed in Derridean inheritance must remain altogether unjustified? Would Derrida's work be improved if such norms were removed? More specifically, relating to the focus of this book, would Derrida's work on democracy be more philosophically robust if he had refrained from endorsing democracy to come? I think the answer to these questions is "No," and the task of the final section of this chapter is to show this to be true. I do so by beginning with a return to Hägglund's interpretation.

As I discussed earlier, Hägglund does acknowledge some legitimacy to Derrida's endorsement of democracy, claiming that it is based on what I have termed the concept's descriptive merit. Democracy can be endorsed because it testifies to an exposure to the future that applies to all political regimes. However, reflecting on this further, it seems clear that such a claim has little use for justifying one's support for democracy. Indeed, promoting this claim seems only to eliminate a reason for choosing democracy, namely its openness to the future, since this is precisely what is claimed of all of its rivals. It is perhaps for this reason that among all the things historically and today to which democrats appeal in order to win support for their position, one will have a hard time finding democracy's superiority as a concept in describing the necessity of openness. It is simply too weak a characteristic to motivate a desire for democracy; it fails to give a reason for choosing democracy over anything else.

It is thus not altogether surprising that when Hägglund himself speaks of the desire for democracy, in the course of his critique of the desire for fullness presupposed by Ernesto Laclau, he says nothing concerning this desire's content. Apart from its not being as Laclau conceives it, all Hägglund states is that it presupposes survival: "To desire democracy cannot be to desire an ideal fullness, since even the ideal state of democracy is temporal and alterable. The desire for democracy presupposes that we are not driven toward an ideal fullness but toward *living on* as finite beings."[47] As with the characteristic of openness, this also fails to distinguish democracy from any other political regime, since Hägglund maintains that the affirmation of survival is presupposed by every desire, without exception. Thus, nothing in Hägglund's account explains why one would desire democracy in the first place.

The challenge, therefore, is to articulate just how it is that a meaningful endorsement of democracy can be legitimately expressed in Derrida's writings, if only ever provisionally, without going so far as to arrive at a position like Lawlor's which relies on oppositional structures that these writings undermine. I have already argued that this occurs in Derrida's practice of inheritance, in his choice to up the ante on the aporias he receives. My task now is to give further precision as to what facilitates this choice and what allows me to claim that it is properly a part of deconstructive analysis.

As a first step in doing so, consider the following remarks from "The Reason of the Strongest." Reflecting on "the obscure status or mode" of the words "democracy to come," Derrida writes:

> "Democracy to come" can hesitate [*hésiter*] endlessly, oscillate indecidably and for-ever, between two possibilities: it can, on the one hand, correspond to the neutral, constative analysis of a concept. . . . This would amount to saying: if you want to know what you are saying when you use this inherited word *democracy*, you need to know that these things are inscribed or prescribed within it; for my part, I am simply describing this prescription in a neutral fashion. . . . But, on the other hand, no longer satisfied to remain at the level of neutral, constative conceptual analysis, "democracy to come" can also inscribe a performative and attempt to win convic-tion by suggesting support or adherence, an "and yet it is necessary to believe it," "I believe in it, I promise, I am in on the promise and in messianic waiting, I am taking action or am at least enduring, now you do the same," and so on. The *to* of the "to come" wavers [*hésite*] between the imperative injunction (call or performative) and the patient *perhaps* of messianicity (nonperformative exposure to what comes, to what can always not come or has already come). (*R*, 91/*V*, 132)

One must be careful in interpreting this passage, for evoked are two different, albeit linked relations. The first involves the relation between two possibilities of the way one might understand Derrida's talk of democracy to come. On the one hand, there is the interpretation that in his discussions of democracy, Derrida is giving a neutral descrip-tion of what is entailed by the concept "democracy to come," providing a purely con-stative analysis. On the other hand, there is a second possibility suggesting that when Derrida says "democracy to come" he may well be endorsing it, through the emergence of a performative force that places him on the side of democracy. He would no longer simply be offering neutral diagnoses of the operation of democracy, but supporting it and calling for others to do the same. Crucially, Derrida does not argue that one of these interpretative possibilities is correct and the other mistaken. He claims that both are inscribed in a further possibility, that of the endless, indecidable oscillation that would move between them. Derrida's point is that this oscillation cannot be arrested, such that only one of these possibilities prevails over the other.

However, there is a second relation in this passage different from the first. This relation is described in the last sentence, holding between "the imperative injunction (call or performative) and the patient *perhaps* of messianicity (nonperformative expo-sure to what comes, to what can always not come or has already come)." The focus now is not on "democracy to come" but more precisely on the "to" embedded in this phrase, and Derrida's claim is that while here it is again a question of the performative, this time it is related to nonperformative exposure. This is different from constative analysis. Thus, while Derrida uses the same word (*hésiter*—translated as "hesitate" in one case and as "wavers" in the other) each time to describe the relation in question, in each case it is a question of a different relation—performative to constative in one, and performative to nonperformative exposure in the other.

The relevant distinction for my present concern is primarily the first, for it is precisely the relation between Derrida's constative analysis of democracy to come and his performative commitment to the notion that I am seeking to explain. What then is this relation? How should one understand Derrida's claim that "'Democracy to come' can hesitate endlessly, oscillate indecidably and forever" between constative analysis and performative commitment? My proposal is that the coemergence of the constative and performative can be traced to the fact that deconstruction in Derrida's texts necessarily takes place in and through language. Language remains. And it remains not as a neutral medium, but as one that comes already differentially infused with contours of value, formed from the particular sedimented history that precedes it. This terrain exerts forces structuring processes of evaluation, forces never fully determining, but that resist or encourage different paths in the evaluative choices one makes. Thus when Derrida speaks of democracy, he never does so from scratch. My first three chapters have emphasized this with respect to the descriptive dimension of Derrida's work. In arguing that his engagement with democracy is necessarily tied to a practice of inheritance, I have demonstrated how this engagement involves a process of sorting between the many different ways democracy has been understood in the past, a wide range of meanings, from the rule of the poor to the protection of human rights, meanings whose only commonality is their shared history of being grouped under the same name. Derrida privileges some and downplays others, and the success of his proposed description—whether, for example, an understanding of democracy as engaged in self-critique through inheritance comes to be more widely accepted—will emerge out of the interplay between the force of his work and the forces differentially distributed through the preexisting terrain of meaning, along with any additional forces his present and future audience will bring to the encounter.

My point here is that a similar phenomenon occurs in terms of value. The term "democracy" has been valued differently at different moments in its history, which any discussion of the term necessarily engages. Thus, the very act of picking out this term for attention, among the many others also describing political structures or having political resonance, brings Derrida's deconstructive writings into relation with this history of value, and with its present distribution. Put simply, in choosing to speak of "democracy to come"—rather than "republic to come," "community to come," "fraternity to come," "classless society to come," or even "fascism to come," structures that would all resemble democracy to come at the fundamental level of spacing—Derrida unleashes a configuration of values shaped by a particular history. At present there is widely shared support of the discourse of democracy, since its positive value today is relatively stable, despite the many different interpretations of its meaning around the world. This being the case, Derrida may very well find himself placed on the side of democracy. Now he could attempt to resist this, and come out forcefully against democracy. One could thus imagine him arguing, on the basis of the many negative characteristics of democracy underlined in "The Reason of the Strongest," that a positive view is mistaken. This would be difficult, precisely because democracy is so highly valued, and so such a position against democracy is likely to meet strong resistance. But it is not an impossible task, especially given the resources contained in a history of political thinking dominated by antidemocratic views. Of course, Derrida did not choose this path, but note that even if he did he would have already moved well beyond providing a simply constative analysis of what is implied in democracy's concept.

Thus Derrida cannot avoid the performative dimension of evaluation in his deconstructive analyses, since the language with which he must necessarily engage is already infused with value in a sedimented history. As sedimented, this history is a multiplicity always involving contours of relative stability and instability. And importantly, these contours will rarely be equally shaped, providing an explanation for the phenomenon of provisional justification. Such justification will depend in a large part on the degree of inherited stability. This can be amplified or diminished in the way the heir takes this inheritance up, and it can always be overturned by an oppositional force in its reception. But this is just to say that any justification would be provisional, not final, not that justification is impossible. And my interpretation also allows for the possibility that a text may be normatively neutral, since it can engage language that has little resonance in a normative register. This explains how Derrida could avoid embracing writing over speech in his early work, mentioned at the beginning of this chapter, since at the time of his writing these terms were not widely seen to embody particular values.[48] But when it comes to a language that does carry such resonance, as with the political and ethical vocabulary Derrida analyzed most in his later work, and in particular the language of democracy, then normativity in his texts will unavoidably arise. For here even if Derrida completely withheld all value judgments, he would leave unchecked the values already at work in the language used.

My interpretation therefore provides a way of understanding the link between the constative and the performative dimensions in Derrida's deconstructive discourse on democracy and so demonstrates the necessity that normative claims be contained within this discourse. And I would suggest that it is not reducible to the framework that Hägglund proposes. The strength of *Radical Atheism* lies in its articulation of a fundamental logic that functions across Derrida's writings. But this carries with it a certain weakness that I would describe as an indifference to language. It doesn't matter to Hägglund which particular term is being shown to follow the logic of deconstruction, whether it be time, hospitality, writing, violence, justice, life, and so on. He abstracts the logic underlying each particular term, leaving their evaluative resonances behind. Having done so, he cannot account for the performative force I have argued Derrida's writings must necessarily contain.

When I first advanced a version of this claim about Hägglund's work, he responded with a spirited defense of his view. Much of this defense rests on an interpretation he offers of the proper place of performative commitments in deconstruction. He writes: "Derrida may indeed oscillate between an analysis *of* the concept of democracy and a performative commitment *to* democracy, but the latter cannot be grounded in the former. Rather, Derrida argues that we make commitments because of the exposition to a future that may come to question or undo these commitments."[49] But this is to mischaracterize the issue. There is no claim being made, by me or by Derrida, that the relation in question is one of grounding. Further, in the alternative he proposes to a relation of grounding, Hägglund leaves out any mention of the constative, focusing only on the second relation raised in the original quote from Derrida, that between the performative and the exposure to the future. This shift in focus remains as Hägglund sums up his position.

> Thus, Derrida draws a clear distinction between performative acts of language and the structure of the event that he describes as unconditional. We necessarily commit ourselves to values through performative acts of language, but Derrida maintains that these acts are exceeded from within by the event that makes them possible. As he puts it in "Typewriter Ribbon": "What happens, by definition, what comes about in an unforeseeable and singular manner, could not care less about the performative" (2002, 146). Derrida's point is that even the most stable commitment can betray itself or turn out to be misguided because of the exposition to unpredictable events. This does not mean that commitments or values are "arbitrary in their justification," as Haddad suggests (2009, 137); it only means that they are based on reasons and considerations that are not grounded in deconstruction. The role of deconstruction is not to ground anything but to think through the implications of the unconditional exposition to time.[50]

Hägglund's claim here is that the distinction between performative acts of language and the unconditional supports his view of deconstruction's independence from justifying commitments or values. On the one side lie performative acts of language, together with the commitments and values that they make possible, and on the other lies deconstruction, which is focused on the structure of the unconditional. Now things are somewhat complicated by the fact that Hägglund implicates the unconditional in the event that makes performatives possible, since this suggests a relation between the two that might compromise the integrity of the division. But Hägglund's description of the relation saves the clarity of the distinction. For he presents the conditioning as going in one direction only—the unconditional conditions performatives, and not vice versa. This unidirectionality is supported by the citation from "Typewriter Ribbon," since in not caring about the performative, the unforeseeable happening (or the unconditional) would be free of what it conditions. The implication of this freedom is that the unconditional can be examined in and of itself. This would not be the case for the performative, since to properly understand it one would need to explore its condition (here the unconditional). But the unconditional itself is said to depend on nothing else. This being the case, deconstruction would be able to go about the task Hägglund sets it and think the unconditional in isolation, uninterrupted as it were by trying to justify values and commitments.

However, the problem with Hägglund's view is that it does not match the view of Derrida. As I quoted above, Derrida states that "the *to* of the 'to come' wavers [*hésite*] between the imperative injunction (call or performative) and the patient *perhaps* of messianicity (nonperformative exposure to what comes, to what can always not come or has already come)" (*R*, 91/*V*, 132). This "wavering" or "hesitation" is a movement of oscillation between the two sides of the division, and so the relation that is thought must go in both directions. Further, it is precisely such a dual relation that Derrida articulates in the very paragraph in "Typewriter Ribbon" from which Hägglund cites. There Derrida seeks to describe "the paradoxical antinomy of performativity and the event." Hägglund isolates one arm of the antinomy, where Derrida speaks of the event exceeding the performative. Equally important is the other arm, to which Derrida refers two sentences earlier: "It is often said, quite rightly, that a performative utterance produces the event of which it speaks."[51] Thus, far from describing the way the event makes performatives possible, as Hägglund asserts, Derrida is here concerned with the opposite phenomenon, with the way performatives make the event possible. Derrida's point is that performatives are the condition of certain kinds of event, at the same time as these events exceed their condition. And crucially, if they are to be in a relation of antinomy (a word that, as I discussed in Chapter 1, can be understood as a synonym for "aporia" in Derrida's writings), then neither performatives nor the events that exceed them can take place without one another. If they could, then the antinomy would be resolved, and this is precisely what Derrida maintains cannot be done.[52]

Now as I noted above, in this account of performative commitments in Derrida's work Hägglund makes no mention of constative analysis. This contrasts with my own interpretation, which is directed toward the relation between the performative and the constative, not the performative and the unconditional. To repeat, I am concerned with understanding how it is that Derrida's constative, descriptive analyses of various phenomena (in particular of democracy) at the same time carry a performative force. This is not to say, however, that I think the unconditional is irrelevant. Doing so would ignore an important part of Derrida's own understanding, since in the original citation from "The Reason of the Strongest" he locates the unconditional in the "to" embedded in the "to come." This means that if the question is what occurs in Derrida's constative analysis of "democracy to come," then Derrida's view is that in addition to the performative commitment this necessarily invokes, the unconditional in the necessary exposure to the unknown future is also at work. There are thus three terms in play, the constative, the performative, and the unconditional. The key point to underline for the view I am proposing is that the relations between all of these terms are ones of mutual interdependence—there is a "hesitation" or oscillation between all the terms involved.[53] As a consequence, there is no moment or dimension of Derrida's analysis that is free from the performative. There is performative commitment when he gives a constative analysis in his texts, and there is performative commitment when the unconditional interrupts or undermines his texts. There is thus no aspect of Derrida's texts that is free of normative force.

My interpretation claims, therefore, that deconstruction necessarily engages a language that is inescapably infused with contours of value, and it is here that the dimension of normativity in this kind of writing can be located. Now to be sure the kind of normativity here in play falls far short of a single set of prescriptions that would constitute a determined politics or ethics. Deconstruction still does not say what is to be done in all cases. But different events of deconstruction will give rise to particular normative claims, for in their inevitable inheritance of language these events engage with and relaunch particular configurations of value. It remains in addition that none of these normative claims lie under the control of a sovereign I. There is an irreducible alterity in the relation of inheritance, both in the past that is engaged and in the future that is promised. The particularity of the claims is thus exposed to this alterity, and any stability they might obtain is always open to destabilization. But this exposure to alteration does not automatically discount the normative force at work.

Finally, this emphasis on the relation between deconstruction and language also opens up a path to pursue in my own analysis, one that enables a better understanding of what is involved in the act of democratic inheritance, which I have argued is one of the central contributions Derrida has to make to contemporary political thinking. For its inescapability means that the language inherited in democratic discourse is one site on which the process of filtering and sorting—the engagement with the aporias of democracy—will be played out. This, at least, is what I aim to demonstrate in the next two chapters. I do so first by examining in Chapter 5 Derrida's most substantial act of democratic inheritance, the book *Politics of Friendship*, in which he engages the discourse of the democratic tradition. Then in Chapter 6 I focus on one aspect of Derrida's democratic discourse that results from this engagement, and seek to expand and enrich it through an interrogation of his use of the vocabulary of birth.

5 *Politics of Friendship* as Democratic Inheritance

I ARGUED IN CHAPTER 3 that Derrida theorizes democracy such that inheritance is a democratic act. To be democratic, one needs to inherit. This interpretation, however, left certain questions unanswered. First, given the tension between Derrida's diagnosis of a fundamental ambivalence in the structures underlying democracy and his simultaneous support for democracy, the place and role of normativity in Derrida's account were left undetermined. Second, it remained unclear just what such a democratic act of inheritance might look like. I addressed the first issue in Chapter 4, concluding that the values at work in the language Derrida engages mark out a space that is already constituted along normative lines. Derrida cannot avoid the possibility that his constative analyses at the same time carry a performative force of normative injunction, and this force is located in the language used. In this chapter, I take up the second question and give further determination to the possible shape of democratic inheritance as understood within the Derridean framework. I do this by examining a text I have already mentioned in passing a number of times, *Politics of Friendship*. In this work Derrida inherits discourses of fraternity and friendship from the democratic tradition. My task, therefore, is to show how this inheritance, in its conformity with the structure I have been articulated, itself constitutes a democratic act.

A Tradition of Friendship

As Geoffrey Bennington remarks, "*Politics of Friendship* is an unusual book for Derrida to have written."[1] Bennington notes that Derrida tends to write essays, sometimes very long ones, which restrict themselves to a reading of one, maybe two authors, even if other names appear in passing. By contrast, the scope of the readings contained within *Politics of Friendship* is enormous—it contains detailed and sustained engagements with Plato, Aristotle, Montaigne, Kant, Nietzsche, Heidegger, and Schmitt, as well as shorter (but still dense) discussions of several other figures, including Cicero, Augustine, Blake, Michelet, Freud, and Blanchot. It is a complicated book, and finding an underlying structure is no easy task. But among all of its twists and turns, one particular thematic constellation emerges in *Politics of Friendship* involving friendship, fraternity, and political belonging. These three notions are connected in a very particular manner across the tradition that Derrida traces in his inquiry, and it is these connections that I will investigate.

Although the distinction between belonging to a tradition and not will never be a firm one in a Derridean text, any attempt to read a tradition must operate according to some criterion of belonging. One must necessarily read some works and not others to advance one's claims. In *Politics of Friendship* Derrida determines the tradition he will investigate by privileging a phrase quoted by Montaigne that is attributed to Aristotle in Diogenes Laertius's *Lives of Eminent Philosophers*—"O my friends, there is no friend [*O phíloi, oudeis philos*]." This statement is quoted by almost all the authors Derrida reads—they all inherit it—binding together the particular tradition of writing on friendship he explores. This phrase is thus the *arkhē*, both origin and principle, of the lineage of thinkers linked in Derrida's analysis. And to name an *arkhē* in a Derridean context is simultaneously to call it into question both as origin and as principle. "O my friends, there is no friend" is questionable first as origin, for it is a phrase that is only ever attributed to Aristotle—it is only ever being said to have been said by him—since it is nowhere found in the writings classified under his signature. It thus may well be a fictive beginning that never took place. Second, the phrase is questionable as a principle, for it appears incoherent, a contradiction, with no obvious meaning. How can a contradiction govern or legislate anything?[2]

Following a pattern I have shown repeatedly in Derrida's work, such instabilities do not render the Aristotelian phrase ineffectual. On the contrary, they are responsible for its particular persistence across time. By citing "O my friends, there is no friend" in one form or another, thinkers ranging from Montaigne to Blanchot each respond to it by giving it an interpretation, making sense of its seeming nonsense. And the fact that there exists no authoritative first record of its utterance only amplifies the freedom and necessity of these citations. The very force of the phrase thus lies in the fact that it exists in no original utterance and in the contradictory status that calls for the responses constituting a whole tradition.

Politics of Friendship is thus an investigation of a certain inheritance, a chain of legacies that traverses the length of what is more or less accepted as the Western philosophical tradition. Now I have argued that for Derrida legacies will always involve aporetic structures, and there are several here at work. But the most prominent is found in the relation between two models of friendship which Derrida argues consistently recur. The first he describes as "the Graeco-Roman model, which seems to be governed by the value of *reciprocity*, by homological, immanentist, finitist—and rather politist—concord" (*PF*, 290/*PA*, 323). This idea of friendship follows a logic of sameness and proximity, where the friends resemble each other and share much in common. It is political insofar as the value of equality lends itself to a democratic reading—the political friendship that is sometimes said to hold between citizens in a democracy has its roots in this model. The second model is the first's opposite, based on a "heterology, transcendence, dissymmetry and infinity, hence a Christian type of logic" (*PF*, 291/ *PA*, 323). Rather than following a law of the same, commonality and similarity, friends according to this model are different from each other, sharing little or nothing in common, and are separated by distance.

Much of *Politics of Friendship* aims to demonstrate the work done by these two models of friendship across the tradition investigated. Derrida argues that the first is dominant, and that it operates most strongly in the theories given by Aristotle, Cicero, Montaigne, and Kant. The presence of the second is more subdued, and Derrida reads its clearest expression in Nietzsche and Blanchot. However, one cannot so easily align one model with one set of thinkers, and the other with another. If these two models constitute an aporia, they must both be at work together, at once. Otherwise the contradiction would not be necessary, and the aporia would be resolved. The challenge therefore is to show how all of these writers in fact engage both models of friendship.

Derrida meets this challenge not through a formal analysis like the one I examined in *Of Hospitality*, where terms are interrogated at a distance from any particular textual context. He does not argue for the conceptual necessity of the contradiction. Rather, he pursues what he describes in "Force of Law" as the other style of deconstruction, one "more historical or more anamnesic, [which] seems to proceed through readings of texts, meticulous interpretations and genealogies" (FOL, 250/FDL, 48), and articulates the relation between the two models of friendship through close readings of each of the authors investigated. Although this does not reveal a single template that is repeated in each instance, an overall pattern emerges, whereby each author, despite his tendency to promote one of the models, nevertheless ends up relying on aspects of the other at certain crucial moments. Thus the authors read testify to the aporetic status of friendship, as all remain caught in the contradictory tension.

Since I cannot examine all of Derrida's readings, I will discuss one of the most important, that of Montaigne, which is exemplary of Derrida's inheritance from the tradition.[3] The bulk of this reading takes place in a long parenthesis appearing after Derrida has referred to the Aristotelian conception of a friend being "one soul in twin bodies" (*PF*, 177/*PA*, 202). In "On Friendship" Montaigne appeals to this definition when discussing what is shared between friends. "Everything is genuinely common to them both: their wills, goods, wives, children, honour and lives; their correspondence is that of one soul in bodies twain, according to that most apt definition of Aristotle's, so they can neither lend nor give anything to each other."[4] This description thus conforms to the dominant model in the tradition, based on commonality and similarity. Between such friends everything is shared, and nothing can be said to be held individually. However, the tranquility of this model is soon disrupted. For having asserted that in such a friendship nothing can be given, Montaigne then goes on to claim that giving is possible, albeit in a pattern that inverts its usual order.

> In the kind of friendship I am talking about, if it were possible for one to give to the other it is the one who received the benefaction who would lay an obligation on his companion. For each of them, more than anything else, is seeking the good of the other, so that the one who furnishes the means and the occasion is in fact the more generous, since he gives to his friend the joy of performing for him what he most desires.[5]

In this new claim, giving is said to take place in a perfect friendship, but it does so only through an exchange of the places of the donor and the donee. What each friend seeks the most is to do good for the other, to give to him. In receiving, the friend allows the other to perform this good. Receiving a gift is thus the greatest gift that a friend can give.

Derrida draws two consequences from these remarks. First, alluding to his own extensive analyses of the gift, Derrida argues that Montaigne's description of giving introduces dissymmetry and difference into the model of perfect friendship. Once the recipient is he who gives, a hyperbolic outbidding—a *surenchère*—is set into motion. Each friend seeks to outdo the other in giving him more opportunities to give through receiving. This "disproportionate inversion of dissymmetry" (*PF*, 179/*PA*, 204) disrupts the common measure, measured reciprocity, and equality that is said to mark the friendship.

Second, Derrida underlines the implication of isolation that follows from Montaigne's account. The description of "one soul in two bodies," together with the extremity of the giving that Montaigne demands, limits the friendship to an indivisible and closed couple. In Montaigne's words, "Each gives himself so entirely to his friend that he has nothing left to share with another."[6] A man can only have one perfect friend, for to that friend he gives all, amplifying the rarity of great friendships of which Montaigne has already spoken ("it is already something if Fortune can achieve it once in three centuries").[7] For Derrida, this singularity introduces another, related aporetic couple into Montaigne's account of perfect friendship, involving a simultaneous relation to the political and the apolitical. On the one hand, the exceptional nature of such a friendship means that "no political project can predict, prescribe or programme it." The two friends are "heterogeneous to political laws," above the law, and so in this respect apolitical (*PF*, 182/*PA*, 208–9). Derrida pushes this exceptionality to a point where the examples of great friendships listed by Montaigne resist inscription into a genealogy: "The unique must be, every time, as is said of genius, a genus: in its own respect its own genus. . . . Hence the obligatory conclusion that spiritual fraternity is a-generic and a-genealogical" (*PF*, 182–83/*PA*, 209). The a-genealogical character of what is here called "spiritual fraternity"— another phrase for perfect friendship to which I will return shortly—goes hand in hand with its apoliticality, reinforcing the link between inheritance and the political.

But, on the other hand, Derrida argues that this resistance to genealogy, and the corresponding resistance to the political, is never quite achieved in Montaigne's text. For at the same time as the singularity of such friendships is emphasized, the fact remains that they are inscribed in a chain, and are in one important respect subordinated to political law. Despite their singularity, these perfect friendships are not free of all restrictions. In particular, Montaigne argues that they must be in accord with reason, with a virtue ruled by reason, and according to Derrida, "Reason and virtue could never be *private*. They cannot enter into conflict with the public realm. These concepts of virtue and reason are brought to bear in advance on the space of the *res publica*. In such a tradition, a virtuous reason or a rational virtue that would not be in essence homogeneous to the best reason of State [*raison d'État*] is unthinkable" (*PF*, 184/*PA*, 211). All of Montaigne's perfect friends are also model citizens, and so their friendship cannot, in Derrida's eyes, avoid being marked as political—marked, that is, as to some extent programmed, prescribed, and calculable by the reason of political law.

Thus from the assumption of the dominant model of friendship, based on symmetry and sameness, Montaigne introduces elements of the other model, based on asymmetry and difference. This interruption arises in Montaigne's discussion of giving and in perfect friendship's (a)political status. In both cases Derrida argues that Montaigne is relying on elements from both logics, despite their contradiction. However, although the tension remains irreducible, and must be so if it can be accurately described as an aporia, it is not the case that the two logics are in perfect balance, with each engaged equally. Derrida argues that there is another thread of similarity underlying the whole of Montaigne's project, binding the contradiction together. This bond is formed in Montaigne's consistent appeals to fraternity. Across the tensions and fissures of this theory of friendship, one constant remains—all of the friends are men. A perfect friendship seems impossible between a man and a woman, and between women. The exclusion of women holds despite the heterogeneity and dissymmetry to which Montaigne appeals, for while friends gain distance from one another and indeed from all law, this distance is never so great so as to cross the division of the sexes. Thus, speaking of the two logics that I have just reviewed as "two times," Derrida writes, "That which ensures the mediation or the solder—in any case, a certain continuity between the two times—that which also relates to the exclusion of woman, if only in the form or the pretext of 'not yet', is the brother, and, more precisely, the name, the name 'brother' and the brother's name" (*PF*, 291/*PA*, 323).

Why does Derrida emphasize the name? In the first instance because Montaigne himself has recourse to the name "brother": "The name of brother is truly a fair one and full of love: that is why La Boëtie and I made a brotherhood of our alliance."[8] Montaigne appeals to the name of brother to capture the value of his friendship with

La Boëtie. Further, the name of this brother, "La Boëtie," appears in two key moments of Montaigne's account. First, in the context of his inheritance of his friend's papers, in particular of his friend's work *The Discourse on Voluntary Servitude* for which "On Friendship" was originally intended as the preface, Montaigne writes: "Yet I am particularly indebted to that treatise, because it first brought us together: it was shown to me long before I met him and first made me acquainted with his name; thus preparing for that loving-friendship between us which as long as it pleased God we fostered so perfect and so entire."⁹ Montaigne came to know his friend first by his name, the name that signed the work whose reading constituted their first encounter. And it is not by chance that this memory returns in a scene of inheritance, when the rights over this name are being passed from one friend to another. For the name lives on after death, and its transmission seals the perfect friendship. Second, Montaigne returns to this initial knowledge of names when searching for an explanation of their friendship's force. "We were seeking each other before we set eyes on each other—both because of the reports we each had heard, which made a more violent assault on our emotions than was reasonable from what they had said, and, I believe, because of some decree of Heaven: we embraced each other by repute [*nous nous embrassions par noz noms*—we embraced each other by our names]."¹⁰ Each possessing a name of renown, the two friends sought each other out with the passion that would characterize their perfect friendship to come.

As Montaigne describes it, friendship, in its highest expression, is thus framed by inherited names and names of renown. And it is precisely this framing that ties the perfect friendship to fraternity and the exclusion of women. For in the tradition in which Montaigne inscribes himself, such names belong to men. Not passed on, and rarely renowned, the names of women would seem to have no place in such a scheme. As Derrida writes, "Under the two forms of this enframing [*arraisonnement*] (inheritance of the name and social renown) *this* history leaves less chance to the woman, to the daughter, to the sister. We are not saying *no* chance, but *less chance*" (*PF*, 292–93/*PA*, 325). It is the name that consolidates the bond between friendship and fraternity. And this, in turn, paves the way for Montaigne's explicit exclusion of women, as when he claims the following: "Women are in truth not normally capable of responding to such familiarity and mutual confidence as sustain that holy bond of friendship, nor do their souls seem firm enough to withstand the clasp of a knot so lasting and so tightly drawn. . . . There is no example yet of woman attaining to it, and by the common agreement of the Ancient schools of philosophy she is excluded from it."¹¹ Strictly speaking, women could be perfect friends, both with each other and with men. But it turns out that in the canonical accounts of Montaigne and those he cites, they are not. One might think at first this exclusion is the result of chance, but this chance is quickly rewritten as necessity. Derrida's reading of Montaigne tracks this transformation of chance into necessity.

It is thus through a constant if sometimes subtle reliance on fraternity in his conception of friendship that Montaigne returns his discourse to an economy of the same.

Even as he introduces elements of dissymmetry and heterogeneity, he remains bound to the name of the brother as a constraint on friendship, implying that women will never be accepted within it. The possibilities offered by the aporetic structure of friendship are thus dramatically closed down—fraternity's dominance results in a deference to similarity over difference. Translated to the political, such a model reinforces women's exclusion, for they can never attain the status of model citizens.

This is the pattern that Derrida uncovers again and again in the tradition that he investigates. For Aristotle friendships of virtue must be between equals, and there is dissymmetry in his claim that it is better to love than to be loved (and he also articulates an aporetic relation between friendship and the political, arguing that friendship is necessary in the polis, while the best friendship lies above justice). Yet amid these complications he similarly excludes women, confining their relation to men within friendships of utility. Kant also negotiates the logics of sameness and difference, avoiding the dangerous fusion of love by promoting distance through respect. But he too appeals to fraternity, using the brother as a figure for the friend of humanity. And Michelet states that "fraternity is the law beyond the law" (cited on *PF*, 182, 237/*PA*, 209, 265), at the same time as he proposes that it is the basis of equality and democracy. But he also claims that women are never fraternal enough.

Given that the authors just listed begin from the model of sameness, one might think of starting instead from an idea of difference. This is the path taken by the Nietzschean approach, and is one for which Derrida has sympathy. But even with its promise of making a break with the tradition that precedes it, Derrida argues that those theorizing this model nonetheless return to an economy of the same in their own appeals to fraternity. Nietzsche thus pursues dissymmetry and distance to the point of inverting the Aristotelian friend into an enemy, yet he keeps the brother in Zarathustra's reversal of Christian values. Schmitt takes up Nietzsche's reversal in placing the enemy at the center of his concept of the political, but he speaks of the absolute enemy through reference to the brother. And Blanchot pushes the Nietzschean understanding of friendship in distance to its most extreme point, while he also retains the brother when describing relations to the other.

Thus, in each his own way, the writers Derrida reads all engage with the aporia of friendship, thinking friends in terms of both sameness and difference, within the law and above the law, symmetrically and asymmetrically, yet all return to the same in granting a privilege to the brother. None breaks with this hegemony, and thinks a friendship across sexual difference.

A Resistance to Fraternity

Politics of Friendship is thus an investigation of a legacy, or more accurately of legacies, that traverse a certain history of Western philosophy. And, of course, Derrida does not occupy a neutral position with respect to this history, merely observing and describing it with a disinterested gaze. In writing this book he is now an active part of this history, inscribing himself in a chain that extends across centuries. Derrida is inheriting from this tradition, just as each writer before him inherited from it in his turn. So what occurs in Derrida's turn? How does he inherit this tradition of friendship? As might be expected, he does so according to the pattern I traced in Chapter 2—he negotiates the aporias in question, maintaining their tension by refusing to resolve them, in a movement of *surenchère* that aims to increase the openness and transformation in play. In particular, Derrida raises the stakes over those coming before him by explicitly questioning fraternity as an appropriate trope for friendship, and, by implication, for a democratic politics. Thus Derrida's question throughout is whether one can think friendship and democracy beyond the principle of fraternity. This is posed at the beginning of the book: "Let us ask ourselves what would then be the politics of such a 'beyond the principle of fraternity'" (*PF*, viii/*PA*, 12). And it is repeated at the end:

> Is it possible to think and to implement democracy, that which would keep the old name "democracy," while uprooting from it all these figures of friendship (philosophical and religious) which prescribe fraternity: the family and the androcentric ethnic group? Is it possible, in assuming a certain faithful memory of democratic reason and reason *tout court*—I would even say, the Enlightenment of a certain *Aufklärung* (thus leaving open the abyss which is again opening today under these words)—not to found, where it is no longer a matter of *founding*, but to open out to the future, or rather, to the "come," of a certain democracy? (*PF*, 306/*PA*, 339)

Derrida thus seeks an understanding of democracy that would break with the history he has examined, a democracy in which the citizen might be thought independent of fraternity. Now in expressing this desire, Derrida is characteristically cautious. He raises this break as being only perhaps a possibility, in the form of questions such as those just cited, and never claims that it could in fact occur. The fleeting invocations of "lovence [*aimance*]" in the text are here instructive. Derrida proposes this term to name what is beyond both love and friendship traditionally understood, suggesting that it is a minimal call to friendship, a call to be heard, at work in every address to another. Perhaps, Derrida intimates, one could think politics wholly otherwise based on such a notion, outside of all the determined figures that are found in the tradition. But while courting this possibility, Derrida ultimately argues against using it to ground a new politics. Doing so, he asserts, would be to attempt to gain certainty and assurance, erasing the very chance that this possibility opens. Further, he emphasizes that the call can never be unequivocal: "We cannot, and we *must* not, exclude the fact that when someone is speaking, in private or in public . . . some force in him or her is also striving *not to* be understood, approved, accepted in consensus" (*PF*, 218/*PA*, 246). This possibility of failure, that a declaration "can always flip into its opposite," is essential and unavoidable. "Without the possibility of radical evil, of perjury, and of absolute crime, there is no responsibility, no freedom, no decision" (*PF*, 219/*PA*, 247). Thus, although Derrida at times speaks approvingly of lovence, seeing in it the chance for a wholly other politics, he holds back from pursuing it further, both in fidelity to its chance and because of the inevitable threat it harbors.

This caution over breaking with the discourse of fraternity is consistent with what I have argued regarding Derridean inheritance, in particular concerning the necessity of the aporias inherited. If it is indeed a question of aporias, then one cannot simply divorce democracy from fraternity, and be done with this aspect of the tradition once and for all. Ignoring the name "fraternity" altogether would not be enough, since this is no guarantee that the brother would not return in another guise. To adapt a Freudian motif that Derrida uses in this text and across his work, such a killing of the brother would allow him to return all the more strongly as a specter. It is thus not a question of making a clean break with this history of democracy—this history so rooted in the fraternal—but rather of how to engage it. And as I have already suggested, Derrida's answer to this question in *Politics of Friendship* is far from neutral. In his inheritance of this tradition Derrida aims to reduce the force of fraternity in democratic discourse, and he does this in two main ways. First, by maintaining the questioning stance I've been discussing, he seeks to weaken the link between fraternity and democracy that so many take for granted. Second, alongside this interrogation Derrida attempts to avoid any endorsement of fraternity emerging from his work, for although the very interrogation of fraternity makes the term appear in his discourse, Derrida does his best to ensure that it never does so favorably. He never issues, for example, a call for a "fraternity to come," analogous to "democracy to come." Derrida thus shows sensitivity to the fact I discussed in Chapter 4 that values are always at work in language. That these values are beyond anyone's sovereign control means that this strategy is not guaranteed to work. It may be that fraternity comes to be positively valued in Derrida's writings, despite his actions. But his questioning stance and his avoidance of endorsement are attempts to prevent such a valuation coming to pass.

Derrida's inheritance in *Politics of Friendship* thus follows a strategy of upping the ante on the tradition that precedes him by calling into question its reliance on fraternity, without ever claiming to make a clean break from this past. Now if one is committed to feminist causes, one has good reason to support Derrida's resistance to fraternity. The very word excludes women from its scope, and historically, as Derrida demonstrates at length, fraternity has been invoked by thinkers who are also explicitly committed to the exclusion of women from politics. Even today, where such an explicit commitment to exclusion is rarely voiced, the discourse of fraternity remains in circulation, especially in France, without very much attention paid to its masculine connotations. This lack of attention makes it all the more likely that its exclusionary force will be allowed to work unchallenged. Thus, in the light of this history, and of this present, one may well share Derrida's hope for a democracy beyond fraternity.

However, on further reflection, it is not altogether clear that Derrida's framework of analysis warrants such a firm stand against the fraternal. Although the concept has a history that is marked by exclusion, and even granting that this force remains at work today, it is far from given that such exclusion is inevitably a part of its use. Indeed, Derrida's understanding of inheritance suggests that it is not, for, as I have argued, inheritance makes possible a transformation in value. What would prevent an inheritance of fraternity transforming its negative connotations? I have already shown how Derrida can be in favor of democracy, without enthusiastic support of the *demos* or the *kratos*, the people or power. In addition, there are aspects of Derrida's reading of fraternity that point to resources one could use to attempt to positively transform it. As I stated above, Derrida argues that the exclusion of women in Montaigne's account is predicated on the masculine dimension of names inherited and of renown. But as Derrida notes, this in itself is not enough to ensure that women have "*no* chance" of attaining a perfect friendship, with each other or with men, only that they have "*less chance*." Further, Derrida also points out that in its history fraternity has been linked to what seems to be exactly the kind of universalizing movement that in part motivates his more positive inheritance of democracy. He claims that "the fraternal figure of friendship will often bestow its features, allegorical or not, on what all revolutionary oaths involve with respect to responsibility to a future" (*PF*, 236/*PA*, 263). How is this future different from the one attached to democracy? Similarly, Derrida describes Michelet's formula "Fraternity is the law beyond the law" as a "hyperbolization of the fraternity concept which extends it not only beyond all boundaries but indeed beyond all juridical, legislative, and political determinations of the law" (*PF*, 237/*PA*, 265). Beyond all law—does this not suggest that this idea of fraternity could be in the same relation to justice as is democracy?

Given these resources, it is thus not altogether clear why one should not a call for a "fraternity to come," even if Derrida himself never issued such a call. Now in raising this question, I do not myself endorse such a call. I count myself among those sharing Derrida's position—I think that political discourse is much better without any reference to fraternity, since the connotations of this word remain powerfully exclusionary. I thus believe that it is strategically better to seek to reduce its force and argue against its recuperation, for I do not see the kind of transformative inheritance that is here required of fraternity actually succeeding. But my point in speaking of the possibility of this inheritance is to highlight that a strong justification for not pursuing it remains lacking in Derrida's account, as I have presented it thus far. That is, there remains a gap in Derrida's resistance to fraternity. In the face of certain promising elements in the fraternal tradition, Derrida still refuses to embrace the term, arguing that "in keeping this word to designate a fraternity beyond fraternity, a fraternity without fraternity (literal, strict, genealogical, masculine, etc.), one never renounces that which one claims to renounce—and which returns in a myriad of ways, through symptoms and disavowals whose rhetoric we must learn to decipher and whose strategy to outwit" (*PF*, 237/*PA*, 265). There is something in this name that resists transformation—it is somehow too heavy, too determined, too set in its meaning to allow one to inherit it otherwise. But what this something is has not yet been articulated.

Although Derrida does not address this concern directly in *Politics of Friendship*, I propose that a response to it is nonetheless contained in this work. The response is that Derrida's resistance to fraternity is justified not only by the masculine associations of the word but also by the connotations of nature that it carries, through its tie to birth. To speak of fraternity evokes the natural relation of being born of the same parents, and this reinforces the appearance of necessity to any exclusion that might be made on its basis. One can see the initial plausibility of such a claim by considering contemporary understandings of citizenship. Every contemporary nation-state, without exception, offers no more than three ways of being a citizen (some states do not offer all three, but these options exhaust the present possibilities). The first two appeal to nature through an appeal to the natural relation of birth—one is a citizen if one is born of citizens or born on the territory of the state. This is citizenship by blood or soil, *jus sanguinis* or *jus soli*. The third way, becoming a citizen through immigration (either by marriage, adoption, or residency within national borders), refers to nature directly in English (and French) in that one speaks of "naturalization" ("*naturalisation*"). Immigrants are spoken of *as if* they were naturally born citizens.[12] Thus all citizenship laws refer to natural birth, and from the point of view that I am suggesting is Derrida's, this is no accident. Nature does important work securing the boundaries of this relation of belonging, and insofar as they are marked natural, such relations carry with them a force of necessity. They appear as determined and irreversible, and their exclusions thus seem irresistible.

This would mean that the problem with fraternity is not simply its exclusion of women, but that through its being a natural relation, via an idea of natural birth, this exclusion appears necessary. However, Derrida's analysis of the link between the fraternal and the natural is not so straightforward, as it is complicated by two further claims. The first can be seen by examining a point I mentioned in passing above, that Montaigne explicitly describes the fraternal relation as spiritual, not natural. As Derrida writes:

> Natural fraternity (Montaigne, like Schmitt and so many others, seems to believe in such a thing) is not indispensable to perfect friendship; it would even be improper to it, as is natural paternity, for there can be no correspondence in the factual family ("Father and son can be of totally different complexion: so can brothers"). Likewise natural friendship can be only one of the attributes which I appreciate in the other, one among others in those "common, customary friendships" which are by definition divisible. Whereas the fraternity of alliance or election, the figure or the oath, the correspondence of convention, the fraternity of the "*covenant*" as one would say in English, the fraternity of spiritual correspondence, is the indivisible essence of "perfect friendship." (*PF*, 181/*PA*, 207)

Montaigne (as well as other thinkers in this tradition) articulates an unnatural fraternity, and this distance from nature is crucial to its value. If it were merely natural, it would fall far short of the perfection it is said to have. It would thus seem that

Montaigne and others like him are seeking to divest fraternity of its naturalistic connotations. The relation between the fraternal and the natural is one of separation, not identification.

The second complication follows from the claim, made by Derrida earlier in this text and in several others, that the nature thus invoked is a fiction. Of so-called natural family relations, he writes:

> A genealogical tie will never be simply real; its supposed reality never gives itself in any intuition, it is always posed, constructed, induced, it always implies a symbolic effect of discourse—a "legal fiction," as Joyce put it in *Ulysses* on the subject of paternity. This is true also—as true as ever, no matter what has been said, down to and including Freud—of maternity. All politics and all policies, all political discourses on "birth," misuse what can in this regard be only a *belief*, some will say: only remain a belief; others: what can only tend towards an act of faith. Everything in political discourse that appeals to birth, to nature or the nation—indeed to nations or to the universal nation of human brotherhood—this entire familialism consists in a renaturalization of this "fiction." What we are here calling "fraternization," is what produces symbolically, conventionally, through authorized engagement, a *determined politics*, which, be it left- or right-wing, alleges a real fraternity or regulates spiritual fraternity, fraternity in the figurative sense, on the symbolic projection of a real or natural fraternity. Has anyone ever met a brother? A uterine or consanguine (distantly related) brother? In nature? (*PF*, 92–93/*PA*, 114)

A genealogical link, Derrida insists, is a fiction. It rests on a belief, a faith in a truth that one never directly perceives. Any seemingly natural fact of birth (that one is born of this father and mother, with these siblings, at this location) requires a legal stamp of approval, a mark of confirmation given by society to ward off the threat of skepticism that may always haunt. As Derrida remarks here and elsewhere in this work (*PF*, 149, 159/*PA*, 171–72, 183–84), one never encounters a brother in nature—brothers are a cultural phenomenon through and through.

Reading these two claims together, that the tradition promotes a spiritual fraternity over the natural and that natural fraternity rests on a legal fiction, gives greater insight into Derrida's understanding of the exclusionary work being done in the political appeal to brotherhood. For if the fraternity so valued by Montaigne and others is not a natural relation, one may well ask, as does Derrida, "Why, then, retain this 'natural' figure? Why this adherence or this reference again to a natural bond, if one has set out to de-naturalize? Why does the natural schema remain?" (*PF*, 191/ *PA*, 205). If nature is unnecessary, then why does it still appear? The answer is that it is not unnecessary, for the spiritual needs the natural bond as a point of contrast to shore up its own purity. This is what constitutes the process of naturalization, such that the natural relation can appear in the first place. In other words, there are no brothers in nature—there are brothers who appear in culture *as* natural, an appearance achieved precisely in the elevation of a universal brotherhood or spiritual fraternity above the merely natural in a hierarchical relation. The political invocation of spiritual fraternity thus brings forth those other fraternal bonds that come to be seen as natural.

But at the same time—and this point is crucial—even as the spiritual relation is differentiated from the natural, this difference is never total. For each relation is named a "fraternity." In sharing the name, spiritual fraternity receives the connotations that adhere to natural fraternity. More precisely, as is suggested in one of the citations above, it is the particular connotation of birth carried in natural fraternity that is carried over to the spiritual. The importance of birth in this respect is underlined in the following passage from *Politics of Friendship*, where Derrida reflects on his inquiry as a whole.

> At stake would thus be a deconstruction *of the* genealogical schema. . . . Wherever it commands in the name of birth, of a national naturalness which has never been what it *was said to be*. It would concern confidence, credit, credence, *doxa* or *eudoxa*, opinion or right opinion, the approbation given to filiation, at birth and at the origin, to generation, to the familiarity of the family, to the proximity of the neighbour—to what axioms too quickly inscribe under these words. (*PF*, 105/*PA*, 128)

The "name of birth" considered as "a national naturalness" is thus one of Derrida's central targets in *Politics of Friendship*. That is, Derrida worries when thinkers appeal through fraternity to a naturalized understanding of birth in order to ground claims concerning political belonging. And just a few pages earlier this worry is shown to be based in the force of necessity carried by such an understanding of birth. Reading Plato's *Menexenus*, Derrida argues that the appeal to nature in Aspasia's discourse implies

> that nature commands law, that equality at birth founds *in necessity* legal equality. . . . This bond between the two ties—this synthetic a priori necessity, if we can speak of it thus—ties what is to what must be, it obliges, it connects the obligation to the tie of birth which we call natural; it is the *obligatory* process of a natural law, the embedding of an "it is necessary" in the filiation of what is, of what is born and what dies. It is the place of fraternization as the symbolic bond alleging the repetition of a genetic tie. (*PF*, 99/*PA*, 121–22)

Natural filiation is a bond tied at birth, and this is what gives it necessity. By association through the sharing of its name, spiritual fraternity would share in this necessity, thereby closing down the possibility of transforming its own boundaries, of opening itself up to other members, to other ways of belonging. "Truth, freedom, necessity, and equality come together in this politics of fraternity. One can hardly see how a *perhaps* could ever stand a chance in such a politics, the chance of an absolute housebreak or hospitality, an unpredictable decision or *arrivance*" (*PF*, 100/*PA*, 122–23).

Derrida's resistance to the use of fraternity is thus justified by the term's connotation of the relation to nature, via its repetition of a tie made at birth. This relation operates in a double movement—there is the casting down of a cultural relation (brothers by blood, filiation) into mere nature, which at the same time aligns the idea of fraternity with the necessity carried by birth. This alignment in place, the bond between spiritual brothers (blood brothers, affiliation) is thereby strengthened to resist transformation. It is in this way that fraternity appears as a term of little promise, precisely because it remains tied to natural birth. And it is thus that fraternity differs greatly from democracy, explaining Derrida's willingness to embrace the latter term but not the former. Although he argues that democracy is also necessarily implicated in acts of exclusion, it remains less determined than fraternity, and in particular is not directly implicated in the naturalizing discourse of birth. Thus, the promise of democracy follows not only from the claims I discussed in Chapter 3, showing just how undetermined it is in its meaning, harboring an absence of sense, bordering on nonsense. There I demonstrated how this poverty in the concept goes hand in hand with an abundance in its history—it is the proliferation of its uses that empties out its meaning, and this emptiness is what allows such proliferation to continue—and from this abundance Derrida inherits free speech, hospitality, and self-critique. The contrast with fraternity brings out the additional point that although Derrida's inheritance of democracy remains aporetic, the distance from nature allows it a certain room to move. Fraternity just does not offer the same possibilities. In its tie to birth it is too heavy a term to be moved otherwise, elsewhere, to a future unforeseen.

Further, with this analysis, one can now understand how the book *Politics of Friendship* is itself an act of democratic inheritance. I have argued that in this work Derrida reads a certain tradition in philosophical thinking that privileges fraternity in its conception of friendship. As a consequence of this privilege, the derived models of political belonging articulated in this tradition remain exclusionary, particularly of women, precisely because the invocation of fraternity produces and is supported by a natural, familial bond grounded in the necessity of birth. Derrida's own inheritance of this tradition follows the logic of the *surenchère*. Those before him distance themselves from natural fraternity, but in retaining the name of the brother they remain tethered to it so as to continue the patterns of exclusion that fraternity entails. Derrida's inheritance of this legacy raises the possibility of going one step further, raising the stakes so as to break from all figures of the brother in political discourse. In this way Derrida ups the ante on current understandings of democracy, issuing a challenge to break with one of the barriers imposed, to break with one of the dimensions of the tradition inherited. Which is not to say that Derrida proposes a break with the tradition *tout court*. His own questioning is loyal to a certain idea also found in the history of democratic theory, namely the injunction to universalize and open democracy up to its others. Thus when he challenges one aspect of the tradition, Derrida does so by deploying another aspect against it. He always works within inheritance, and it is in his particular way of doing so that this work can be seen to be a democratic act.

An Exclusion of Women

Politics of Friendship is thus an example of the kind of work that can follow from the claim that inheritance is essential to democracy. Of course, it is not the only way one might respond to this claim, since the heterogeneity of the legacies of the past opens them up to multiple receptions, none of which can be predicted in advance. Further, it is by no means an example that is beyond interrogation. In any work of inheritance, certain choices are made at the expense of others, and certain elements of a tradition are conserved so that others can be overturned. To close this chapter, I wish to draw attention to one such choice made by Derrida in this particular inheritance of democracy. It concerns the way women appear in *Politics of Friendship*. As I have highlighted, one of Derrida's central arguments in this text focuses on the absence of women in the models of friendship proposed in the tradition that he investigates. Time and again when friendship is theorized, women are excluded from its scope. It is precisely for this reason that Derrida resists fraternity, calling for a democracy that would break with all discourse of the brother. In this respect *Politics of Friendship* can be characterized as a feminist text. Nonetheless, one might wonder whether Derrida is also complicit with the very exclusion he at the same time resists. For Derrida to a great extent invents the tradition he discusses—he chooses to read a particular configuration of thinkers, and not another, from the history of Western philosophy. This configuration is a rich one, and as I suggested at the beginning of this chapter, *Politics of Friendship* is distinct among Derrida's texts in the large number of authors given detailed attention in its pages. But when surveying these pages, one might well say of them what Derrida says of Schmitt: "That which a macroscopic view is able to align, from afar and from high above, is a certain desert. Not a woman in sight. An inhabited desert, to be sure, an absolutely full absolute desert, some might even say a desert teeming with people. Yes, but men, men and more men" (*PF*, 155–56/ *PA*, 179). Derrida makes this claim to underline the absence of "a figure of woman, a feminine silhouette" in Schmitt's political theory, and it is certainly the case that such figures are not lacking in own Derrida's text—he precisely outlines the silhouettes of women in the very movement of their exclusion from the tradition read. But they are only silhouettes, and it remains that every author of remarks on friendship and political belonging examined in *Politics of Friendship*, whether briefly or at length, is a man. No women appear.[13]

This can be seen as part of a broader tendency in Derrida's work as a whole to avoid reading women philosophers. As Penelope Deutscher points out, although one can trace in Derrida's oeuvre a long-standing, if somewhat intermittent, engagement with feminism and feminist issues (of which *Politics of Friendship* is an important part), very few women appear in the vast array of philosophers, writers, and artists that he reads. And when women do appear as the object of his focus, as in the case of the one woman whose work he has engaged at significant length, Hélène Cixous, it is never in the capacity of their being philosophers—Derrida treats women exclusively as "writers" or "thinkers," not as representatives of the discipline or tradition of philosophy.

Deutscher argues that this is not just an oversight on Derrida's part. Rather, it follows from his vision of the nature of philosophy, as expressed in the following citation from the 2002 film, *Derrida*:

> Question: If you had a choice what philosopher would you like to have been your mother?
>
> Derrida: . . . I have no ready answer for this, give me some time. My mother? Good question, it's a good question in fact. I'll try to tell you why it's impossible for me to have any philosopher as a mother. My mother, my mother couldn't be a philosopher. A philosopher couldn't be my mother. That's a very important point. Because the figure of the philosopher is, for me, always a masculine figure. This is one of the reasons I undertook the deconstruction of philosophy. All the deconstruction of phallogocentrism is the deconstruction of what one calls philosophy which since its inception, has always been linked to a paternal figure. So a philosopher is a Father, not a Mother. So the philosopher that would be my mother would be a post-deconstructive philosopher, that is, myself or my son. My mother as a philosopher would be my granddaughter, for example. An inheritor. A woman philosopher who would reaffirm the deconstruction. And consequently, would be a woman who thinks. Not a philosopher. I always distinguish thinking from philosophy. A thinking mother—it's what I both love and try to give birth to.[14]

In his response Derrida describes an exclusivity in philosophy's association with the masculine. The philosopher has always been a paternal figure for Derrida, and he can place his mother in this tradition only as his own heir. Further, even in this "impossible genealogy," as Deutscher describes it, this woman who would follow is stripped of her philosophical status—named first "a woman philosopher who would affirm the deconstruction," she is immediately transformed into "a woman who thinks. Not a philosopher."

Now Deutscher argues that this does not necessarily mean that women philosophers cannot exist in the Derridean framework. She supports this claim by citing remarks Derrida makes on other occasions where he warns of both feminism and women writers promoting phallologocentrism, sometimes against their best intentions. There is nothing about being a woman that can necessarily prevent this from happening, and so women could be philosophers, provided they inhabit a masculine position. Nonetheless, Deutscher draws attention to the fact that, while it is raised, this possibility of women being philosophers is never actualized in Derrida's writings: "Derrida above all avoided a close look at the woman philosopher. . . . If he took the deconstruction of phallogocentrism to be the deconstruction of philosophy then to engage in the former with respect to the women writers he admired would have converted them into philosophers. He seems to have preferred aversion, in the sense of the averted look."[15] For Derrida women can be philosophers insofar as they can be paternal figures. Yet it just so happens that he never reads them as such.

In the light of this avoidance, Deutscher questions the value of affirmative ascription Derrida gives to his mother-granddaughter, the thinker who would be untouched by the masculine taint of the philosophical enterprise. As I have emphasized in my analysis, Derrida insists throughout his work that what is to come is always the chance and the threat, what is desirable and what is not, and here Derrida explicitly occludes the negative dimension of the future. But is this really a good thing? As Deutscher argues, "Subordinated to Derrida's imaginary genealogy, we are offered a remarkably conditional vision of women's futures. . . . The thematization of women is too conditional unless it includes their status as subjects of the potential worst as well as the potential best."[16] To place his mother in a purely positive future is thus to place her in a status diminished vis-à-vis that of men.

Further, the features of Derridean inheritance that I articulated in Chapter 2 provide another reason to question the position of the woman in this fantastic family scene. There I argued against the possibility, on occasion intimated by Derrida himself, that one can be done with an inheritance once and for all, putting it to death such that it could never return. This would be equivalent to resolving an aporia, something Derrida insists is strictly impossible. Yet this is precisely what Derrida seems to propose in his desire to give birth to his own mother. This is a sovereign dream, to erase one's dependence and debt on every other, to be free of every determining aspect that is found in one's past. Pure activity, the source of everything to come—there would no longer be a past from which a legacy could arrive in the future that would place Derrida once more in the position of an heir. And this erasure of inheritance would hold for all those coming after, including the mother-granddaughter Derrida here names. Despite Derrida's claim to the contrary, she in fact could not be an inheritor, on his understanding of the word, since there would be no more aporias left for her to receive. Opposed to such a dream, the theory of Derridean inheritance shows why it could never be realized. To be is to inherit—"the *being* of what we are *is* first of all inheritance, whether we like it or know it or not" (*SOM*, 54/*SDM*, 94). There is always a trace of the past that remains, always a legacy to come. The place Derrida gives to his mother-granddaughter is thus no place at all.

Returning now to *Politics of Friendship*, one sees that it conforms to this pattern characterizing Derrida's work more generally. Women are nowhere to be found among the actors in the tradition Derrida invents, even as he challenges this tradition's exclusion of women from friendship. He is yet another man, in a long line of men, discussing women and "woman" among themselves. One could thus describe *Politics of Friendship* in terms of a structure that Deutscher identifies in Derrida's writings on hospitality. Examining several examples he uses, Deutscher draws attention to the way Derrida demonstrates that the "woman is not the agent of hospitality (nor in the actual examples provided by Derrida the recipient), but the means of conduit in an exchange entre-hommes often occurring at her expense."[17] Such a demonstration can provide a useful model for certain forms of feminist critique, and Deutscher uses it criticize

Derrida's failure to mention women philosophers such as Harriet Taylor and Mary Wollstonecraft when he discusses the democratic autoimmunity of the expansion of women's political rights. My point is that this criticism also applies to Derrida's inheritance of friendship and fraternity. In this inheritance women are passed from the tradition to the heir, without ever occupying either position themselves.

The inheritance of democracy that takes place in *Politics of Friendship* is thus one that perpetuates a certain exclusion of women. Now this exclusion results from a choice that Derrida makes, and it is a choice that is far from necessary. For there is a wealth of material written by women on both friendship and political belonging that could be engaged along the lines of Derrida's inquiry. Such an engagement is by no means guaranteed to produce a break with the discourse of fraternity and the general privilege of the masculine—as mentioned above, texts written by women can be just as phallogocentric as those of men. But at the very least it would break with the particular masculine economy Derrida perpetuates, where women are simply the means by which a discussion takes place among men. Challenging this aspect of Derrida's inheritance of democracy would thus involve a turn outside his text, opening it up to elements in the tradition that he himself ignored. This is precisely the turn that Deutscher takes in the two essays from which I have been citing.

While supporting such a strategy of inheriting from Derrida's work, for my part I wish to maintain a position internal to his oeuvre, and pursue a further line of inquiry that arises from within. For even on their own terms Derrida's writings are far from uniform or complete, and their internal instabilities provide further possibilities for a transformative inheritance to take place. In the final chapter, therefore, I will focus on one such instability in Derrida's inheritance of democracy, which is located in and around his use and understanding of the concept of birth. I argued above that in the tradition examined in *Politics of Friendship*, birth is understood as carrying a mark of necessity, as it stands for an event that takes place only once and is beyond all revision. This is what in the end explains Derrida's resistance to fraternity—it is not so much that fraternity is traditionally associated with men, but that as a familial bond rooted in birth this association takes on a necessity that drastically reduces the possibility of its transformation. Birth anchors the fraternal bond such that it appears necessarily tied to its traditional understanding. However, at odds with this conception of birth is another I have just discussed, contained in Derrida's response to the question of his mother as a philosopher. In his fantastical wish to give birth to his mother, Derrida challenges the very necessity of the event of his birth. Now I have suggested that Derrida's desire is strictly impossible. To give birth to his mother would be to be done with inheritance, and I have already shown that this can never take place in a choice made by a sovereign I. Nonetheless, Derrida's very wish raises the possibility of calling into question the necessity of birth's determination as necessary. Is being a natural necessity the only possible meaning of birth? Or is it just one element of a more rich tradition that Derrida inherits in *Politics of Friendship* without question, without any attempt to relaunch it otherwise? My view is that, contrary to what is implied in Derrida's resistance to fraternity, the meaning of birth is multiple. It is a term that contains more possibilities than Derrida allows in *Politics of Friendship*, and these possibilities can in turn open the idea of democracy as inheritance beyond the horizon delimited in this text. Further, in addition to the one response that I cited above, there are a number of invocations of birth that occur across Derrida's writings implying that there is indeed much more to this notion than being a simple necessity. It is thus to these appearances that I now turn.

6 Inheriting Birth

In "The Reason of the Strongest," Derrida again takes up the question of fraternity, this time in relation to the work of Jean-Luc Nancy. The possibility of this reading had been raised in a long footnote in *Politics of Friendship*, where Derrida questioned the appeal to brotherhood in the inheritance of the Nietzschean understanding of community by Bataille, Blanchot, and Nancy (*PF*, 46–48/*PA*, 56–57). In the later essay Derrida pursues this question, examining Nancy's use of fraternity in *The Experience of Freedom*.[1] Derrida again expresses his reservations about the deployment of the word and summarizes his position at the end of his analysis thus:

> I am simply concerned that when it comes to politics and democracy this fraternalism might follow at least the temptation of a genealogical descent back to autochthony, to the nation, if not actually to nature, in any case, to birth, to *naissance*. I would wish to put this crucial word from the same family, this word *naissance*, before any other, before nature and before nation. . . . The theme of birth is not in and of itself worrisome or something to be suspicious of. The experience of birth, with all it implies, does indeed call for a singular thought—singular first of all because it does not reduce birth to either genesis or creation or beginning or origin. . . . Similarly, the theme of filiation or genealogy is not itself something to be suspicious of. But these two themes become "critical," they call for a critical and deconstructive deciphering, when their intersection becomes political, when a particular model, figure, or hegemony—for example the paternal, fraternal, or maternal—ends up getting politicized. (*R*, 61/*V*, 92)

This passage repeats the concerns raised in *Politics of Friendship*—the problem with using fraternity in political discourse is that it too easily connotes birth. This time, however, Derrida presents a more nuanced warning, qualifying his remarks in a number of ways. First, he avoids making a strict identification between birth and nature. Unlike many of the writers examined in *Politics of Friendship*, Nancy does not simply assert or assume that birth is natural, and so Derrida cannot level this charge against him. The coupling of birth with nature is thus not here the root of Derrida's worry. Second, Derrida concedes that birth and the related terms of filiation and genealogy, in and of themselves, are not automatically problematic. Rather, suspicion should arise when these themes intersect and become "political." It is when figures such as the paternal, fraternal, and maternal end up "getting politicized" that the problems start.[2]

The earlier concerns of *Politics of Friendship* are thus here modified, but the basic message is the same—there is something troubling about the politicization of fraternity, as it returns the discourse to an idea of birth. But if one pauses to reflect more closely on this passage, one might well raise some questions. For the qualifications made here are in fact rather strange. How should one understand birth, or each of the related terms of filiation or genealogy, "in and of itself"? Is there a sense in which these terms could be understood before they become "critical"? How could birth not intersect with filiation or genealogy? And does it make sense for Derrida to thereby suggest that these figures could ever *not* be "politicized"?

From a Derridean perspective, these are odd claims to make, and one can easily imagine Derrida interrogating another thinker who advanced them. It may be that part of their strangeness is due to the fact that Nancy was sitting in the audience at the time they were first delivered. When reading the work of his friends, especially in their presence, Derrida often cloaks the force of his readings behind caveats and qualifications. But in addition to this, I would suggest that these remarks signal an instability in Derrida's resistance to the use of fraternity. As I argued in Chapter 5, this resistance relies on a very particular understanding of birth, one that necessarily ties it to nature and necessity. Here Derrida would seem to acknowledge that such a reduction is unsatisfactory, when he states that "the experience of birth, with all it implies, does indeed call for a singular thought." Similarly, a couple of years earlier in his conversation with Roudinesco, Derrida asks, "But what is it 'to be born'? If we distinguish it rigorously from the origin, the beginning, provenance, etc., 'birth' is perhaps a question of the future and of arrival, a newly arrived question [*une question d'avenir, une question toute neuve*]" (*FW*, 40/*DQ*, 74). These remarks suggest that birth need not be understood in only one way and that how it is to be understood remains a task for thinking. It is this task that I undertake in the analysis that follows.[3]

Birth as Positive

That there is more to the notion of birth is supported by statements elsewhere in Derrida's writings. For unlike fraternity, which he never embraces in his own name, Derrida does invoke birth in a positive manner. I already cited one instance of this at the end of the last chapter, when Derrida expresses his desire to give birth to his own mother.

Of interest to me here are other appearances of birth in Derrida's work, appearances occurring in contexts that are overtly political. For example, in the 1993 interview "The Deconstruction of Actuality," Derrida is questioned with regard to the rise of xenophobia in the immigration debate in France. Such a turn, the interviewer suggests, is surprising. In response, Derrida contrasts this occurrence with what takes place in an event. Whereas French xenophobia can be analyzed more or less thoroughly after the fact and so lose its element of surprise, "an event that remains an event is an arrival, an arrivance: it surprises and belatedly resists analysis." As occurs, he states, with the birth of a child.

> With the birth of a child—the first figure of the absolute arrivant—one can analyze the causalities, the genealogical, genetic, and symbolic premises, or the wedding preparations. But even if such an analysis could ever be completed, one can never reduce the element of chance [*aléa*], the place of the taking-place; there will be someone who speaks, someone irreplaceable, an absolute initiative, another origin of the world.[4]

The birth of a child is here presented as a figure for the event. No matter how much one may prepare for it, no matter how keenly it is anticipated, there is always something that surprises. A child might be welcomed into the world, but as someone who speaks, it never quite fits as expected. The child is another, and an other, origin of the world.[5]

Continuing, Derrida returns this idea to the issue at hand, the immigration debate in France.

> The immigration in which the history of France is rooted, its culture, its religions, and its languages, was first the history of all the children, whether or not they were the children of immigrants, who were such absolute arrivants. The task of a philosopher—and therefore of anyone, and of a citizen, for example—is to take the analysis as far as possible to try to make the event intelligible up to the moment when one comes to the arrivant.[6]

Those who wish to study the history of immigration in France, which in many ways constitutes the history of France itself, must thus find a way of giving place to the recurring dimension of absolute surprise found in the birth of children.

In these remarks, Derrida would appear to make exactly the move against which he warns in his reading of Nancy. Discussing immigration and characterizing the history of France as a history of those who are born, he crosses birth with the genealogical in a political context. Further, this is not the only time that Derrida had done this. The child also appears as a figure for the arrivant in *Aporias*, dating from around the same time (1992).

> The absolute *arrivant* as such is, however, not an intruder, an invader, or a colonizer, because invasion presupposes some self-identity for the aggressor and for the victim. Nor is the *arrivant* a legislator or the discoverer of a promised land. As disarmed as a newly born child, it no more commands than is commanded by the memory of

some originary event where the archaic is bound with the *final* extremity, with the finality par excellence of the *telos* or of the *eskhaton*. (*A*, 34/*AP*, 66)

Here the newly born child is proposed as a figure for what exceeds a determined political situation, that which lies beyond all calculation and predictability. It lies outside the sphere of sovereignty, neither commanding nor commanded, to the point where its self-identity is called into question.

Finally, a third appearance is found in one of Derrida's last public discourses, "A Europe of Hope," delivered in May 2004, which he closes with the following words:

> Thus this is my dream. I thank you for helping me, not only to dream this dream, to dream, as Ramonet said, that "an other world is possible," but also for giving us the strength to do everything in our power so that it may actually become possible. Billions of men and women in the world share this dream. Slowly, with the labor pains of birth, they will bring it to the light of day, one fine day.[7]

These words resonate with the remarks from the early 1990s. Again at issue is the possibility of another world and of what might be to come in an overtly political context, and again Derrida invokes birth as a figure approximating this event. Now there is a difference between this citation and the last two, which is that here there is an appeal to birth without the accompanying mention of the child. Thinking about this difference reveals more of what is at stake in Derrida's discourse. What work is done by speaking of the birth of a child, rather than just the act of birth alone? I would suggest that the image of the child places Derrida's words in a more positive and hopeful light. In terms of the argument I made in Chapter 4, this is to say that the value carried by the child in past and present discourse is positive, and Derrida inherits this value in his use of such language. To speak of a child being born is to speak of a positive possibility. And this positivity is only amplified when this birth is placed in the future.[8] This occurs first through birth's association with the arrivant, which already operates to name the "to come" in Derridean discourse, and then in the future tense used in "The Deconstruction of Actuality," where Derrida writes that "there will be someone who speaks, someone irreplaceable, an absolute initiative, another origin of the world." Of course, this does not mean that the child is necessary for producing this effect. It is alternatively achieved in the citation from "A Europe of Hope" in the tone of the text's title, in the future tense used in the phrase "with the labor pains of birth, they will bring it to the light of day," and in Derrida's invocation of the birth occurring "one fine day." No child is named, but a similar result in the value communicated is achieved through the work of these other positive signs.

In speaking positively of birth, Derrida's remarks in these citations thus stand in stark contrast to the discourse of birth I tracked in *Politics of Friendship*, which as I noted is taken up again in "The Reason of the Strongest." There would, therefore, seem to be a clear division in the meaning and value given to birth in Derrida's later writings. On the one hand, he identifies it narrowly with nature and necessity, and this identification grounds his resistance to the use of fraternity in political discourse. Birth understood in this sense is thus marked as negative, since it is said to be at work in a discourse whose force Derrida wishes to diminish. On the other hand, Derrida himself has recourse to birth as a figure for the arrivant, as that which comes and exceeds all calculation and determination, precisely in political contexts. Here Derrida imparts a positive value to birth, insofar as he invokes the figure of the child or its substitutes, suggesting he endorses an openness to the arrivant. Derrida's work would thus appear to contain two births, with two meaning and two values.

How to understand this division? The dates of publication prevent a narrative of evolution or change in Derrida's thought, since he invokes each kind of birth in both the early 1990s and the early 2000s. However, there is a further difference between the appearances of these two understandings of birth. As I have noted, when Derrida speaks positively of birth he places it in the future, through its association with the arrivant and the use of the future tense. By contrast, when Derrida states his concerns over fraternity he places it in the past, speaking of "a national naturalness which has never been what it *was said to be*" (*PF*, 105/*PA*, 128), and of a "genealogical descent back to . . . birth" (*R*, 61/*V*, 92). In these cases birth is something that has already happened, something that has occurred in the past.

This temporal division has the potential to save Derrida's discourse from contradiction, for differences in meaning and value can be tolerated if they are diffused across time. There is no tension in holding that the meaning and value of birth in the past is different to that of birth in the future. But, given all I have argued, one would expect that this division cannot be sustained. With respect to time, this book has been devoted to showing the relation between the past and future carried in the figure of inheritance. So it would be odd if all of a sudden one could coherently read Derrida's work as maintaining a clean opposition between these two temporal tenses. Similarly, on the question of value, I have shown at length that for Derrida the unforeseeable future is always ambivalent, containing possibilities of both chance and threat. While the passages linking birth to the arrivant thus appear to present birth as positive, it ought not be so unambiguously. Even in the seemingly innocent image of a newborn child—an image that in our culture stands for innocence itself—one would expect that all threats cannot be averted.

Birth as Ambivalent

The next step in my analysis is thus to show that the division drawn between these two understandings of birth is indeed unstable. The point of doing so is not to oppose Derrida's position, as if he had a single, clear stance on the matter, since I will make this demonstration by appealing to other passages in his writings. Rather, through examining and exploiting the instabilities in Derrida's multiple appeals to birth, I aim to develop a richer and more satisfactory understanding of this notion. The seeds for doing so are in fact already contained in "The Deconstruction of Actuality." In a passage I cited earlier, immediately after placing birth firmly in the future, Derrida complicates the temporal schema: "The immigration in which the history of France is rooted, its culture, its religions, and its languages, was first the history of all the children, whether or not they were the children of immigrants, who were such absolute arrivants."[9] As a part of history, the children lie in the past, but as arrivants, they are still to come. One could thus read this sentence as suggesting that the status of these children as arrivants is activated through inheriting them from the past, in a movement that opens up their previous determination to an unknown future. In this way, Derrida opposes the xenophobic right by capitalizing on the fact that these events of birth are never fully past—through inheriting these births otherwise he points to an alternative history of France. At stake here is thus not simply the future, but that future that enfolds the past through a relation of inheritance.

Further, this challenge to temporal separation can be seen to open a space for a challenge to value. This can be detected in the ease with which Derrida moves, as the interview progresses, from the discourse of birth to that of the ghost. Following Derrida's appeal to the incalculable event, his interlocutor asks, "But doesn't philosophy also struggle at the same time with the idea that something, possibly the worst, could always return?" Derrida answers immediately with a "Yes," and, articulating ways in which this struggle might take place, he invokes "a law of the spectral that resists both ontology . . . and a philosophy of the subject. . . . Yes, a ghost can return as the worst, but without this revenance, and if one challenges this irreducible originality, one is also depriving oneself of memory, legacy [*héritage*], and justice, of everything that matters beyond life."[10] While the invocation here of the worst should be read in the light of my analysis in Chapter 4, it is clear that the event, linked earlier to birth as a positive figure for the arrivant, is at the same time tied to a negative force in a past that returns. The link to the ghost thus also points to a temporality of inheritance, and rather than being simply positive, birth starts to appear as more ambivalent.

"The Deconstruction of Actuality" thus gestures also to an alternative understanding of birth—one that stands for contingency, but with an ambivalent value and involving both past and future linked by inheritance. However, these remarks are fleeting, and at best merely suggestive. So to develop this understanding further, I turn to other appearances of birth in Derrida's writings. The first is Derrida's most famous invocation of birth, found in the final paragraph of his early essay "Structure, Sign, and Play in the Discourse of the Human Sciences." Having invoked two interpretations of interpretation, one associated with Rousseau, the other with Nietzsche, Derrida writes:

> For my part, although these two interpretations must acknowledge and accentuate their difference and define their irreducibility, I do not believe that today there is any question of *choosing*—in the first place because here we are in a region (let us say, provisionally, a region of historicity) where the category of choice seems particularly trivial; and in the second, because we must first try to conceive of the common ground, and the *différance* of this irreducible difference. Here there is a

kind of question, let us still call it historical, whose *conception, formation, gestation,* and *labor* we are only catching a glimpse of today. I employ these words, I admit, with a glance toward the operations of childbearing [*l'enfantement*]—but also with a glance toward those who, in a society from which I do not exclude myself, turn their eyes away when faced by the as yet unnamable which is proclaiming itself and which can do so, as is necessary whenever a birth is in the offing, only under the species of a nonspecies, in the formless, mute, infant [*infante*], and terrifying form of monstrosity.[11]

It is important to note that this image of childbearing does not appear out of nowhere. Two pages earlier Derrida speaks positively of Claude Lévi-Strauss's suspicion of history, since this is "a concept which has always been in complicity with a teleological and eschatological metaphysics, in other words, paradoxically, in complicity with that philosophy of presence to which it was believed history could be opposed." Nonetheless, Derrida at the same time warns against the danger in such a suspicion of "falling back into an ahistoricism of a classical type," and he charges Lévi-Strauss of doing exactly this in that for him "the appearance of a new structure, of a new system, always comes about . . . by a rupture with its past, its origin, its cause."[12] This is evident in the following lines from Lévi-Strauss's *Introduction to the Work of Marcel Mauss,* which Derrida then cites: "Whatever may have been the moment and the circumstances of its appearance on the scale of animal life, language could only have been born in one fell swoop [*n'a pu naître que tout d'un coup*]. Things could not have set about acquiring signification progressively."[13] Lévi-Strauss here invokes a birth that occurs in an instant, with no relation to the past—"on the model of catastrophe," as Derrida describes it[14]— in order to characterize the appearance of the new phenomenon that is language.

It is thus in this context that Derrida's talk of birth in "Structure, Sign, and Play" is to be understood. Attempting to avoid both teleological and catastrophic understandings of the appearance of events to come, Derrida takes up and transforms—he inherits—Lévi-Strauss's vocabulary of birth. This suggests a kind of middle path that might avoid either extreme. But most relevant to my present concern is the relationship posited here between the child to come and the monstrous. Determining this is difficult, given the very strange optics staged in this passage.[15] Derrida speaks of a glance toward childbirth, and a glance toward those, including himself, who do not look at the monstrous. So how many glances are there? Three?—one toward a child, another toward those others, including himself, and the third the failed glance to the monstrous? Does the third count? Or do all three constitute a single glance? What about just two? And how many "things" are glanced at? One, two, or three? That is, are these three things kept separate, or is the child carried in those others, including himself, that are glanced at, and is the monstrous somehow there too in its failure to be seen? Or again, are only two out of three united?

The text does not say. Leaving the others (including Derrida) aside, and focusing on the child and the monstrous, on the most straightforward reading these would be two different things, two objects of two looks. Which would be to say that Derrida is describing two separate possibilities being carried in the pregnancy, implying that *either* a child *or* the monstrous will be born: "I employ these words, I admit, with a glance toward the operations of childbearing—*but also* with a glance toward those who . . . turn their eyes away when faced by . . . monstrosity" (my emphasis). The "but also" here is crucial, for it subtly implies a division, seeming to mark the child and the monstrous as two distinct possibilities that are contained in the birth to come. If this is indeed the case, then while the pregnancy would be ambivalent, the value of each of its possible outcomes would remains untouched by the other. This reading would thus preserve the child as positive and so reinforce what I have argued above is the value dominating Derrida's later invocations of this figure.

However, the indetermination of the optics makes possible another interpretation. For if there is only one glance occurring, and only one "thing" seen, then the future the pregnancy portends might consist of not either the child or the monstrous, but of a monstrous child. This is given further support in Derrida's qualification of the monstrosity as "infant [*infante*]," for in addition to amplifying the idea of speechlessness implied by its Latin root, this one word also places the child within the possibility of the monstrous. Thus, on this second interpretation, the two possibilities of the child and the monstrous cannot be separated so cleanly, and the one contaminates the other.

Given this second interpretation—the one I wish to privilege—the question then becomes just what the value of the monstrous is, in order to understand the kind of contamination taking place. "Structure, Sign, and Play" alone provides very little information in answer to this question. It would seem to present the monstrous as more or less negative, since it is glossed as a "species of a nonspecies . . . formless, mute, infant, and terrifying form." But this passage should not be read in isolation. As is often noted, it echoes another, equally famous paragraph from Derrida's early work, that which closes *Of Grammatology's* Exergue.

> Perhaps patient meditation and painstaking investigation on and around what is still provisionally called writing, far from falling short of a science of writing or of hastily dismissing it by some obscurantist reason, letting it rather develop its positivity as far as possible, are the wanderings of a way of thinking that is faithful and attentive to the world irreducibly to come which proclaims itself in the present, beyond the closure of knowledge. The future can only be anticipated in the form of an absolute danger. It is that which breaks absolutely with constituted normality and can only thus proclaim itself, *present* itself, as a species of monstrosity. For this world to come and for that within it which will have made tremble the values of sign, speech, and writing, for that which here guides our future anterior, there is as yet no exergue.[16]

While childbirth is absent, the correspondence with "Structure, Sign, and Play" is clear. But here the monstrous carries a more ambivalent value. For the first sentence of the paragraph has a more hopeful tone, and that against which the monstrous is cast—the "constituted normality" and "the values of sign, speech, and writing" that it will have made tremble—are things the reader has been given to understand ought to be called into question. Thus, even as monstrosity remains a danger, it is a danger that carries hope. Further, the use of and reference to the future anterior in the paragraph from *Of Grammatology* can also be read to prefigure a temporality of inheritance, as it is no longer just a question of the future, but of the past enfolded in the future.

Thus, read in this manner, these early texts of Derrida can be seen to testify to the contamination between the possibilities of a child and a monster—of a monstrous child—mixing the values of positivity and ambivalence, as well as the temporal tenses of past and future. However, I have advanced this interpretation against what is perhaps a more plausible alternative, which preserves the child as positive (and note that the end of "Structure, Sign, and Play" places this child more squarely in the future, without reference to a past). So to provide more support for my interpretation, I will now examine another chain of citations from Derrida's work. This chain begins with a phrase I have cited but not yet discussed, the description of the birth of a child as "another origin of the world." As far as I am aware, "The Deconstruction of Actuality" is the only text in which Derrida describes birth in this way, and he provides no further explanation as to what it might mean.[17] But it echoes another phrase in his oeuvre, one to which he does appeal on a few occasions and which I mentioned in Chapter 4, "the end of the world." This is inscribed in the French title of what was first published in English as *The Work of Mourning—Chaque fois unique, la fin du monde*. In the preface of this book, Derrida claims that death "does not announce an absence, a disappearance, the end of *this or that* life, that is, of the possibility for a world (always unique) to appear to *some* living being." Rather,

> death declares each time *the end of the world in totality*, the end of every possible world, and *each time the end of the world as unique totality, thus irreplaceable and thus infinite*. As if the *repetition* of the end of an infinite whole was still possible: the end of the world *itself*, of the only world that would be, each time. Singularly. Irreversibly.[18]

Just how one is to understand this definition of death is not clear, and Derrida does not expand on it here. But he closes the preface by suggesting that another text he published at the same time, "Rams," would be "a true introduction to this book," noting that "it circles around a line from Celan which has not left me for years: *Die Welt ist fort, ich muß dich tragen* [The world is gone, I must carry you]."[19]

Following this lead, I will thus turn to "Rams." First delivered in 2003 as a lecture in memory of Gadamer, it offers a reading of Celan's poem from which this line comes. Early in the lecture Derrida repeats the formulation of the end of the world articulated in *Chaque fois unique*. But this time a new element is introduced.

> For each time, and each time singularly, each time irreplaceably, each time infinitely, death is nothing less than an end of *the* world. Not *only one* end among others, the

end of someone or of something *in the world*, the end of a life or of a living being. Death puts an end neither to someone in the world nor to *one* world among others. Death marks each time, each time in defiance of arithmetic, the absolute end of the one and only world, of that which each opens as a one and only world, the end of the unique world, the end of the totality of what is or can be presented as the origin of the world for any unique living being, be it human or not.[20]

In the final sentence a direct link is made between "the origin of the world" and "the end of the world" which is Derrida's focus.[21] Derrida does not comment further on this link, and the phrase "the origin of the world" does not reappear in "Rams." However, something akin emerges in this text's closing pages, when Derrida discusses the particular line from Celan, "*Die Welt ist fort, ich muß dich tragen.*" He organizes his interpretation into five points: two focused on the meaning of *tragen*, and three on the meaning of *Welt*. Concerning *tragen*, Derrida first speaks of the *dich*, the "you" who is carried. He initially suggests that this "you" could be the possible addressee of the poem, and then raises another possibility: "The *dich* can also designate a living being *to come*. The *I must* (*ich muß*) must necessarily be turned toward the future." With the future on the table, Derrida passes easily to the child.

> *Tragen*, in everyday usage, also refers to the experience of *carrying* a child prior to its birth. Between the mother and the child, the one in the other and the one for the other, in this singular couple of solitary beings, in the shared solitude between one and two bodies, the world disappears.[22]

Derrida thus reiterates the association between the child and the "to come." And in line with the tendency that I am seeking to amplify, here too the value of this child falls short of being unambiguously positive. For now birth does not mark the origin of the world, but its end. Under such a light, "the end of the world" certainly appears less threatening, for its coupling with the image of the child keeps the negative force of death somewhat at bay. But at the same time, this association also works to undermine the value in the other direction, since in being linked to the end of the world instead of its origin, the innocent image of childbirth takes on a different hue. This ambivalence is reinforced as Derrida moves immediately to a second possible meaning of *tragen*.

> But, to continue, if *tragen* speaks the language of birth, if it must address itself to a living being present or to come, it can also be addressed to the dead, to the survivor or to the specter, in an experience that consists in carrying the other in the self, as one bears mourning—and melancholy.[23]

In the discussion that follows, the theme of loss dominates. Derrida examines *Welt* in Freud on mourning and melancholy in which one attempts to internalize the dead other, in Husserl on the alter ego eluding pure presence in phenomenological intuition, and in Heidegger on the departure of the world. This turn to loss is to be expected given the memorial context of the lecture. But rather than follow Derrida in this turn and leave birth behind, I want to remain in the interchange that has taken place here between birth and death. Uniting them in the line from Celan, Derrida ties the "to come" understood in the carrying of the child in pregnancy to the past of the specter carried in the survivor. This tie reveals more of what is at stake in Derrida's radical interpretation of death as "the end of the world." For it implies that if the world as a totality ends each time there is death, then each time there is death, there is also birth. Indeed, this must be so. In marking it as "the end of *the* world," as opposed to *a* world, Derrida suggests with death the world does not *continue*, that it does not *go on*. Nonetheless, it remains that *there is* the world. Which is to say that with each death, each time the world ends, it—the one and only world—also begins. Each death is thus a birth. It is at the same time the end and the origin of the world. Birth and death are inseparable.

Gathering these citations together—from Derrida's early remarks in "Structure, Sign, and Play" and *Of Grammatology*, to some his very last statements in *Chaque fois unique* and "Rams"—one is left with a significantly different understanding of birth than the one I proposed first emerges out of Derrida's more positive invocations in "The Deconstruction of Actuality," *Aporias*, and "A Europe of Hope." As a figure simultaneously of the world's origin and end, birth now carries both the good and the bad, the chance and the threat. Its value is ambivalent. And confirmed again is one of the central claims of my interpretation as a whole, that the "to come" is not cut off from the past. Rather, the "to come" arises precisely through an interaction with the past, through an act of inheritance. For birth in the future carries a trace of the past, naming simultaneously the survivor and the specter. To express it in alternative Derridean terminology, every arrivant is a revenant—what is to come is at the same time a return of what has been.

However, even as I have challenged a simple understanding of birth in the future that would cut it off from the past and leave its value positive, untouched thus far is the other conception of birth that I have argued is found in Derrida's writings. This other conception is that implied in Derrida's resistance to fraternity, that which lies in the past, standing for nature and necessity, and is assigned a negative value. In the light of my interpretation, can such an understanding maintain its integrity? There is good reason to think that it cannot. For, as I argued in Chapter 2, in the Derridean schema there is no past that is beyond the reach of repetition through inheritance. Every past, in being named past, remains open to the possibility of being inherited in the future. Indeed, the very act of naming something as being in the past, of pointing to it as such, is itself an act of inheritance, as minimal as it is. As such, this other birth marked as nature or necessity, in also being marked as past, is at the same time marked as able to be transformed through inheritance.

This being the case, a change in the meaning and value that is ascribed to this birth ought to be possible. It is cast as necessary because it is placed in a past understood as immune to all revision. The possibility of inheritance calls this into question, shifting the necessity associated with this birth to a contingency. It would not necessarily be the case that birth will stand for necessity. Such a claim depends on its not being inherited otherwise, a state that cannot be assured. In its turn, this revision in meaning can lead to a revision in value, for it can no longer be maintained that such a birth will always be negative. With the possibility of inheritance, of being turned elsewhere in the future and so of disrupting its necessity, it is possible that a positive value might also accrue to this figure. The birth formerly of nature and necessity would thus move from being purely negative, to being ambivalent. In this way, what first seemed to be two conceptions of birth operating in Derrida's writings would collapse into one. Both the birth Derrida opposes in traditional political discourse, and the one he invokes in his attempts to think politics otherwise, would be equally contingent in their meaning, ambivalent in their value, and crossing past and future in a time of inheritance.

Birth as Aporetic

My final task, therefore, is to demonstrate that birth as necessity can indeed be inherited otherwise, and in the course of this be transformed in its meaning and value. To do so, I will turn to a text rarely discussed in the literature, "The Night Watch," which Derrida wrote as the preface to the 2001 republication of Jacques Trilling's *James Joyce ou l'écriture matricide*.[24] Across "The Night Watch" Derrida is explicit in acknowledging the place he occupies as an heir to Trilling's work, making inheritance one of his central themes. This is perhaps nowhere more apparent than in the text's opening paragraphs.

> In a word, in brief, as befits a preface, I will speculate about a working hypothesis, one that will remain for me, to be sure, the object of a risky choice. It is a deliberate selection that I intend to sign, a boldly assumed sorting out, a *tri*, I might even say an essay, a trial run, an experimental attempt, a *try* (a word that apparently has the same etymology as *tri*).
>
> To what hypothesis am I referring? The author of this book, so well known and so well-versed in literature, psychoanalysis, music, and a few other arts, here proposes, he too, he first of all, to sort things out, to *trier*. My own *tri* would thus raise the stakes [*surenchérir*] or speculate upon his own. For Jacques Trilling would have proposed a *tri* or sorting out between the *mother* and *maternity*.
>
> To distinguish between the mother and maternity, to sort them out [*trier*], to draw an infinitely fine but indivisible line between them, even when the thing seems undecidable—that, I would say, is Trilling's decisive gesture, his critical operation, his *krinein*. And this operation takes place at the very moment he reminds us of the inevitability or fatality for the one who writes, and par excellence for Joyce, of a certain matricide.
>
> But here is the aporia that never fails to appear—and far from paralyzing the matricidal desire this aporia actually exacerbates it, begins by motivating it, and opens the way for it: if one distinguishes between [*trier*] the mother and

maternity, it follows that one can dream of doing away with the mother, some particular mother, though one will never be done with the maternity of the mother. (NW, 87–88/LV, 7–8)

This passage mobilizes all the characteristics of the Derridean model of inheritance I articulated in Chapter 2. Derrida presents his preface as focused on Trilling's work of sorting out (*trier*), attempting to distinguish between the mother and maternity in his reading of Joyce. Trilling assumes a separation between the mother and maternity. This takes place in his articulation of all writers as bearing a matricidal wish, where every writer's dream is to begin with a blank and virgin page, free of debt to anything in the past. On Derrida's reading, for Trilling the matricide may well succeed in killing a particular mother, but would leave untouched the structure of maternity itself.[25] It is precisely this separation that Derrida will challenge. Performing an act of sorting out in his turn, Derrida is going to up the ante or raise the stakes (*surenchérir*) on Trilling's assumed distinction. Maternity and the mother cannot be cleanly divided, for they remain, he will argue, in an aporetic relation. At the beginning of this preface Derrida thus announces that he will sort through strands of the legacy he receives, raising the stakes by bringing attention to an aporia that Trilling fails to acknowledge. Derrida will inherit from Trilling, in the precise Derridean understanding of this term.

In addition, inheritance is seen also at work in "The Night Watch" in the parallel that can be drawn between it and Montaigne's "On Friendship." Both are prefaces written in homage by one friend to another who has passed away. This parallel is already suggested in the above citation's emphasis on the text's status as an "essay" and is made clear in Derrida's description of how he first met Trilling:

This piece of writing watched over [*veillait*] the birth of a friendship. Jacques Trilling generously sent it to me more than a quarter of a century ago, no doubt so that I might recognize, among so many other things, a few complicitous winks, particularly with regard to the *Phaedrus* and "Plato's Pharmacy," not far from a nod toward our friend Hélène Cixous, who was already the author of the first great reading of Joyce in France. We had not yet met, Jacques and I. (NW, 89/LV, 10)

Compare to Montaigne's words: "Yet I am particularly indebted to that treatise, because it first brought us together: it was shown to me long before I met him and first made me acquainted with his name," and later, "we embraced each other by repute [*nous nous embrassions par noz noms*]."[26]

In the light of my discussion of gender in the previous chapter, one can see that in one respect Derrida's preface is an improvement on Montaigne's. For in the latter the subject examined was friendship, and it was theorized in such a way as to exclude women from its scope. By contrast, Derrida chooses to focus on the figures of the mother and maternity in Trilling's work, placing them at the center of their encounter. Far from being excluded, these images of women are for Derrida the key to understanding Trilling's reading of Joyce. Now one might balk at the fact that this focus comes at what may seem to be an extraordinarily high price, since the mother only appears in the context of her attempted murder. What good is a discussion of a woman in which she is the object of a murderous wish? Without erasing such a concern, I would also suggest that this price can also be read as a certain mark of respect. For recall one of Penelope Deutscher's charges against Derrida's reading of women, that I discussed in Chapter 5. Deutscher argues that Derrida on occasion casts women and women's issues solely in a positive light, avoiding any exploration of the potential negativity that they might harbor in their future. This is seen in particular in Derrida's assimilation of women's rights to democracy's perfectibility, without an accompanying acknowledgment of the pervertibility that this entails. It is also present in Derrida's desire to give birth to his mother as a thinker, not a philosopher, who would thus be untainted by the phallogocentrism of the philosophical tradition. In both cases Deutscher argues that "the thematization of women is too conditional unless it includes their status as subjects of the potential worst as well as the potential best."[27] The present discourse on matricide can be seen to counter this tendency, for at the very least, the appearance of the mother in this discourse of murder places her on an equal footing with the father. She is powerful enough to provoke the matricidal desire, she is worthy of being killed, just as the father is worthy of being killed in the patricidal desire that is that of deconstruction.

Now this does not mean that Derrida's invocation of maternity and the mother in "The Night Watch" is immune to all critique. It remains exposed to the other charge that I received from Deutscher and leveled against *Politics of Friendship*, that concerning the absence of women read. For the distinction between maternity and the mother is the conduit through which Derrida's inheritance of Trilling takes place—yet again, Derrida discusses a figure of woman with another man, without any women being granted the status of either legatees or heirs.[28] One might also question the need of both Trilling and Derrida to use such violent imagery in the first place, regardless of the gender of the figure to which it is aimed.[29] All of which is to say that Derrida's inheritance of the matricide from Trilling is complex when considered with an eye on gender. Neither clearly pro- nor antifeminist, "The Night Watch" thus calls for a certain vigilance as one proceeds to engage its claims.

With this in mind, I now turn to examine the details of these claims. As Derrida states, Trilling's focus on the figure of the matricide is to be understood in terms of his engagement with and challenge to psychoanalytic theory. Trilling's "Joycean knowledge . . . is always put in the service of the revolution within the psychoanalytic revolution: the matricide rather than Oedipus, the matricide who weaves his ruses into the act of writing, the matricide who hounds the mother since he cannot have his way with maternity" (NW, 90/LV, 11). Derrida also claims that there is some uncertainty as to whether for Trilling the matricide targets a particular mother or maternity itself. The distinction between the mother and maternity is thus not always clearly marked in Trilling's text. Nevertheless, Derrida argues that this distinction can be drawn on the basis of Trilling's analysis, for the key difference between the two terms lies in their relation to substitution. The mother remains open to substitution: "It is indeed possible to kill the mother, to replace her, to substitute one 'womb' for another. This is more possible today than ever, though the possibility is ageless" (NW, 91/LV, 12–13). In contrast, for Trilling maternity would resist this possibility. Derrida justifies this interpretative claim by drawing attention to Trilling's gloss of maternity as "the ineluctability of birth, of the marked hour, always already inscribed."[30] It is the link to birth, specifically to a unique birth that has already taken place, which renders maternity immune to erasure or replacement. "But what is impossible to expunge is birth, dependency upon an originary date, upon an 'act' of birth before any birth act or certificate" (NW, 91/LV, 13).

Derrida goes on to develop this thought of ineluctability by associating it with Job's curse against his own birth.[31] Such a curse "remains powerless," since the "evil" it wants to erase "remains the very condition for such a wanting," and so in its utterance it "confirms, repeats, reproduces, and makes endure that which it would like to repress" (NW, 91/LV, 13). In its display of powerlessness, the curse would only reinforce the necessity of one's having been born. Discussing Job's curse also allows Derrida to amplify the singularity of being born, for the particularity of its paradox serves to distinguish it from everything else. To curse one's own birth is not simply to oppose just any being, or any origin, but one's own being and origin. The matricidal desire is tied to an infanticide and a suicide. Derrida thus suggests that "matricide puts us on the path of a birth irreducible to all ontology, to all ontological or phenomenological thinking about originarity. Being born [*naître*], the event of 'being born,' has *already* come in place of the origin" (NW, 92/LV, 15).[32] Prior to being and any phenomenon, this unique birth that names maternity would seem to be beyond the reach of the matricide.

It is thus by upping the ante of maternity's tie to the ineluctability of birth that Derrida marks the distinction between maternity and the mother in Trilling's text. As the most extreme figure of immovable necessity, the event of one's birth, and by association, maternity, would remain resistant to substitution. In terms of the analysis that I have been pursuing, the birth contained in "The Night Watch" thus corresponds to that found in Derrida's resistance to fraternity. Birth is said to lie in the past as an event whose necessity would be immune to all revision. However, I suggested above that such a conception cannot ultimately be sustained in the Derridean framework, and this is confirmed as Derrida continues his reading. The cracks can be discerned in passages I have already cited, for in stating that Job's curse "confirms, repeats, reproduces, and makes endure that which it would like to repress," Derrida signals that iterability is already at work from the very beginning, even in this beginning before all beginnings that is birth. Otherwise put, "Writing comes to be inscribed in this repetition" (NW, 91/LV, 13), and writing opens birth up to the endless possibility of repetition with difference. Further, Derrida quickly links this work of writing to the presence of the specter. "Writing is a killer; one is never done with it. Even if the mother dies, even if a son kills her . . . the mother reappears in maternity, and it is no doubt for this reason that Trilling must so often evoke the 'specter of the mother,' the 'ghost of the mother'" (NW, 92–93/LV, 15–16). Thus, the murder of the mother does not result in her absolute erasure. Rather, she reappears in the incessant return of maternity, which "always survives, by coming back, by returning to its haunts [*en revenante*]" (NW, 94/LV, 18).

In this way, Derrida begins to challenge the distinction between the mother and maternity. As a revenant, maternity would seem to give itself over to repetition, and so would not be immune to all substitution. Maternity thus starts to take on characteristics initially thought to belong only to the mother. However, as in the passages just cited, for most of "The Night Watch" Derrida only hints at this challenge, and he suspends his analysis each time he gets close to the aporia. It is only addressed more directly toward the end of the text. There Derrida recasts the question of separating the mother and maternity as a contest between two logics at work in Trilling's text. The first holds that "while paternity would always be a problematic attribution . . . a 'legal fiction' . . . and thus a sort of speculative object susceptible to substitution, the maternity of the mother is [would be] unique, irreplaceable, an object of perception." This, according to Derrida, is the "classic" logic, shared by Freud, Joyce, and Lacan, and is "in the end, *commonsensical*" (NW, 99/LV, 26–27). By contrast,

> The other logic, the one toward which I myself would risk leaning here, would subject the mother (I'm not saying "maternity" in Trilling's sense of the word) to the *same* regimen as the father: possible substitution, rational inference, phantasmatic or symbolic construction, speculation, and so on. If today the unicity of the mother is no longer the sensible object of a perceptual certitude, if maternities can no longer be reduced to, indeed if they carry us beyond, the carrying mother, if there can be, in a word, more than one mother, if "the" mother is the object of calculations and suppositions, of projections and phantasms, if the "womb" is no longer outside all phantasm, the assured place of birth, then this "new" situation simply illuminates in return an ageless truth. The mother was never only, never uniquely, never indubitably the one who gives birth—and whom one sees, with one's own eyes, give birth. If the word "maternity," as it is interpreted and deployed by Trilling, gestures toward the unicity of a mark and of a birth date that has already taken place, if there is, undeniably, maternity in this sense, then every determination of this maternity by the figure of a mother, indeed of a date, of an indisputable trace (this one and not that one), becomes the effect of a phantasm and a speculation. The mother is also a speculative object and even a "legal fiction." (NW, 99–100/LV, 27–28)

In this second logic, the mother would no longer be resistant to substitution, for just like the father she is considered a legal fiction. This is a repetition of the claim in *Politics of Friendship* that I discussed in the previous chapter, where Derrida extends this status of legal fiction, via its attribution to the mother, to all genealogical ties, specifically to that of the brother (*PF*, 92–93/*PA*, 114). However, on the face of it, this claim might not seem enough to disrupt the distinction between the mother and maternity. Indeed, by insisting that maternity is not submitted to this regime ("I'm not saying 'maternity' in Trilling's sense of the word"), Derrida would seem to use this second logic to reinforce the division between the two terms, and so agree with Trilling on this point. How then is maternity dislodged from its position of safety? The answer lies in its relation to the mother, noted above in Derrida's reference to "every determination of this maternity by the figure of the mother, indeed of a date, of an indisputable trace." The point is that maternity is nothing outside of such a determination. Having no force, meaning, or value without its inscription in such figures, be it in the mother or the event of birth, it is necessary that maternity be thus inscribed, that it be thus written. Otherwise, why use this word "maternity" and not another? Or in Derrida's words, "What are we to make of a maternity that would not be the maternity of a mother? And why necessarily associate with the maternity of the mother 'the ineluctability of birth, of the marked hour, always already inscribed?'" (NW, 100/LV, 28). These questions echo those that Derrida asked of Montaigne and his heirs with respect to their use of fraternity, which I also discussed in Chapter 5: "Why, then, retain this 'natural' figure? Why this adherence or this reference again to a natural bond, if one has set out to de-naturalize? Why does the natural schema remain?" (PF, 191/PA, 205). In both cases the same implication holds, that a notion supposedly divorced from all relation to any particular inscription (maternity from the mother in Trilling, spiritual fraternity from natural fraternity in Montaigne), remains, in sharing the name, necessarily tied to this inscription.

Now to insist on this necessity of inscription is not to collapse maternity into the mother. That is, it is not thus the case that maternity is open to substitution in the same way as is the mother. Rather, the relation is one of an impossible necessity, where the two terms can never be fully separated, at the same time as they elude identification. "There is thus no possible *tri*, no real sorting out, between the mother and maternity. And yet this sorting out is necessary, for maternity will never be reducible to the mother and this ontological difference opens up the possibility of a *tri* or a sorting out in general" (NW, 101/LV, 30). In other words, the relation between maternity and the mother is one of aporia.

Caught in an aporia, maternity thus remains open to inheritance. This movement of inheritance is precisely what I have been tracking in "The Night Watch," as Derrida retrieves maternity from a position seemingly beyond all contact, engaging and redeploying it into an unknown future. Most relevant for my purposes is the fact that this is simultaneously an inheritance of birth, the figure of ineluctability that Derrida reads in Trilling as tied to maternity. This birth in the past too lies in an aporia, not fully reducible to a logic of substitution yet at the same time inevitably tied to substitutable determinations. Thus, through the action of inheritance, this birth remains exposed to alternations in its meaning and its value. Such a change cannot be fully determined, since the aporia ensures that there is always a remainder eluding the grasp of the heir. And it is precisely this indeterminacy that is displayed in the ending of "The Night Watch." Or rather I should say in its endings, since Derrida effectively ends the text twice through the writing of a postscript. Both endings testify to the impossibility of mastering the aporia's essential ambivalence. In the first, which closes the text proper, Derrida returns to Job's matricidal desire. The lesson of this inheritance has been that maternity can never be done away with, that the specter or the trace always returns. Job's curse is thus a desire

> to be done with the trace of the trace, with birth itself. To kill oneself by killing one's birth, in other words, the maternity of one's mother. So as to entertain the suicidal illusion, yet again, of giving birth to oneself. On one's own, freely, to one-self. . . . Auto-parthenogenesis of a writing, for example, that would like to deny or—for this amounts to the same thing—to appropriate without remainder the entirety of one's heritage. One writes, but it would be necessary to do otherwise in order to redo or remake oneself. In order to be in the end, as Joyce would have wanted, "father and son of his works." Even if it means running the risk—for who could deny it?—of finding oneself at the end of the road, at the moment of signing, done in [*refait*]. (NW, 101–2/LV, 30–31)[33]

The matricidal desire is thus a desire to be done with inheritance. To be free of the past, either through eradicating it altogether or through its complete and total incorporation. To have never been born or to have given birth to oneself. To write with no reference to the past or to write all of the past without remainder. Each of these possibilities comes to the same, for each aims to move beyond all inheritance. And with the description of this desire to be "father and son of his works," Job's curse can be connected to Derrida's wish, discussed at the end of Chapter 5, to give birth to his own mother. For there too it was a question of the son as father, erasing the debt to his mother by becoming her source, giving birth to a thinker unlike any seen before. I argued that this desire also amounted to putting an end to inheritance, and that because of the impossibility of doing so demonstrated in Chapter 2, this wish was strictly impossible. By showing that the desire expressed in Job's curse "to be done with the trace of the trace, with birth itself" is impossible, Derrida here can be read as providing a critique of his own sovereign wish. There is no beyond to inheritance that can be achieved through the actions of a sovereign I.

All heirs are thus condemned to matricide, to endlessly desiring to destroy the past without ever attaining this goal. And a lesson of Trilling's text is that this violent impulse is inscribed in the very act of writing. To write is to try to kill the mother, to try to destroy one's heritage, and yet since this killing and destruction never fully or finally takes place, the matricidal desire always returns. In the light of such inevitability, the second, final ending of "The Night Watch" can be better understood. Dated July 15, 2000—Derrida's seventieth birthday—the postscript begins with a mention of *Memoirs of the Blind*, where Derrida "used and abused the 'name of nobody' (*outis*), which Ulysses gives to himself or remakes for himself" (NW, 102/LV, 31).[34] This is a reference to the scene in *The Odyssey* when Ulysses drives a stake into the eye of the Cyclops, an attack enabled by the ruse of Ulysses naming himself "Nobody." It is a scene of extreme violence, yet another murderous wish toward another, made possible by a certain violence against the self in the erasure of one's own name. The first paragraph of the postscript thus remains in the orbit of the violence that saturates the preceding text.

Immediately, however, Derrida tries to move beyond this violence. Referring to the talk he had just given to the States General of Psychoanalysis (later published as "Psychoanalysis Searches the State of Its Soul"),[35] he speaks of "a beyond of cruelty, a beyond of sovereignty, a beyond of the death drive," and associates this thought with a renunciation of writing.

> It is as if I had thought I could hear a silent lesson from Jacques Trilling, the one whose hypothesis I just advanced. As if I had said to myself, in short, yet one more time but once and for all, for good and forever: from now on, no more writing, especially not writing, for writing dreams of sovereignty, writing is *cruel*, murderous, suicidal, parricidal, matricidal, infanticidal, fratricidal, homicidal, and so on. Crimes against humanity, even genocide, begin here, as do crimes against *generation*. (NW, 102/LV, 31)

If one wishes to be done with writing's murderous violence, then one must be done with writing. Never write again, and so never kill again. Derrida continues by pursuing this "nostalgia for retirement," translating it as a command "to begin finally to love life, namely birth. . . . A new rule of life: to breathe from now on without writing, to take a breath beyond writing." And yet, as Derrida develops this thought, the hope of leaving writing behind shows itself unsustainable: "But I want to want, and decidedly so, I want to want an active and signed renunciation of writing, a reaffirmed life." Chasing the desire to be done with writing, Derrida starts to stumble. He cannot want it, but merely want to want it, and he can only express this wish in a language of writing and repetition—the renunciation would be "signed," such a life "reaffirmed." It is thus no surprise when a few sentences later Derrida renounces his renunciation, expressing his wish now as one for a "writing without writing. The other writing, the other of writing as well, altered writing, the one that has always worked over my own in silence, at once simpler and more convoluted, like a counter-witness protesting at each and every sign against my writing through my writing" (NW, 102–3/LV, 31–32). The renunciation cannot be made, writing remains inevitable, and the best Derrida can hope for is a counterwriting within his own that would fight the matricidal desire. The best he can hope for is a violence against violence.

Pursuing the desire to be done with all violence, Derrida thus remains in an aporia. Such a desire requires a renunciation of writing, once and for all, and yet Derrida's writing testifies to this renunciation's impossibility. Now as I have stressed throughout this book, facing an aporia need not lead one to be paralyzed. There are choices one can make in inheriting it, and here Derrida makes the choice that I have argued is consistently his. For in the next paragraph he performs one more *surenchère*, upping the ante on the contradiction in which he finds himself caught. And in doing so he invokes a figure that perhaps will not surprise.

> If the *tri* or the sorting out between the mother and maternity remains at once ineluctable and illusory, if matricide becomes so inevitable [*fatal*] that it exonerates one guilty of it, wouldn't one have to be an absolute monster of innocence to go on writing? A child? An ingénue? Better, an *innate* monster of innocence?
>   Is writing without matricide still possible? (NW, 103/LV, 32)

Here the aporia is heightened yet again—at once ineluctable and illusory, the simultaneous impossibility and necessity of sorting between the mother and maternity leaves Derrida committing a violence so inevitable that he can perhaps be relieved of all guilt. For if one must commit violence, if it is an absolute necessity, is not one thereby released of any responsibility for it? Could one not be considered as innocent as a child? The answer to these questions is "No," since the presence of such pure innocence would resolve the contradiction, allowing an escape from the aporia. There is thus no longer any question of a child appearing alone, pure in its innocence, as seemed to be the case in texts I cited at the beginning of this chapter. At best, Derrida can only hope that a monstrous innocence might be born. Fused to its ambivalent and undetermined other, the monstrous child that might arrive in the future carries the good and the bad, the chance and the danger. The result of Derrida's inheritance thus remains without form and fundamentally ambivalent.

And finally, one last time but not once and for all, such ambivalence is reasserted in the postscript's closing lines.

> J'avais commencé par un vœu, en voici un autre, et vous pourrez toujours dire qu'il est pieux: écrire sans tuer personne (signé Ulysse).
>   —Jacques Derrida (LV, 32)

> I began with a wish. Here is another one, and it may always strike you as being pious, and little more than a pipe dream: to write and kill nobody (signed Ulysses).
>   —Jacques Derrida (NW, 103)

I cite both the French and the English to highlight the astonishing density of Derrida's prose, as well as the elegance of Brault and Naas's translation from which I have been quoting. As the latter remark in a note, "Derrida is playing on the expression 'vœu pieux'—literally, a pious wish, but, figuratively, a hollow or empty wish. Read as a noun rather than an adjective, *pieux* is the plural of *pieu*, a stake or sharpened stick of the kind Ulysses used to strike out the eye of the Cyclops" (NW, 108n50). To write and kill nobody appears a pious wish, a dream of writing in a way that has left violence behind. But, signed Ulysses, this dream is shown for what it also is—a pipe dream. For killing nobody is to kill someone, the very self who is thus named. As Derrida blows out the candles of "The Night Watch," his birthday wish remains suspended, both a pious dream and a pipe dream, a violent wish for the end of violence.

Returning now to the concern that motivated my turn to this text, one sees that Derrida's analysis thus demonstrates that there can be no birth located in a past that is beyond all retrieval. Derrida transforms precisely such an understanding in his inheritance of Trilling's work—he takes up the birth associated with maternity which would be immune to all attack and shifts its location to the heart of an aporia. This inheritance does not thereby subject birth to the full control of the heir, as is testified in Derrida's failed attempts to place it beyond all violence. But birth has been shaken from its position of a necessity out of reach, and brought within the orbit of repetition and engagement. Which is also to say that there are not two kinds of birth: one lying in the past to be resisted and another found in the future that Derrida would embrace. In all cases, birth is contingent in its meaning, ambivalent in its value, and located in a time between past and future. Birth is aporetic, and so calls for an inheritance.

Conclusion

Inheriting Derrida's Legacies

T HE POINT THAT my analysis reaches at the end of the last chapter may seem far from the central concern of this book. On the face of it the themes and figures of maternity and the mother, of matricide and the monstrous child, have little connection to democracy. However, if one recalls the role birth plays at the foundation of democratic citizenship, one gets a glimpse of how one might take this analysis forward such that it returns to what is more recognizably the sphere of political philosophy. This would be to fold this alternative understanding of birth back into democratic discourse, substituting it at the base for the traditional concept of natural necessity, and see what, if any, transformations might occur.[1]

Such would be one way, among others, of continuing the Derridean project, of inheriting its past and so encountering its future. And in the end, this is perhaps the most important message my analysis could hope to communicate. For while my focus has been on Derrida's inheritance—both on the idea of inheritance that is developed in his work, and on his own inheritance from the democratic tradition—the most pressing question that remains is how one might inherit from Derrida in turn. My own development of Derrida's fragmented discourse on birth gives one answer to this question. After examining *Politics of Friendship* as an example of democratic inheritance, I demonstrated how "birth" remains an unstable term in Derrida's oeuvre. He seems to fix its meaning in different contexts, aligning it negatively with the past in his resistance to fraternity, and positively with the future as a sign of the arrivant. But at the same time, there are resources in this oeuvre for challenging this very distinction. I showed how Derrida's writings contain another discourse on birth that demonstrates that the future cannot be clearly valued as positive, nor the past cut off from a trans-forming act of inheritance, and that birth is aporetic, in all of its appearances. Now while the resources for this development are found from within Derrida's own text, and he acknowledges that birth is a singularity calling for further thought, his writings do not pursue this thought very far, falling well short of thinking through the many meanings that birth can have. In other words, Derrida's texts contain the seeds of a response to the inadequacy of his theorization of birth, but I would maintain that this response could only take place through an intervention, an inheritance, by someone to some extent outside these texts themselves.

This strategy of engagement provides a template for what I would suggest in clos-ing is a promising way to inherit from Derrida's writings. My approach is based on two fundamental claims. First, in his own inheritance of past thinking, Derrida can only ever destabilize certain notions by stabilizing others. I have shown this to be true in one aspect of Derrida's inheritance of democracy, where the meaning of birth is held firm in order to justify a strong resistance to any appeal to fraternity in democratic discourse. More generally, I propose that one can find a similar phenomenon at work in all of Derrida's writings. For example, I would wager that one could demonstrate that his understanding of aporia, as outlined in Chapter 1, relies on a very particular understanding of law as commandment in order to show the necessity of the contra-diction. This would be true even as Derrida's analysis challenges this very conception in his theorization of the unconditional law—indeed, his challenge relies on it for its force. Derrida stabilizes law as commandment in order to destabilize so many of those ethical, political, and religious concepts that he shows to be aporetic in his later work. A deconstructive reading cannot challenge everything at once, with the stability of some terms providing the point from which any particular intervention is launched.

The second claim assumed in my approach is, as I argued in Chapter 4, that the meanings and values in language lie beyond the sovereign control of an individual. Derrida cannot decide on what his terms mean, and on the value that they carry, as this depends on forces that elude his grasp. As a consequence, the stabilizations that Derrida performs are not immune to challenge or change. They remain open to desta-bilization in turn, to being opened up and transformed in both their meaning and their value. This can be brought about by mobilizing resources from within Derrida's own oeuvre, as I have done with birth, and in many cases this body of work will be rich enough to allow such an internal destabilization to take place. But one might also choose to follow a path different from the one in this book, and bring the work of oth-ers to bear on the terms being used. In the specific case of birth, this might be done through pursuing the exchange between Derrida and Nancy to see if the latter's writ-ings contain possibilities that elude the Derridean matrix, or turning to the work of Hannah Arendt, who appeals to birth in her own way in a very rich theorization of politics. Yet another alternative would be to engage the large and diverse literature on motherhood and reproduction found in contemporary feminist philosophy and queer theory. Beyond birth, one could follow a similar strategy of moving outside the confines of Derrida's text to examine the broader implications of his claims about democracy. I stated in the Introduction that I thought it important to provide an internal and sustained reading of Derrida on democracy, given the complexity of his position. Now that I have done this, an alternative step forward would be to relate this position to those circulating in contemporary democratic theory. Particularly appropriate to what I have explored in this book would be to engage other accounts of democracy's relation to its past, as found, for example, in the now large literature on intergenerational justice. To pursue these paths by following my particular strategy of inheritance would involve in each case putting pressure on the assumptions Derrida makes in order to advance the readings he proposes. This always carries the risk of undermining these readings, at the same time that it offers the chance of opening them up to further articulation, and further responses.

Such, then, is the inheritance of Derrida that I propose: to engage Derrida's work at the level of its language and exploit the richness that this language possesses by testing the limits within which his claims currently reside. This testing might be performed through an internal reading as I have here undertaken, or through bringing external forces—the work of other thinkers, new experiences and phenomena—to bear on the Derridean text. We are far from being done with Derrida. We have not solved the riddle of his oeuvre or decoded the logic of his position. Rather, his texts remain unstable, shifting, in themselves and in their engagement with the world. The task of Derrida's heirs today is to remain within this instability, enhancing it at times, defusing it at others, following and transforming the contours of the language that is its medium.

Notes

Introduction: Derrida's Legacies

1. Jacques Derrida, "As If It Were Possible, 'Within Such Limits,'" in *Paper Machine*, trans. Rachel Bowlby (Stanford: Stanford University Press, 2005), 81, originally published as "Comme si c'était possible, 'within such limits' . . . ," in *Papier machine* (Paris: Galilée, 2001), 295. Throughout the text all references to works by Derrida that are available in both English and French refer first to the English pagination, then to the French. Unless stated otherwise, translations of works that are available only in French are mine.

2. "As for the phrase you just cited ('learning to live finally [*apprendre à vivre enfin*]'), it came to me once the book [*Specters of Marx*] was finished. It plays first of all, though in a serious way, on its everyday meaning. *Apprendre à vivre* means to mature, but also to educate: to teach someone else and especially oneself. When you address someone and say '*je vais t'apprendre à vivre*,' it sometimes has a threatening tone, meaning not only 'I am going to teach you how to live' but 'I'm going to teach you a lesson,' 'I'm going to get you to shape up or whip you into shape.' . . . So, to finally answer your question, no, I never *learned-to-live*. In fact not at all!" And later: "It is necessary in each situation to create an appropriate mode of exposition, to invent the law of the singular event, to take into account the presumed or desired addressee; and, at the same time, to make as if this writing will determine the reader, who will learn to read (to 'live') something he or she was not accustomed to receiving from anywhere else. One hopes that he or she will be reborn differently, determined otherwise, as a result. . . . Each book is a pedagogy aimed at forming its reader" (Jacques Derrida, *Learning to Live Finally*, trans. Pascale-Anne Brault and Michael Naas [Hoboken, NJ: Melville House, 2007], 23–24, 31, originally published as *Apprendre à vivre enfin* [Paris: Galilée, 2005], 23–24, 31–32).

3. Jacques Derrida, *Rogues: Two Essays on Reason*, trans. Pascale-Anne Brault and Michael Naas (Stanford: Stanford University Press, 2005), originally published as *Voyous: Deux essais sur la raison* (Paris: Galilée, 2003). Hereafter referred to as *R/V*. "The Reason of the Strongest" was first delivered in July 2002 at the Cerisy conference on Derrida's work titled "The Democracy to Come."

4. Geoffrey Bennington, *Interrupting Derrida* (New York: Routledge, 2000), 31.

5. Matthias Fritsch, "Derrida's Democracy to Come," *Constellations* 9, no. 4 (2002): 578.

6. Pheng Cheah, "The Untimely Secret of Democracy," in *Derrida and the Time of the Political*, ed. Pheng Cheah and Suzanne Guerlac (Durham, NC: Duke University Press, 2009), 79–80.

7. Judith Butler, "Finishing, Starting," in Cheah and Guerlac, *Derrida and the Time of the Political*, 300.

8. Aletta J. Norval, *Aversive Democracy: Inheritance and Originality in the Democratic Tradition* (Cambridge: Cambridge University Press, 2007), 146. The passage Norval cites is from *R*, 85/*V*, 125.

9. Ananda Abeysekara, *The Politics of Postsecular Religion: Mourning Secular Futures* (New York: Columbia University Press, 2008), 11, 2–3.

10. Jacques Derrida, *Specters of Marx: The State of the Debt, the Work of Mourning, and the New International*, trans. Peggy Kamuf (New York: Routledge, 1994), originally published as *Spectres de Marx: L'état de la dette, le travail du deuil et la Nouvelle Internationale* (Paris: Galilée, 1993). Hereafter referred to as *SOM/SDM*. Jacques Derrida and Elisabeth Roudinesco, *For What Tomorrow . . . : A Dialogue*, trans. Jeff Fort (Stanford: Stanford University Press, 2004), originally published as *De quoi demain . . . : Dialogue* (Paris: Fayard/Galilée, 2001). Hereafter referred to as *FW/DQ*.

11. Leonard Lawlor, *This Is Not Sufficient: An Essay on Animality and Human Nature in Derrida* (New York: Columbia University Press, 2007); Martin Hägglund, *Radical Atheism: Derrida and the Time of Life* (Stanford: Stanford University Press, 2008).

12. Jacques Derrida, *Politics of Friendship*, trans. George Collins (London: Verso, 1997), originally published as *Politiques de l'amitié* (Paris: Galilée, 1994). Hereafter referred to as *PF/PA*.

1. The Structure of Aporia

1. Jacques Derrida, *Aporias: Dying—Awaiting (One Another at) the "Limits of Truth,"* trans. Thomas Dutoit (Stanford: Stanford University Press, 1993), published in French as *Apories* (Paris: Galilée, 1996). Hereafter referred to as *A/AP*.

2. See, for example, Jacques Derrida and Anne Dufourmantelle, *Of Hospitality*, trans. Rachel Bowlby (Stanford: Stanford University Press, 2000), originally published as *De l'hospitalité* (Paris: Calmann-Levy, 1997). Hereafter referred to as *OH/DH*.

3. Jacques Derrida, "Faith and Knowledge: The Two Sources of 'Religion' at the Limits of Reason Alone," trans. Samuel Weber, in *Acts of Religion*, ed. Gil Anidjar (New York: Routledge, 2002), originally published as "Foi et savoir," in *Foi et savoir, suivi de Le siècle et le pardon* (Paris: Le Seuil, 2000). Hereafter referred to as *FK/FS*. Jacques Derrida, "Autoimmunity: Real and Symbolic Suicides," trans. Pascale-Anne Brault and Michael Naas, in *Philosophy in a Time of Terror: Dialogues with Jürgen Habermas and Jacques Derrida*, ed. Giovanna Borradori (Chicago: University of Chicago Press, 2003), published in French as "Auto-immunités: suicides réels et symboliques," in *Le concept du 11 septembre: Dialogues à New York (octobre–décembre 2001) avec Giovanna Borradori*, by Jacques Derrida and Jürgen Habermas (Paris: Galilée, 2004); Derrida, *Rogues*.

4. This practice of Derrida's is somewhat of a tradition in the addresses he gave at the Cerisy conferences devoted to his work. At "The Ends of Man" Derrida points to the places where the end that is the apocalypse has appeared in his writings; at "The Autobiographical Animal" he lists his own bestiary; and at "The Democracy to Come" he refers to all of his past uses of this phrase. See Jacques Derrida, "On a Newly Arisen Apocalyptic Tone in Philosophy," trans. John Leavey Jr. in *Raising the Tone of Philosophy*, ed. Peter Fenves (Baltimore: Johns Hopkins University Press, 1993), 161–62, originally published as *D'un ton apocalyptique adopté naguère en philosophie* (Paris: Galilée, 1983), 83–89. Jacques Derrida, *The Animal That Therefore I Am*, trans. David Wills (New York: Fordham University Press, 2008), 37–41, originally published as *L'animal que donc je suis* (Paris: Galilée, 2006), 60–64. And see *R*, 81–91/*V*, 119–33. I discuss this practice of self-citation examining the particular case of "The Reason of the Strongest" (in *Rogues*) in Samir Haddad, "Reading Derrida Reading Derrida: Deconstruction as Self-Inheritance," *International Journal of Philosophical Studies* 14, no. 4 (2006).

5. Jacques Derrida, *The Other Heading: Reflections on Today's Europe*, trans. Pascale-Anne Brault and Michael Naas (Bloomington: Indiana University Press, 1992), originally published as *L'autre cap* (Paris: Minuit, 1991). Derrida cites from pages 76–81/75–79 of this work.

6. There is in fact an ambiguity here as to whether in discussing this plural logic Derrida is referring to the citations he has just made from *The Other Heading* or whether he is commenting on the aporias in all of his previous texts. In either case, my claims would hold and are indeed strengthened if the second is true.

7. The relation between the singularity of aporias and death is given a different twist when one follows the subtle yet insistent theme of the secret in *Aporias*. Earlier in the text Derrida distinguishes an aporia from a problem. The latter has connotations of "*projection* or *protection*, that which one poses or throws in front of oneself . . . like a shield (*problēma* also means shield, clothing as barrier or guard-barrier) behind which one guards oneself *in secret* or *in shelter* in case of danger." By contrast,

an aporia takes place "in the very place where *it would no longer be possible to constitute* a *problem, a project, or a projection,* that is, at the point where the very project or the problematic task becomes impossible and where we are exposed, absolutely without protection" (*A*, 11–12/*AP*, 30–31). The implication here is that in an aporia the secret is exposed, but not as something that could be deciphered, decoded, or solved. Rather, an aporia is something like an absolute secret—an essential absence. Resonating with this theme is Derrida's earlier brief allusion to the death of Oedipus (*A*, 7–8/*AP*, 26). This encourages a connection to *Of Hospitality*, where Derrida again takes up Oedipus's death, this time discussing it at length precisely around the figure of the secret (*OH*, 93–121/*DH*, 85–107).

8. A similar point is made with respect to "the" aporia of time by Geoffrey Bennington in his review of Richard Beardsworth's *Derrida and the Political* (New York: Routledge, 1996): "For Beardsworth, Derrida gives us *the* aporia of time, in the singular, and this singularising gesture, operat[es] on what Derrida will *always* make plural" (Bennington, *Interrupting Derrida*, 175).

9. Further, Derrida suggests that hospitality has the potential to be exemplary for many more, perhaps all, of the concepts that he discusses. Of the "contradiction (atopical: madness, extravagance, in Greek: *atopos*)" of hospitality, he writes that it "produces or registers this autodeconstruction in every concept, in the concept of concept: not only because hospitality undoes, should undo, the grip, the seizure (the *Begriff*, the *Begreifen*, the capture of the *concipere, cum-capio,* of the *comprehendere,* the force or the violence of the taking [*prendre*] as comprehending [*comprendre*]), hospitality is, *must be, owes to itself* to be, inconceivable and incomprehensible, but also because in it—we have undergone this test and ordeal so often—each concept opens itself to its opposite, reproducing or producing in advance, in the rapport of one concept to the other, the contradictory and deconstructive law of hospitality. Each concept becomes hospitable to its other, to an other than itself that is no longer *its* other" (Jacques Derrida, "Hostipitality [Seminar]," trans. Gil Anidjar, in *Acts of Religion*, 362). (There are two separate texts by Derrida published in English under the title "Hostipitality," one the transcript of four seminars given in 1997 and the other a talk delivered in Istanbul dating from the same time. I will distinguish the two by inserting "Seminar" or "Talk" into the title.) Michael Naas makes a related point when he proposes understanding deconstruction itself as hospitality, precisely through relating the aporia of hospitality to the practice of reading developed in Derrida's early texts. This is a move that implicates inheritance. See Michael Naas, *Taking on the Tradition: Jacques Derrida and the Legacies of Deconstruction* (Stanford: Stanford University Press, 2003), 164–69, and Michael Naas, *Derrida from Now On* (New York: Fordham University Press, 2008), 28–33. For another instance of the same claim see A. J. P. Thomson, *Deconstruction and Democracy: Derrida's Politics of Friendship* (London: Continuum, 2005), 98–100.

10. Although Derrida does not make this choice exclusively. He also refers at times to the antinomy as an aporia, for example when he states, "This is definitely where this aporia is, an antinomy" (*OH*, 77/*DH*, 73).

11. This dual strategy characterizes Derrida's work as a whole, as he states in "Force of Law": "Deconstruction is generally practiced in two ways or two styles, and it most often grafts one on to the other. One takes on the demonstrative and apparently ahistorical allure of logico-formal paradoxes. The other, more historical or more anamnesic, seems to proceed through readings of texts, meticulous interpretations and genealogies" (Jacques Derrida, "Force of Law: The 'Mystical Foundation of Authority,'" trans. Mary Quaintance, in *Acts of Religion*, 250, originally published as *Force de loi* [Paris: Galilée, 1994], 48. Hereafter referred to as FOL/FDL).

12. In what follows I analyze the aporia of hospitality as Derrida articulates it using the language of unconditionality and conditionality. At other moments he runs a very similar argument using the vocabulary of visitation and invitation. See Derrida, "Autoimmunity," 128–29/187–88; Derrida, "As If It Were Possible," 194–95n11/296–97n1; Jacques Derrida, "Hospitality, Justice and Responsibility," in *Questioning Ethics: Contemporary Debates in Philosophy*, ed. Richard Kearney and Mark Dooley (New York: Routledge, 1999), 70–71; Derrida, "Hostipitality [Seminar]," 360–62; Jacques Derrida,

"Une hospitalité à l'infini," in *Manifeste pour l'hospitalité*, ed. Mohammed Seffahi (Grigny: Paroles d'aube, 1999), 103–4; *FW*, 59–60/*DQ*, 100–102. In Jacques Derrida, "Hostipitality [Talk]," *Angelaki* 5, no. 3 [2000]: 17 (originally published as "Hostipitalité," in *Pera Peras Poros*, edited by Ferda Keskin and Önay Sözer [Istanbul: Yapi Kredi Yatinlari, 1999], 43–44), Derrida suggests that these two sets of terms are interchangeable: "Thus, the distinction between invitation and visitation may be the distinction between conditional hospitality (invitation) and unconditional hospitality."

13. See also Jacques Derrida, *Adieu to Emmanuel Levinas*, trans. Pascale-Anne Brault and Michael Naas (Stanford: Stanford University Press, 1999), 35, originally published as *Adieu à Emmanuel Lévinas* (Paris: Galilée, 1997), 59. There Derrida writes that a "possible hospitality to the worst is necessary so that good hospitality can have a chance, the chance of letting the other come, the *yes* of the other no less than the *yes* to the other." See also Derrida, "Hostipitality [Talk]," 17/44: "If I accept the coming of the other, the arriving [arrivance] of the other who could come with the best or worst of intentions: a visitation could be an invasion by the worst. Unconditional hospitality must remain open with horizon of expectation, without anticipation, to any surprise visitation."

14. Derrida, "Hospitality, Justice and Responsibility," 70. Derrida explores the necessary threat of the deprivation of mastery in a number of ways, focusing on the ambiguity of the French word "*hôte*" (meaning both "host" and "guest") as well as reading the inversion between the host and guest as it is staged in Klossowski's *Les lois de l'hospitalité*. See, for example, *OH*, 123–25/*DH*, 109–11; Derrida, *Adieu*, 41–42/79–81; Derrida, "Hostipitality [Talk]," 9/28–29; and Jacques Derrida, "Responsabilité et hospitalité," in Seffahi, *Manifeste pour l'hospitalité*, 118–19.

15. Derrida, "Une hospitalité à l'infini," 100.

16. Derrida, "Hostipitality [Seminar]," 361. A similar claim is made in Jacques Derrida, "On Cosmopolitanism," in *On Cosmopolitanism and Forgiveness* (New York: Routledge, 2002), 16, originally published as *Cosmopolites de tous les pays, encore un effort!* (Paris: Galilée, 1997), 42. See also Jacques Derrida, "The Principle of Hospitality," in *Paper Machine*, 66, originally published as "Le principe d'hospitalité," in *Papier machine*, 273.

17. Note, however, that this still does not explain why one has to address this issue through the particular configuration of the unconditional and conditional laws. Why do these regimes of law in particular necessarily arise? Here it is a question of inheritance—one negotiates hospitality in these terms and not others to the extent that one inherits hospitality in this form. That this is the inherited form of hospitality receives support from that other aspect of Derrida's analysis of hospitality that I have not discussed, his readings of texts in the Western tradition that testify to this aporetic structure. I will return to the issue of inheritance at the end of this chapter and, of course, throughout the book.

18. In *Rogues*, Derrida writes that the distinction between "sovereignty" and "unconditionality" "presupposes that we think at once the unforeseeability of an event that is necessarily without horizon, the singular coming of the other, and, as a result, a *weak force*. This vulnerable force, this force without power, opens up unconditionally to what or who *comes* and comes to affect it" (*R*, xiv/*V*, 13). For related references to the idea of a weak force, see *R*, 36, 41, 74/*V*, 61, 66, 109, and Jacques Derrida, *Limited Inc.*, trans. Samuel Weber (Evanston, IL: Northwestern University Press, 1988), 137, 149, published in French as *Limited Inc.* (Paris: Galilée, 1990), 253, 275–76. Jacques Derrida, "The University without Condition," in *Without Alibi*, trans. Peggy Kamuf (Stanford: Stanford University Press, 2002), 206, originally published as *L'université sans condition* (Paris: Galilée, 2001), 18. And see Jacques Derrida, "For a Justice to Come: An Interview with Jacques Derrida," in *The Derrida-Habermas Reader*, ed. Lasse Thomassen (Chicago: University of Chicago Press, 2006), 267–69, and *SOM*, 55/*SDM*, 91.

19. This sentence is missing from the English translation. It should appear on page 83. I should note that Derrida does not consistently use the word "*mander*" when speaking of the action of the unconditional law. He also states that this law "commands." But this need not prevent the exploitation

of the connotations of writing to open up different possibilities for thinking the status of the unconditional law.

20. Derrida, "Signature Event Context," in *Margins of Philosophy*, trans. Alan Bass (Chicago: University of Chicago Press, 1982), 315, originally published as "Signature Événement Contexte," in *Marges de la philosophie* (Paris: Minuit, 1972), 375.

21. Ibid., 320/381.

22. As Derrida says in "Hostipitality [Talk]," 7/25, we have "the law of iterability at the heart of every law of hospitality."

23. I include this parenthetical remark as a reminder that the two arms of the aporia cannot be mapped onto an ideal law and its empirical instantiation, for, as Derrida writes, what is at stake here is "the frontier between two regimes of law, both of them non-empirical" (*OH*, 77–79/*DH*, 73). Both regimes of law, to the extent that they are laws, are nonempirical.

24. Of course, Derrida argues that all moments have this feature, insofar as there is no moment that can be conceived as a pure presence. That is, all moments of time are aporetic. See Jacques Derrida, "*Ousia* and *Grammē*: Note on a Note from *Being and Time*," in *Margins of Philosophy*, originally published as "Ousia et grammè: Note sur une note de Sein und Zeit," in *Marges de la philosophie*. For my purposes simply asserting this point is not all that illuminating. Of more interest to me here and throughout this book is to examine precisely how this aporetic structure plays out in different contexts. Issues concerning temporality will become more apparent in the next chapter when my discussion turns to inheritance.

25. Derrida invokes urgency and the here and now in his discussions of a wide number of normative concepts, discussions that have much in common with the one I have been investigating. See with respect to democracy *R*, 84/*V*, 122–23; Derrida, *Other Heading*, 78/76; Jacques Derrida, "Nietzsche and the Machine," trans. Richard Beardsworth, in *Negotiations: Interventions and Interviews, 1971–2001*, ed. Elizabeth Rottenberg (Stanford: Stanford University Press, 2002), 242; Jacques Derrida, "Not Utopia, the Im-possible," in *Paper Machine*, 130 (originally published as "Non l'utopie, l'im-possible," in *Papier machine*, 359); *PF*, 105/*PA*, 129; with respect to justice: *SOM*, 31/*SDM*, 60; Derrida, "Autoimmunity," 134/194 FOL, 255–57/*FDL*, 57–61; ethics: Jacques Derrida "Ethics and Politics Today," trans. Elizabeth Rottenberg, in *Negotiations*; the event: Jacques Derrida, "The Deconstruction of Actuality," trans. Elizabeth Rottenberg, in *Negotiations*, 93 (originally published as "La deconstruction de l'actualité," *Passages* 57 [1993]: 64); the decision: Derrida, *Adieu*, 115/199; and forgiveness: Derrida, "On Forgiveness," trans. Michael Hughes, in *On Cosmopolitanism and Forgiveness*, 51 (originally published as "Le siècle et le pardon," in *Foi et savoir, suivi de Le siècle et le pardon* [Paris: Le Seuil, 2000], 125).

26. The insertions in square brackets are Derrida's. I have included in this citation the sentence "A call which mandates without commanding," which, as I noted above, is missing in the English translation. Immediately following this parenthesis is a footnote where Derrida refers the reader to his essay "Passions: 'An Oblique Offering,'" trans. David Wood, in *On the Name*, ed. Thomas Dutoit (Stanford: Stanford University Press, 1995), originally published as *Passions* (Paris: Galilée, 1993), for more on the logic of this "law without duty" (*OH*, 159n2/*DH*, 77n1). "Passions" is Derrida's central point of self-reference when it comes to this question of a duty beyond duty, and he makes the same referral in *A*, 17/*AP*, 38 and *SOM*, 35/*SDM*, 65.

My present concern is with those moments in which Derrida's discussion of hospitality invokes Kantian language, but it is worth noting that Kantian terminology appears regularly across Derrida's writings engaging a number of different ethical and political concepts: sometimes it is a question of the categorical imperative and at other times a regulative Idea. In each case Derrida invokes an unconditional injunction that is beyond all calculation and mastery, and then both acknowledges his proximity to Kant and at the same time suggests that what he is saying is not simply reducible to Kant. See, in the context of the gift, Jacques Derrida, *Given Time: I. Counterfeit Money*, trans. Peggy Kamuf (Chicago: University of Chicago Press, 1991), 29–30 (originally published as *Donner le temps.*

1: *La fausse monnaie* [Paris: Galilée, 1991], 46); of justice: Derrida, "Autoimmunity," 133–35/193–96; FOL, 254/FDL, 55–56; of affirmation against apartheid: Derrida, *Limited Inc.*, 152/281; of ethical negotiation in politics: Derrida, "Ethics and Politics Today," 304; and of democracy: *R*, 83–85/*V*, 122–24; and *PF*, 105/*PA*, 128–29. This is not the place for it, but I would suggest that an in-depth analysis of these passages would show that Derrida in fact moves away from embracing the Kantian terminology, especially since in the more recent works, "The Reason of the Strongest" and "Autoimmunity," the relevant passages (which are virtually identical to one another) strongly emphasize the differences over the similarities between Derrida's and Kant's positions.

27. I will discuss this strategy of "upping the ante" more in Chapter 2 when I examine the work done by the notion of *surenchère* (which can be translated as "upping the ante") in Derrida's understanding of inheritance. In "On Cosmopolitanism," 20–23/50–58 and *Adieu*, 87–101/155–76, Derrida makes a similar move, this time with respect to Kant's discussion of hospitality itself rather than the formal structure of the categorical imperative. There he discusses Kant's remarks in "Toward Perpetual Peace" calling for a universal hospitality, and argues that this amounts to a conditional hospitality. So again, Derrida raises the stakes of the analysis—Kant outlines what might be seen as already an extreme position, and Derrida admonishes him for not going far enough. For helpful discussions of Derrida's reading of Kant on hospitality, see O. Custer, "Making Sense of Derrida's Aporetic Hospitality," in *Jacques Derrida: Critical Assessments of Leading Philosophers*, ed. Zeynep Direk and Leonard Lawlor (New York: Routledge, 2002); Marguerite La Caze, "Not Just Visitors: Cosmopolitanism, Hospitality, and Refugees," *Philosophy Today* 48, no. 3 (2004); and the briefer account in Naas, *Taking on the Tradition*, 162–63.

28. An almost identical argument is made in one of the other aporetic contexts cited above, that of the gift. In *Given Time* (156/197–98) Derrida argues that the unconditionality of the gift calls for a law beyond obligation, a law that would refuse determination. In this case Derrida stops one step short of the extremity advocated in *Of Hospitality*, arguing that for the gift it is a question of a "law or a 'you must' without duty, in effect, if that is possible" (whereas the passage cited above speaks of a "law without law"). But the two analyses do converge on the law's status as an outlaw (in *Given Time* Derrida calls the gift "a stranger [or foreigner—*étranger*] to the law").

I should also note that this moment in which the unconditional law interrupts itself and obliges one to pass over to the conditional laws can be aligned with what Bennington describes as deconstruction's structure of "interrupted teleology." Bennington argues that what is particular to deconstruction is that it diagnoses the auto-interruptive moment in a telos, in which it must undermine its own goal and thus own nature as a telos. He discusses this most often precisely in the context of relating Derrida to Kant (in particular in the essay "Almost the End," but his "R.I.P" and "X" also examine related issues in Kant, and "Is it Time?" argues for a similar structure, this time in contrast to Hegel. All of these essays are found in Bennington, *Interrupting Derrida*).

Bennington's twist is to argue that Kant himself, in the *Critique of Judgment*, also diagnoses the same auto-interruptive moment to the telos. Kantian critique, he claims, is thus more deconstructive than one thinks. In this way, Bennington's argument aims to show not that Kant and Derrida are all that different, but that they are in fact very similar; it is just that Kant should be viewed as closer to Derrida rather than Derrida as closer to Kant.

29. Richard Kearney, "Desire of God," in *God, the Gift, and Postmodernism*, ed. John D. Caputo and Michael J. Scanlon (Bloomington: Indiana University Press, 1999), 133. These remarks come from the discussion following Kearney's paper and are also made in part in response to comments offered by John Caputo.

30. Derrida, "Une hospitalité à l'infini," 99–100. See also Derrida, *Adieu*, 34–35/68–69.

31. Derrida, "Une hospitalité à l'infini," 105.

32. This argument is made by Matthias Fritsch in "Derrida's Democracy to Come," 588, referring explicitly to the goal of reducing violence: "it cannot be guaranteed in advance for all contexts

that the violence resulting from unconditional hospitality is less than the one resulting from conditional hospitality, laws, institutions, rights, and so on. . . . Political openness must be open to decide against openness: surely, there are singular situations where openness to the other is inadvisable, where a reduction of violence is to be expected not from unconditional hospitality but from (further) conditions, demands, and normative expectations placed on the other." It is also one of the central claims advanced in Hägglund, *Radical Atheism*. I will examine the question of violence, addressing specifically the issue of whether the notion of pursuing a lesser violence makes sense within the Derridean framework, in Chapter 4.

33. As he states in one discussion, "Today this is a burning issue: we know that there are numerous what we call 'displaced persons' who are applying for the right to asylum without being citizens, without being identified as citizens. It is not for some speculative or ethical reasons that I am interested in unconditional hospitality, but in order to understand and to transform what is going on today in our world" (Derrida, "Hospitality, Justice and Responsibility," 70).

34. This is explicitly acknowledged in Derrida, "Derelictions of the Right to Justice (But What Are the 'Sans-Papiers' Lacking?)," trans. Elizabeth Rottenberg, in *Negotiations*, 140.

35. Jacques Derrida, "What Does It Mean to Be a French Philosopher Today?" in *Paper Machine*, 116, originally published as "Qu'est-ce que cela veut dire d'être un philosophe français aujourd'hui?" in *Papier machine*, 342.

36. Derrida, "Hostipitality [Talk]," 13/37.

37. Derrida, "Une hospitalité à l'infini," 98.

2. Derridean Inheritance

1. It would be remiss, especially given my topic, not to note those works of commentary that have helped me refine my understanding of Derridean inheritance. The first is Geoffrey Bennington's *Interrupting Derrida*, a collection of essays across which inheritance is a persistent theme. While maintaining his analysis on a level less detailed than mine, Bennington offers several rich suggestions, in particular analyzing the relationship between inheritance and politics, including democracy (18–33), clarifying Derrida's early readings in the 1960s as engaged with the issue of negotiating legacies (36–38), and insisting that the passivity entailed by the alterity of inheritance must always be thought together with the activity in Derrida's relation to tradition (139). A second work to mention is Michael Naas's *Taking on the Tradition*. Naas also presents Derridean inheritance as a combination of passivity and activity, but he differs from Bennington in explicitly avoiding general remarks. Rather than attempting "to survey the Derridean corpus from above in order to develop a general theory about it" (xxii), Naas presents a series of patient readings of texts involving the themes of inheritance and donation, justifying his approach by appeal to the performative nature of Derrida's writings. In seeking to provide more detail than Bennington on the actual operation of inheritance, yet nonetheless aiming for a generality that Naas eschews, my own analysis lies somewhere in between these two approaches and is much closer to that followed by Matthias Fritsch in *The Promise of Memory: History and Politics in Marx, Benjamin, and Derrida* (Albany: State University of New York Press, 2005). Fritsch compares Benjamin's and Derrida's respective inheritances of Marx, explicitly theorizing their own conceptions of inheritance in the context of the role played by memory and history in political action. Of particular value are Fritsch's detailed analysis of iterability as the fundamental structure underlying inheritance, and his very careful and thorough exposition of Derrida's readings of both Marx and Benjamin.

2. For more on the relationship between finitude and selectivity in inheritance, see Fritsch, *Promise of Memory*, 95–96.

3. I should note here the slide between Marxism and Marx when discussing the source of this inheritance. This reflects Derrida's own strategy in the book as a whole, for the target of his analysis is not just Marx, but Marxism, in its instantiation in the French Marxists who are his contemporaries, particularly Althusser and his students. And the fact that these Marxists are his contemporaries challenges any clean division one might try to make between generations in the transmission of legacies. On Derrida's understanding inheritance is not something that can be easily understood as a cross-generational phenomenon, something that will be confirmed below in the discussion in *For What Tomorrow* and in my analysis of spacing. For an interesting reflection on Derrida's relation to Althusser as it is expressed in *Specters of Marx*, see Etienne Balibar, "Eschatology versus Teleology: The Suspended Dialogue between Derrida and Althusser," in Cheah and Guerlac, *Derrida and the Time of the Political*.

4. The third meaning of "conjuration" is that of a pact or alliance (*SOM*, 40–41/*SDM*, 73), which Derrida also uses to emphasize the complicity between Marx and his opponents in the resistance to specters. For all their differences, there is agreement in wanting to banish the specter, for example, of communism—Marx and Engels want to be done with the specter so as to have it real, while the "Holy Alliance" wants to be done with it so as to have every trace of it disappear.

5. This connects with Derrida's brief remarks at the very beginning of *Specters of Marx* concerning the meaning of the phrase "*I would like to learn to live finally*," which, as I noted in my Introduction, he takes up again in his final interview: "If it—learning to live—remains to be done, it can happen only between life and death. Neither in life nor death *alone*. What happens between two, and between all the 'two's' one likes, can only *talk with or about* some ghost. . . . And this being-with specters would also be, not only but also, a *politics* of memory, of inheritance, and of generations" (*SOM*, xviii–xix/*SDM*, 14–15).

6. For some critics, it is too late in the game. Terry Eagleton remarks, for example, that "there is something pretty rich, as well as movingly sincere, about this sudden dramatic somersault onto a stalled bandwagon" (Terry Eagleton, "Marxism without Marxism," in *Ghostly Demarcations: A Symposium on Jacques Derrida's* Specters of Marx, ed. Michael Sprinker [London: Verso, 1999], 83–84). But see also Derrida's response in Jacques Derrida, "Marx & Sons," in *Ghostly Demarcations*, ed. Sprinker, 227–28, published in French as *Marx & Sons* (Paris: PUF/Galilée, 2002), 33–34.

7. It is again interesting to note the impossibility of cleanly distinguishing among generations in such discussions. In his response to Roudinesco's opening question, Derrida seems to have no hesitation including Deleuze and Lyotard in the heritage to which he was responding even though they are thinkers more readily classified as his contemporaries (*FW*, 6/*DQ*, 19).

8. The translator of this text, Jeff Fort, notes that "*héritage*" can be rendered into English equally as "heritage," "inheritance," and "legacy," and that he has "chosen one of these three translations based on context, connotation, and consistency" (*FW*, 197). As I have done here, I will on occasion modify this choice.

9. Jacques Derrida, *Limited Inc.*; Jürgen Habermas, *The Philosophical Discourse of Modernity: Twelve Lectures*, trans. Frederick Lawrence (Cambridge, MA: MIT Press, 1987); Luc Ferry and Alain Renaut, *French Philosophy of the Sixties: An Essay on Antihumanism*, trans. Mary S. Cattani (Amherst: University of Massachusetts Press, 1990).

10. Derrida also appeals to this combination of love and aggression when discussing his relation to the French language: "I have the feeling that everything I'm trying to do involves a hand-to-hand struggle with the French language, a turbulent but *primal* hand-to-hand struggle. . . . I have for this language an anxious, jealous, and tormented love. . . . I would dare claim that between the French language and me there will be, there will have been, more love" (*FW*, 14/*DQ*, 30–31).

11. For a comprehensive interpretation of Derrida's understanding of survival, see Hägglund, *Radical Atheism*. I will discuss this book in Chapter 4, and give a more detailed account of why pure life and pure death are beyond the sphere of subjective choice.

12. For more on this word and its importance in Derrida's writings, see Samuel Weber, "La Surenchère—(Upping the Ante)," in *Le passage des frontières* (Paris: Galilée, 1994). This paper appears in English in Anselm Haverkamp, ed., *Deconstruction Is/in America* (New York: New York University Press, 1995), but some of Weber's remarks on the notion of *surenchère* have not been retained in this later, shorter version.

13. Derrida, "As If It Were Possible," 81/295.

14. At the beginning of *Specters* the same pattern recurs, where, speaking of the question "Whither Marxism?" (the title of the colloquium at which the first version of the book was delivered), Derrida writes, "Now if this question, from the moment it comes to us, can clearly come only from the future [*l'avenir*] . . . what stands *in front of* [devant] it must also precede it like its origin: *before* [avant] it. Even if the future is its provenance, it must be, like any provenance, absolutely and irreversibly past. 'Experience' of the past as to come [*à venir*], the one and the other absolutely absolute, beyond all modification of any present whatever" (*SOM*, xix–xx/*SDM*, 16). Note that here both the future and the past are described as "absolute."

15. Of course, to take these phrases to be speaking of temporality still requires an interpretative decision, since "*le temps*" already has multiple meanings, just as does the English "time."

16. See, for example, Fritsch's thorough account of the disrupted time of inheritance, which he articulates through reference to Derrida's understanding of the promise, iterability, and quasi-transcendentality, in *The Promise of Memory*, 66–72.

17. "*Devant*" is also the present participle of "*devoir*" (to owe), so Derrida's claims concerning a legacy lying "before" an heir always carry an echo of the obligation to respond that inheritance entails. This is stated explicitly in *For What Tomorrow*: "Even before [*avant*] saying that one is responsible for a particular inheritance, it is necessary to know that responsibility in general ('answering for,' 'answering to,' 'answering in one's name') is first assigned to us, and that it is assigned to us through and through, as an inheritance. One is responsible before what comes before one but also before what is to come, and therefore *before oneself*. A double *before*, one that is also a debt, as when we say *devant ce qu'il doit: before* what he *ought to do* and *owing* what he *owes*, once and for all, the heir is doubly indebted [*On est responsable devant ce qui vient avant soi mais aussi devant ce qui à venir, et donc encore* devant *soi. Devant deux fois, devant ce qu'il doit une fois pour toutes, l'héritier est doublement endetté*]" (*FW*, 5–6/*DQ*, 18).

18. Jacques Derrida, *Of Grammatology*, trans. Gayatri Chakravorty Spivak (Baltimore: Johns Hopkins University Press, 1976), 68, originally published as *De la grammatologie* (Paris: Minuit, 1967), 99.

19. This signals a complicated issue that is beyond the scope of the present inquiry. In his early writings Derrida is constantly searching for a way to speak of time otherwise than based on a metaphysics of presence. At times, he seems to suggest this is possible, such as when he claims that the structure of *Nachträglichkeit* in Freud's work forms a temporality that is indeed irreducible to presence. Spacing is theorized here as "the fundamental property of writing," and Derrida goes so far as to claim that "it is not a question of a negation of time, of a cessation of time in a present or a simultaneity, but of a different structure, a different stratification of time" (Jacques Derrida, "Freud and the Scene of Writing," trans. Alan Bass, in *Writing and Difference* [Chicago: University of Chicago Press, 1978], 217, 219, originally published as "Freud et la scène de l'écriture," in *L'écriture et la différence* [Paris: Minuit, 1967], 321, 325). However, more frequently Derrida argues against the possibility of another structure of time, and is much more cautious in describing such a structure as "temporal." Thus, in *Speech and Phenomena* he writes, "What we are calling time must be given a different name—for 'time' has always designated a movement conceived in terms of the present, and can mean nothing else" (Jacques Derrida, *Speech and Phenomena and Other Essays on Husserl's Theory of Time* [Evanston, IL: Northwestern University Press, 1973], 68, originally published as *La voix et le phénomène* [Paris: PUF, 1967], 77). Similarly, in *Of Grammatology* Derrida claims, "Since past has always

signified present-past, the absolute past that is retained in the trace no longer rigorously merits the name 'past.' Another name to erase, especially since the strange movement of the trace proclaims as much as it recalls: differance defers-differs [*diffère*]. With the same precaution and under the same erasure, it may be said that its passivity is also its relationship with the 'future.' The concepts of *present, past,* and *future*, everything in the concepts of time and history which implies evidence of them—the metaphysical concept of time in general—cannot adequately describe the structure of the trace. . . . It is the problem of the deferred effect [*Nachträglichkeit*] of which Freud speaks. The temporality to which he refers cannot be that which lends itself to a phenomenology of consciousness or of presence and one may indeed wonder by what right all that is in question here should still be called time, now, anterior present, delay, etc." (66–67/97–98). Finally, in "*Ousia* and *Grammē*," after reading Aristotle, Kant, and Hegel from the standpoint of Heidegger's analysis of temporality in *Being and Time*, Derrida offers the following famous hypothesis: "Perhaps there is no 'vulgar concept of time.' The concept of time, in all its aspects, belongs to metaphysics, and it names the domination of presence. Therefore we can only conclude that the entire system of metaphysical concepts, throughout its history, develops the so-called 'vulgarity' of the concept of time (which Heidegger, no doubt, would contest), but also that an *other* concept of time cannot be opposed to it, since time in general belongs to metaphysical conceptuality. In attempting to produce this *other* concept, one rapidly would come to see that it is constructed out of other metaphysical or ontotheological predicates" (63/73). These citations all suggest that what is being described under the name of spacing has a relation to what is called "temporal," but may not itself be best described this way. For opposing readings of this issue, see Bennington, *Interrupting Derrida*, 172–79, and Hägglund, *Radical Atheism*, 208n5.

20. "Before the law, the man is a subject of the law in appearing before it. This is obvious, but since he is *before* it because he cannot enter it, he is also *outside the law* (an outlaw). He is neither under the law nor in the law. He is both a subject of the law and an outlaw" (Jacques Derrida, "Before the Law," trans. Avital Ronell, in *Acts of Literature*, ed. Derek Attridge [New York: Routledge, 1992], 204, originally published as "Devant la loi," in Jacques Derrida et al., *La faculté de juger* [Paris: Minuit, 1985], 122).

21. The citation is from Emmanuel Levinas, *Totality and Infinity*, trans. Alphonso Lingis (Pittsburgh: Duquesne University Press, 1969), 89.

22. "If I were to say that I know nothing more just than what I call today deconstruction (nothing more just—I am not saying nothing more legal or legitimate), I know that I would not fail to surprise or shock not only the determined adversaries of said deconstruction or what they imagine under this name, but also the very people who pass for or take themselves to be its partisans or its practitioners" (FOL, 249/FDL, 46–47). In saying this, Derrida, as is often the case, places himself against what he takes the standard interpretation to be. What is not always noted is that he immediately follows this statement with the words "And so, I will not say it, at least not directly and not without the precaution of several detours" (FOL, 249/FDL, 47). This movement of retraction or hesitation, which Derrida often performs when making such provocative statements (for example, he introduces the phrase "*Deconstruction is justice*" as part of a paradox he "would like to submit for discussion" [FOL, 243/FDL, 35]), needs to be taken into account when discussing these matters. I would suggest that in the present context it renders Derrida's statements concerning the relation between deconstruction and justice as hypotheses to be tested, which could turn out to be wrong, rather than axioms whose truth can be taken for granted.

3. Inheriting Democracy to Come

1. For one of Derrida's last defenses of the claim that his work has always been engaged with political questions, see *R*, 39/*V*, 64. Almost every sympathetic reading of Derrida on politics makes

such a claim. Two of the more developed accounts are found in Bennington's essay "Derrida and Politics" in *Interrupting Derrida*, and in Beardsworth, *Derrida and the Political.*

2. Derrida, *Other Heading*, 9/16.

3. Ibid., 28–29/32–33. For a reading of Derrida's inheritance of the idea of Europe, particularly as it relates to the concept of responsibility, see Rodolphe Gasché, "European Memories: Jan Patočka and Jacques Derrida on Responsibility," in Cheah and Guerlac, *Derrida and the Time of the Political.*

4. Derrida, *Other Heading*, 78/76.

5. Jacques Derrida, "Sauf le nom," trans. John P. Leavey Jr., in *On the Name*, ed. Thomas Dutoit (Stanford: Stanford University Press, 1995), 83, originally published as *Sauf le nom* (Paris: Galilée, 1993), 108.

6. Something very like this idea also appears in a third text dating from around the same time. In the introductory chapter of his *Du droit à la philosophie*, speaking of "thinking" (in distinction from "science" or "philosophy"), Derrida writes the following: "There *is no* pure instance. 'Thinking,' a word that entitles only the possibility of this 'no,' must even, in the name of a democracy still *to come* as the possibility of this thinking, unremittingly interrogate the de facto democracy, critique its current determinations, analyze its philosophical genealogy, in short, deconstruct it: in the name of the democracy whose being to come is not simply tomorrow or the future, but rather the promise of an event and the event of a promise. An event and a promise that constitute the democratic: not presently but in a here and now whose singularity does not signify presence or self-presence" (Jacques Derrida, "Privilege: Justificatory Title and Introductory Remarks," in *Who's Afraid of Philosophy? Right to Philosophy I*, trans. Jan Plug [Stanford: Stanford University Press, 2002], 42, originally published as "Privilège: Titre justificatif et remarques introductives," in *Du droit à la philosophie* [Paris: Galilée, 1990], 70).

I should also note that another notion to which Derrida links democracy in the early 1990s is free speech, through a relation to literature. I will not be discussing this here, but see, for example, Derrida, "Passions," 28/68. Alex Thomson analyzes this relation in *Deconstruction and Democracy*, 32–37.

7. Jacques Derrida, "Avances," preface to *Le tombeau du dieu artisan—sur Platon*, by Serge Margel (Paris: Minuit, 1995). Hereafter referred to as AV. I cite from "Avances" because the characteristics of the promise articulated there are identical to central features of democracy, but one can articulate Derrida's understanding of the promise in other ways. For an account that is based on *différance*, precisely in order to articulate the meaning of "democracy to come," see Fritsch, "Derrida's Democracy to Come," 575–77. Fritsch develops his analysis of the promise more comprehensively in *The Promise of Memory*, there tying it explicitly to inheritance.

8. There is another aspect of Derrida's analysis in "Avances" which, while it does not bear directly on democracy, is worth noting because it relates the promise to inheritance. Derrida writes: "Margel's interpretative commentary clarifies that, while untenable for the Demiurge, the promise must be renewed by us, by a human race that inherits the (untenable) promise of another and makes itself responsible in this way. But this second promise confirms at the same stroke, it seems to me, the *untenable promise*. It confirms the inherited *promise* in renewing it, but it also confirms, alas, that it is and it remains, in its very structure, *untenable*. It is a question here of a responsibility—as always taken in the name of another—of our own as of another, of a human responsibility which in sum takes on the survival of the cosmos or in any case of our world. Is it a problem more 'current'? More current, that is more present, more urgent but also more pressing and more acute in a new form of the question 'what to do?' What are we going to do, what ought we do with the earth and with the human earth?" (AV, 27). The fact that the promise is untenable places it in a cycle of inheritance, bearing all of its characteristics—the element of alterity and responsibility, the structure of survival, the emphasis on urgency, and so on.

9. That the title of the Cerisy conference, "The Democracy to Come," would have been set far in advance of September 11, 2001, makes one realize just how tightly Derrida's theorization of

democracy was tied to current events. What might I be writing about "democracy to come" in the present chapter had the conference been scheduled a year earlier?

10. The figure of the *tour* is present throughout "The Reason of the Strongest." Although Derrida's main focus is on the turns (*tour*, masculine) in democracy, both the return to the self of auto-determination and the taking turns of democratic governance, the shadow of the towers (*tour*, feminine) of the New York World Trade Center is never far away. Not to mention the tour (*tour*, masculine) that Derrida himself performs around his own previous writings on democracy at this conference on "The Democracy to Come."

11. Derrida claims that "the only and very few regimes, in the supposed modernity of this situation, that *do not present themselves* as democratic are those with a theocratic Muslim government" (*R*, 28/*V*, 51–52). This has the effect of aligning these regimes with the dominant antidemocratic tendency of the Western philosophical tradition, which Derrida later mentions (*R*, 41/*V*, 66). For more on Derrida's remarks concerning Islam and democracy, see Alex Thomson, "Derrida's *Rogues*: Islam and the Futures of Deconstruction," in *Derrida: Negotiating the Legacy*, ed. Madeleine Fagan et al. (Edinburgh: Edinburgh University Press, 2007).

12. Jean-Jacques Rousseau, *On the Social Contract*, in *The Basic Political Writings*, trans. Donald A. Cress (Indianapolis: Hackett, 1987), 181. Cited on *R*, 74/*V*, 108.

13. Ibid. Cited on *R*, 75/*V*, 110.

14. Autoimmunity does appear in Derrida's publications before 1996, but in these instances it is mentioned in passing and not used as a central term of analysis. In *Specters of Marx* Derrida writes that the "living ego is auto-immune, which is what they do not want to know. To protect its life, to constitute itself as unique living ego, to relate, as the same, to itself, it is necessarily led to welcome the other within (so many figures of death: differance of the technical apparatus, iterability, non-uniqueness, prosthesis, synthetic image, simulacrum, all of which begins with language, before language), it must therefore take the immune defenses apparently meant for the non-ego, the enemy, the opposite, the adversary and direct them at once *for itself and against itself*" (*SOM*, 141/*SDM*, 224). In *Politics of Friendship*, Derrida claims that the "modality of the possible, the unquenchable *perhaps*, would, implacably, destroy everything, by means of a sort of self-immunity [*auto-immunité*] from which no region of being, *phúsis* or history would be exempt," and speaks of the "imminence of a self-destruction by the infinite development of a madness of self-immunity [*auto-immunité*]" (*PF*, 75–76/*PA*, 94).

15. Thus in "The Reason of the Strongest" Derrida writes that autoimmunity consists "not only in committing suicide but in compromising *sui-* or *self*-referentiality, the *self* or *sui-* of suicide itself. Autoimmunity is more or less suicidal, but, more seriously still, it threatens always to rob suicide itself of its meaning and supposed integrity" (*R*, 45/*V*, 71).

16. In "Force of Law," Derrida makes a similar statement in his reading of divine violence in Benjamin, describing this as a violence made "in the name of life, of the most living of life [*du plus vivant de la vie*], of the value of the life that is worth more than life" (FOL, 289/FDL, 126).

17. Derrida invokes the example of Algeria without discussing any of its details. For a more comprehensive account, see Thomson, "Derrida's *Rogues*." Samuel Weber questions Derrida's use of this example: "Given the highly undemocratic character of the FLN, even if it was 'elected' prior to 1992, this example strikes me as unfortunate and not entirely appropriate" (Samuel Weber, "Rogue Democracy," *Diacritics* 38, nos. 1–2 [2008]: 112).

18. Derrida does not restrict himself to the example of Algeria to illustrate this point. He also cites the situation in France with Le Pen (*R*, 30/*V*, 53–54), and claims that a similar process was at work when the fascists and Nazis came to power in Europe: "There is something paradigmatic in this autoimmune suicide: fascist and Nazi totalitarianisms came into power or ascended to power through formally normal and formally democratic electoral processes" (*R*, 33/*V*, 57–58).

19. A similar statement is made in Derrida, "Autoimmunity," 95/146–47: The attack "comes, *as from the inside*, from forces that are apparently without any force of their own but that are able to find

the means, through ruse and the implementation of *high-tech* knowledge, to get hold of an American weapon in an American city on the ground of an American airport. Immigrated, trained, prepared for their act in the United States by the United States, these *hijackers* incorporate, so to speak, two suicides in one: their own . . . but also the suicide of those who welcomed, armed, and trained them."

20. This receives a more extensive treatment in "Autoimmunity," 94–106/145–60, where Derrida inscribes the attacks against the World Trade Center within a greater logic of the Cold War.

21. Earlier in "The Reason of the Strongest" Derrida states this idea in a condensed form, linking this directly to the "freedom in the concept of democracy" (*R*, 25/*V*, 48). He also makes similar statements in interviews and discussions given around this time. See Derrida, "Autoimmunity," 121/178; Derrida, "Not Utopia, the Im-possible," 130/360; Jacques Derrida, "'Others Are Secret Because They Are Other,'" in *Paper Machine*, 139, originally published as "Autrui est secret parce qu'il est autre," in *Papier machine*, 371; *FW*, 130/*DQ*, 209.

22. While Derrida's invocation of excluded groups in this context is made in a supportive tone, Penelope Deutscher questions whether this is unambiguously so in the case of women. See Penelope Deutscher, "'Women, and So On': *Rogues* and the Autoimmunity of Feminism," *Symposium: Canadian Journal of Continental Philosophy* 11, no. 1 (2007). I discuss Deutscher's claims in Chapter 5.

23. Derrida makes this connection explicit when he writes, "In its constitutive autoimmunity, in its vocation for hospitality (with everything in the *ipse* that works over the etymology and experience of the *hospes* through the aporias of hospitality), democracy has always wanted by turns and at the same time two incompatible things: it has wanted, on the one hand, to welcome only men, and on the condition that they be citizens, brothers, and compeers [*semblables*], excluding all the others, in particular bad citizens, rogues, noncitizens, and all sorts of unlike and unrecognizable others, and, on the other hand, at the same time or by turns, it has wanted to open itself up, to offer hospitality, to all those excluded. In both cases, let us recall, and here is a problem I take up elsewhere, this hospitality remains limited and conditional" (*R*, 63/*V*, 95).

24. For more on freedom and equality as aporias, see *R*, 34, 48–50, 53–54/*V*, 58, 75–76, 79–82.

25. Jacques Derrida, "Politics and Friendship," trans. Robert Harvey, in *Negotiations*, 181.

26. It is worth noting that Derrida made the above remark in an American context, and that the distinction between "democracy" and "republic" may well play out differently in the context of French politics. However, French republican discourse seems to be of little importance in Derrida's writings on democracy. For brief discussions on the distinction between "democracy" and "republic" in French politics, see Derrida, "Others Are Secret," 139/371, and the transcription of Derrida's comments in Seffahi, *Manifeste pour l'hospitalité*, 143–46.

Concerning the possibility of ceasing to appeal to democracy, Derrida of course in fact did the opposite, increasing references to democracy up until his death. But it is also the case that an increase in use does not necessarily mean an increase in support. While Derrida's appeals to democracy throughout the 1990s seem predominantly to give it a positive value, "The Reason of the Strongest," as shown above, is much more evenhanded, highlighting the dangers equally, if not more, than the chances this term contains. It is thus unclear if Derrida would have continued to invoke "democracy" as a strategically useful term had he not passed away. This uncertainty is captured perfectly in the final line of this text: "Democracy to come—fare well! [*La démocratie à venir, salut!*]" (*R*, 114/*V*, 161). Since, as the translators note, "*Salut* must be understood as both a greeting and a farewell" (*R*, 171), "The Reason of the Strongest" is here marked equally as a first and last word on democracy to come.

27. Derrida, "Politics and Friendship" 182.

28. Similarly, earlier Derrida writes that "the legacy and the allegation, the legibility of the legend or inscription . . . only put off until later or send off elsewhere [*ne font que renvoyer à plus tard ou ailleurs*]. This sending or putting off gestures toward the past of an inheritance only by remaining to come" (*R*, 9/*V*, 28). One could challenge whether this last statement is in fact endorsed by Derrida

since it appears within a "confession" that he hesitates to embrace, but in my opinion it accurately describes what is in play in democracy to come.

29. Fritsch, "Derrida's Democracy to Come," 581–82. Fritsch's remarks predate the publication of "The Reason of the Strongest," in which the elements he defines as less important do receive more attention. Nevertheless, the claim remains valid, since in this work Derrida still promotes these aspects of democratic thinking less than those Fritsch identifies as central to his conception.

30. Derrida, "As If It Were Possible," 81/295.

31. Here I am in agreement with both Fritsch and Bennington, each of whom suggests in his own way that this sentence is to be understood through reference to inheritance. See Bennington, *Interrupting Derrida*, 31–33, and Fritsch, "Derrida's Democracy to Come," 578.

32. Derrida, "Politics and Friendship," 182.

33. Derrida, "Autoimmunity," 113/168–69.

34. Claude Lefort, "The Question of Democracy," in *Democracy and Political Theory*, trans. David Macey (Minneapolis: University of Minnesota Press, 1988), 16. Derrida was in the audience when Lefort first delivered this paper in January 1982 at Lacoue-Labarthe and Nancy's Centre for Philosophical Research on the Political. According to the published summary, Derrida was an active participant in the discussion that followed and was focused precisely on the distinction Lefort draws between democracy and totalitarianism. See Claude Lefort, "La question de la démocratie," in *Le retrait du politique*, by Philippe Lacoue-Labarthe, Jean-Luc Nancy, et al. (Paris: Galilée, 1983), 86–88.

4. Questioning Normativity

1. This is the case even as writing is associated with democracy in Plato's text. See Jacques Derrida, "Plato's Pharmacy," in *Dissemination*, trans. Barbara Johnson (Chicago: University of Chicago Press, 1981), 144–45, originally published as "La pharmacie de Platon," in *Dissemination*, (Paris: Seuil, 1972), 180–81.

2. Hägglund, *Radical Atheism*, 33.

3. Earlier versions of some of the arguments in this chapter are contained in Samir Haddad, "Language Remains," *CR: The New Centennial Review* 9, no. 1 (2009). In a response to my articulation in that article of his understanding of the chance/threat couple, reproduced here, Hägglund agrees that the chance and the threat do specify two different possibilities, but resists my gloss of the chance as one of living on, and the threat as one of dying: "In fact, this formulation is not quite correct, since the threat can be the threat of living on and the chance can be the chance of not living on. As I argue in *Radical Atheism*, it does not follow from the unconditional affirmation of survival that one necessarily prefers that a given entity survives rather than is killed off" (Martin Hägglund, "The Challenge of Radical Atheism: A Response," *CR: The New Centennial Review* 9, no. 1 [2009]: 251n2). It's not clear to me that Hägglund's argument can sustain this modification, but in any case I would argue that the formulation as I have presented it is dominant in *Radical Atheism*, and is the one at work in Hägglund's specific discussion of democracy.

4. Hägglund, *Radical Atheism*, 32.

5. Ibid., 185.

6. Ibid., 32.

7. Ibid., 33.

8. Ibid., 231n4.

9. Ibid., 171.

10. Ibid.

11. Ibid., 171–72.

12. Ibid., 195–96.

13. Ibid., 19.

14. Two other commentators who appeal to a lesser violence to account for normativity in Derrida's work are Richard Beardsworth in *Derrida and the Political* and Matthias Fritsch in "Derrida's Democracy to Come" and *The Promise of Memory*. Hägglund discusses and critiques their positions in *Radical Atheism*, 170–71, 231n4, as do I in Samir Haddad, "A Genealogy of Violence, from Light to the Autoimmune," *Diacritics* 38, nos. 1–2 (2008): 135–41. Some of the arguments against a lesser violence that I make below appeared in an earlier form in that essay.

15. Leonard Lawlor, "Jacques Derrida," *Stanford Encyclopedia of Philosophy* http://plato.stanford.edu/entries/derrida/. Although I have not discussed it, animality plays a role in Derrida's analysis of democracy in "The Reason of the Strongest" and is central to the extended analysis of political sovereignty in Jacques Derrida, *The Beast and the Sovereign*, vol. 1, trans. Geoffrey Bennington (Chicago: University of Chicago Press, 2009), originally published as *Séminaire: La bête et le souverain volume I (2001–2002)* (Paris: Galilée, 2008), and Jacques Derrida, *The Beast and the Sovereign*, vol. 2, trans. Geoffrey Bennington (Chicago: University of Chicago Press, 2011), originally published as *Séminaire: La bête et le souverain volume II (2002–2003)* (Paris: Galilée, 2010).

16. Lawlor, *This Is Not Sufficient*, 37, 23.

17. Ibid., 119.

18. Ibid., 110.

19. Missing from the second series in parentheses is a term that would be opposed to forgiveness, but this may be because Lawlor seems to assimilate forgiveness quite strictly to the other terms: "Once again, the more sufficient response is the friendly response: unconditional friendship. And unconditional friendship is unconditional forgiveness since all the others, all the animals, are defective." And shortly after: "The reversal, then, is an experimentation on the equality of violence, which means that all living beings, no matter how violent, are treated equally in the sense of hospitality: all are welcome. Unconditional hospitality is forgiveness. We could say at this moment, 'O my enemies, there are no enemies'" (ibid., 109, 111).

20. Ibid., 73, 81, 101.

21. Another mark of the difference between Hägglund's and Lawlor's positions is their respective interpretations of spacing. As discussed above, Hägglund sees spacing as a necessary structure underlying all things in time. It is an inescapable feature of everything. Lawlor, by contrast, equates spacing with *mondialisation*, and sees it as only one possibility among others: "When Derrida says in *The 'Concept' of September 11* that '*mondialisation* is not taking place,' he means that spacing is not taking place. Spacing *must* happen in order to institute not a war without war but a peace without peace" (ibid., 19, citing Derrida, "Autoimmunity," 123/181).

22. Ibid., 110–11. See also 32–36.

23. Ibid., 23.

24. Ibid., 9, 23, 26, 40, 66, 71.

25. Related to this confusion is another slide that Lawlor makes in the text. Discussing the worst in the context of Derrida's analysis of globalization and the war on terror, Lawlor writes the following: "Let me repeat this crucial comment: 'A new violence is being prepared and in truth has been unleashed for some time now, in a way that is more visibly suicidal [*plus visiblement suicidaire*] or autoimmune than ever.' What does it mean to be 'more suicidal'? To be more suicidal is to kill oneself *more*" (ibid., 20, citing *R*, 156/*V*, 214). But "more visibly suicidal" is not equivalent to "more suicidal"—the "more" qualifies "visibly," not "suicidal." This renders doubtful the analysis that Lawlor pursues in the subsequent few pages.

26. In this text the words "the worst" appear only in passing: "This unthinkable gives itself to (be) thought in the age when a nuclear war is possible: a, or rather, from the outset, *some* sendings, many sendings, missiles whose distinerring and randomness may, in the very process of calculation and the games that simulate the process, escape all control, all reassimilation or self-regulation by

a system that they will have *precipitously* (too rapidly, in order to avert the worst) but irreversibly destroyed" (Jacques Derrida, "No Apocalypse, Not Now: Full Speed Ahead, Seven Missiles, Seven Missives," trans. Catherine Porter and Philip Lewis, in *Psyche: Inventions of the Other* [Stanford: Stanford University Press, 2007], 1:405, originally published as "*No apocalypse, not now*: à toute vitesse, sept missiles, sept missives," in *Psyché: Inventions de l'autre*, 2nd ed. [Paris: Galilée, 1998], 1:413).

27. Ibid., 400/408.

28. Ibid., 400, 403/409, 411.

29. Ibid., 408/416.

30. Ibid., 402–3/411.

31. See Jacques Derrida, *Chaque fois unique, la fin du monde* (Paris: Galilée, 2003), 9–11; Jacques Derrida, "Rams: Uninterrupted Dialogue—Between Two Infinities, the Poem," trans. Thomas Dutoit and Philippe Romanski, in *Sovereignties in Question: The Poetics of Paul Celan* (New York: Fordham University Press, 2005), 140, originally published as *Béliers: Le dialogue ininterrompu: Entre deux infinis, le poème* (Paris: Galilée, 2003), 23. In the first work the phrase appears in the title and preface of the French edition, and is not thus highlighted in the earlier, English text *The Work of Mourning*, ed. and trans. Michael Naas and Pascale-Anne Brault (Chicago: University of Chicago Press, 2001).

32. Lawlor, *This Is Not Sufficient*, 23.

33. Hägglund, *Radical Atheism*, 47. Hägglund justifies this identification by omitting some crucial words in a passage cited above from "No Apocalypse," when he immediately claims "As Derrida puts it, 'I live this anticipation [of my own death] in anguish, terror, despair, as a catastrophe that I have no reason not to equate with the annihilation of humanity as a whole.'" By omitting the beginning of the cited sentence—"Images, grief, all the resources of memory and tradition, can cushion the reality of that death, whose anticipation remains therefore interwoven with fictionality, symbolicity, or, if you prefer, literature; *and this is so even if* I live this anticipation . . . " (my emphasis)—Hägglund elides the very contrast that Derrida makes.

34. Derrida makes the same association between the worst and the final solution in passing in FK, 91/FS, 84.

35. Jacques Derrida, *Archive Fever: A Freudian Impression*, trans. Eric Prenowitz (Chicago: University of Chicago Press, 1996), 10, 19, originally published as *Mal d'archive* (Paris: Galilée, 1995), 24, 38.

36. In my discussion of the worst I have left out Derrida's remarks in the September 11 interview, when he describes the chemical, bacteriological, or nuclear terrorist attacks as threats "of the worst *to come*." This is related to his claim a few pages later that the actions and discourse of "'the bin Laden effect' . . . *open onto no future and . . . have no future*" (Derrida, "Autoimmunity," 97, 113/149–50, 168–69). For the same reasons that I resisted the latter remarks in Chapter 3, I think it is clear that these events do not coincide at all with the worst, since they in no way involve the complete eradication of the structure of the trace. For similar statements concerning the future threats, see R, 104–5/V, 148–49. The confusion could be avoided by translating "*pire*" in these passages as "worse" rather than "worst," although this would perhaps be a betrayal of Derrida's text.

37. Indeed, Derrida can be read to claim as much in another context. Discussing the erasure of the trace in Lacan's comments about the animal in *The Beast and the Sovereign*, vol. 1, he writes: "It is in the nature of a trace that it always effaces itself and is always able to efface itself. But that it efface *itself*, that it can always efface *itself*, from the first moment of its inscription, through and beyond repression, does not mean that anybody, God, man, or beast, is its master or sovereign subject and can have the power to efface *it* at its disposal. On the contrary. In this respect, man has no more sovereign *power* to efface his traces than the so-called 'animal.' To efface his traces *radically*, hence just as *radically* to destroy, deny, put to death, even put himself to death" (131/182). If one takes Derrida's reference to the radical effacement of the trace at the end of this citation to be a reference to the worst, then here he is precisely arguing that this state is beyond the reach of the sovereign I.

38. I should also note that if my interpretation of the meaning of the worst in Derrida is correct, then some of Hägglund's claims might well need modification. In particular, Hägglund might want to give up his understanding of the fundamental threat in spacing as a threat of the worst, that is, of the total cessation of the trace structure constituting an entity, in favor of a more moderate conception of a threat of destruction, or death, which would nonetheless leave a trace and so enable a living on in some form. I say that he might want to do this, for he need not—the worst, as an impossibility, can still be seen to threaten all of mortal life. But I would suggest that maintaining this would in fact weaken Hägglund's argument, since the worst is so rare that some of its threatening force is diminished.

39. Lawlor, *This Is Not Sufficient*, 24, 26–27, 40.

40. Jacques Derrida, "Violence and Metaphysics: An Essay on the Thought of Emmanuel Levinas," in *Writing and Difference*, trans. Alan Bass (Chicago: University of Chicago Press, 1978), 313n21, originally published as "Violence et métaphysique: Essai sur la pensée d'Emmanuel Levinas," in *L'écriture et la différence* (Paris: Seuil, 1967), 136n1.

41. Ibid., 117/172–73.

42. It is also worth pausing over the eccentricity of the contrast Derrida here draws, in which he does not cast *"pire* [worse/worst]" against it direct opposite, *"meilleur* [better/best]," but against *"moindre* [lesser/least]" (which is not its opposite). This confirms Hägglund's reading of the best and the worst discussed above—*le pire* and *le meilleur* would name the same thing, so cannot be used as opposites—and further supports my resistance to the overly oppositional logic implied by the translation of *"la moindre"* as "the least."

43. The full passage reads as follows: "Discourse, therefore, if it is originally violent, can only *do violence to itself*, can only negate itself in order to affirm itself, make war upon the war which institutes it without ever *being able* to reappropriate to itself this negativity, to the extent that it is discourse. *Necessarily* without reappropriating it, for if it did so, the horizon of peace would disappear into the night (worst violence as previolence). This secondary war, as the avowal of violence, is the least possible violence [*la moindre violence possible*], the only way to repress the worst violence, the violence of primitive and prelogical silence, of an unimaginable night which would not even be the opposite of day, an absolute violence which would not even be the opposite of nonviolence: nothingness or pure non-sense" (ibid., 130/190–91).

44. Ibid., 117/172.

45. Ibid., 313n21/136n1.

46. I should note that despite his criticism of appeals to a lesser violence that attempt to ground a normativity in Derrida's work, Hägglund seeks to retain the notion, arguing that "all decisions made in the name of justice are made in view of what is judged to be the lesser violence" (Hägglund, *Radical Atheism*, 83 [the same claim is repeated on 171]). Viewed this way, Derrida's statement about choosing a lesser violence in "Violence and Metaphysics" would thus presumably be a description of this fact about all decisions made in the name of justice. Although Hägglund does not develop this point at length, I have doubts about its plausibility, since it is unclear to me that all claims to justice are in fact made in the name of a lesser violence. A system of justice based on retribution observing strict equality in the measurement of punishment vis-à-vis the crime, for example, would seem to be involve an economy of violence that does not ever need to appeal to the concept of a *lesser* violence.

47. Ibid., 202.

48. But note that this neutrality is itself not completely stable. Since one of the aims of Derrida's early work is to show precisely how the notions of speech and writing are infused with value in the philosophical tradition, in spite of a widespread blindness on the matter up to that point, the success of his analysis results in a destabilization of the previously perceived neutrality of value. As a consequence, anyone writing after Derrida on this issue thus has to engage the normativity that these terms are henceforth recognized to carry.

49. Hägglund, "Challenge of Radical Atheism," 236–37. I am leaving aside other disagreements that Hägglund expresses with my interpretation, some because they are not relevant to my present concern, but others because they are based on a misreading of my position. Concerning the latter, I will simply here note that one of Hägglund's main claims is that I make a "general assertion that there cannot be a descriptive level of analysis because of the inherited nature of language" (236). I never make this assertion, in the argument's previous instantiation (to which Hägglund is responding) or in the present chapter. All I have ever claimed is that there cannot be a *purely* descriptive level of analysis because of the inherited nature of language.

50. Ibid., 237. The citations are from Jacques Derrida, "Typewriter Ribbon: Limited Ink (2)," in *Without Alibi*, trans. by Peggy Kamuf (Stanford: Stanford University Press, 2002), 146, originally published as "Le ruban de machine à écrire: *Limited Ink II*," in *Papier machine*, 128, and Haddad, "Language Remains," 137.

51. Derrida, "Typewriter Ribbon," 146/128.

52. In a subsequent publication, Hägglund clarifies and expands his interpretation. There he is explicit in stating that he does not "think deconstruction is a 'pure description' (a phrase I have never used) or a value-free enterprise that does not engage in performative acts of commitment," and he makes clear that, contrary to what I have charged above, his view is that the unconditional and the performative are inseparable. However, the claims Hägglund makes to support this assertion imply the contrary, that the unconditional is indeed independent of the performative. He writes: "Derrida even provocatively emphasizes that the unconditional exposure to the event 'couldn't care less about the performative.' The unconditional is thus the spacing of time that does not depend upon performative commitment, since it is the condition for all performative acts, and it cannot be embraced as something good in itself, since it is the source of every chance *and* every threat. For the same reason, the unconditional exposure to time is inseparable from ('calls for') conditional, performative responses that seek to discriminate between the chance and the threat. As Derrida clearly underlines, the exposure to the event—an 'exposure without horizon, and therefore an irreducible amalgamation of desire and anguish, affirmation and fear, promise and threat'—is 'the condition of praxis, decision, action, and responsibility'" (Martin Hägglund, "The Radical Evil of Deconstruction: A Reply to John Caputo," *Journal for Cultural and Religious Theory* 11, no. 2 [2011]: 137, 138. The first citation within this passage is, as before, from Derrida, "Typewriter Ribbon," 146/128, and the last two from Derrida, "Marx & Sons," 249/70). In claiming that the unconditional "does not depend upon performative commitment," Hägglund again makes it clear that he reads this fragment from "Typewriter Ribbon" as testifying to a unidirectional relation (whereas, as I have shown, the original passage theorizes a dual relation, in fact emphasizing the dependence of the event on the performative). And the words he quotes from "Marx & Sons" that are supposed to justify the claim of inseparability simply repeat the same relation. Also, just a page earlier Hägglund writes that "Derrida insists that there is a 'non-performative exposure' to what happens, which he dissociates from the notion of an 'imperative injunction (call or performative)'" (137). "Dissociates" suggests an uncoupling of these terms, as if one can be thought without the other. So my charge is that even though in this later essay Hägglund claims the unconditional and the performative are inseparable, everything he says about them suggests the opposite.

53. I say "between all the terms involved" since, even though Derrida does not mention it, there would be a similar oscillation occurring between the constative and the unconditional. As a speech act, constative analysis is similarly exposed to an unknown future that can undermine it at any moment, even as this exposure is unthinkable apart from being embedded in such an act.

5. *Politics of Friendship* as Democratic Inheritance

1. Bennington, *Interrupting Derrida*, 111.

2. It is also worth noting that the very syntax of the phrase in Diogenes Laertius's text is questionable, since, as Derrida discusses, including an iota subscript on the 'O [ω]' significantly changes its meaning (*PF*, 207–10/*PA*, 234–37). This is how it is taken by Hicks in the standard English translation, who renders the phrase as "He who has friends can have no true friend" (Diogenes Laertius, *Lives of Eminent Philosophers*, trans. R. D. Hicks [Cambridge, MA: Harvard University Press, 1925], 465), but it has not been understood thus by Montaigne and others in the tradition Derrida reads (which happens not to contain any Anglophone philosophers). In any case, Derrida argues that the two versions, despite their apparent differences, both involve constative and performative dimensions and so partake in similar paradoxes (*PF*, 212–14/*PA*, 240–42).

3. In what follows I am not concerned with the accuracy of this reading of Montaigne as I am more interested in the position Derrida occupies vis-à-vis the relations between fraternity, friendship, and democracy, generated (in part) by this reading. Of course, one way to challenge Derrida's position is to challenge the reading on which it relies—if one were to show that Montaigne's view is not as Derrida states, then one might be able to argue that these three terms lie in an alternative configuration. This is always a possibility in the face of deconstruction, precisely because of its intimate tie to inheritance.

4. Michel de Montaigne, "On Affectionate Relationships," in *The Complete Essays*, trans. M. A. Screech (London: Allen Lane, Penguin Press, 1991), 214. Concerning the title of this essay, Screech argues that "On Affectionate Relationships" is a more accurate rendering of what is implied in Montaigne's account. I will, however, refer to it by its more traditional name in English, "On Friendship."

5. Ibid.

6. Ibid., 215.

7. Ibid., 207.

8. Ibid., 208.

9. Ibid, 207.

10. Ibid., 212.

11. Ibid., 210.

12. On the basis of Derrida's argument outlined below regarding the fiction of the genealogical link, one could deconstruct in a rather classical style the distinction between a "natural" and a "naturalized" citizen—the devalued term (the naturalized) becomes a generalized name that governs the logic of both sides of the distinction.

13. I should note that in Chapter 4 of *Politics of Friendship* Derrida does rely heavily on Nicole Loraux's work on Athenian democracy in the course of his reading and interrogation of Schmitt. But this does not contradict the claim above, since Derrida does not read Loraux as a part of the tradition of writing on friendship and politics investigated.

14. Kirby Dick and Amy Ziering Kofman, *Derrida: Screenplay and Essays on the Film* (New York: Routledge, 2005), 97. Cited in Deutscher, "'Women, and So On,'" 105, 113–14. Deutscher also discusses Derrida's avoidance of reading women in her "Derrida's Impossible Genealogies," *Theory and Event*, 8, no. 1 (2005), in which part of this citation appears as an epigraph.

15. Deutscher, "'Women, and So On,'" 105–6.

16. Deutscher, "Derrida's Impossible Genealogies," 26–27. In both of the essays I have been citing Deutscher makes this point in greater detail with respect to the way feminist struggles appear only as purely positive possibilities in Derrida's analysis of democracy. She argues that this too deprives women of the full potential, both positive and negative, that strictly speaking the Derridean view ought to grant them.

17. Ibid., 13.

6. Inheriting Birth

1. Jean-Luc Nancy, *The Experience of Freedom*, trans. Bridget McDonald (Stanford: Stanford University Press, 1993). Since my interest lies in the general claim made here concerning the relationship between fraternity and birth, I will not be pursuing the details of Derrida's reading of Nancy. Such a task would take me too far afield, given the complexity of these two thinkers' relationship, as well as the complexity of their respective oeuvres. For an analysis of Derrida's reading of Nancy in *Rogues* that does give attention to Nancy's work in its own right, see Peter Gratton, "Questioning Freedom in the Later Work of Derrida," *Philosophy Today* 50, Supp. (2006). Gratton also notes the link to birth in Derrida's resistance to fraternity. For a thorough analysis of Nancy's conception of birth, see Anne O'Byrne, *Natality and Finitude* (Bloomington: Indiana University Press, 2010), chap. 5.

2. Conscious of issues related to the exclusion of women that I discussed in Chapter 5, one should no doubt add the sororal to this list. For a theorization of the possibility of a sororal relation as a figure for democratic belonging, see Bonnie Honig, *Democracy and the Foreigner* (Princeton: Princeton University Press, 2001), chap. 3.

3. As far as I'm aware, no one has provided a comprehensive analysis of birth in Derrida's writings. For two recent books that provide rich analyses of the meaning of birth in several other thinkers in the Continental tradition, see Lisa Guenther, *The Gift of the Other: Levinas and the Politics of Reproduction* (Albany: State University of New York Press, 2006), and O'Byrne, *Natality and Finitude*.

4. Derrida, "Deconstruction of Actuality," 104/70.

5. This invocation of birth is not made by Derrida without reserve. Just a few pages earlier he prefaces similar remarks with a hesitation: "Indeed, birth itself, which is similar to what I am trying to describe, is perhaps unequal to this absolute 'arrivance.' Families prepare for a birth; it is scheduled, forenamed, caught up in a symbolic space which dulls the arrivance. Nevertheless, in spite of these anticipations and prenominations, the uncertainty will not let itself be reduced: the child that arrives remains unpredictable; it speaks of itself as from the *origin* of another world, or from an-*other* origin of this world" (ibid., 95/66). But note that the hesitation here is not expressed because the invocation of birth is itself seen to be problematic, it is due rather to a concern as to whether this figure captures everything about the event that Derrida wants to describe.

6. Ibid., 104/70.

7. Jacques Derrida, "A Europe of Hope," trans. Pleshette DeArmitt, Justine Malle, and Kas Saghafi, *Epoché* 10, no. 2 (2006): 411, originally published as "Une Europe de l'espoir," *Le Monde Diplomatique* (November 2004): 3.

8. For a powerful diagnosis of the dominant, virtually irresistible positive value that the birth of children in the future carries in contemporary society, emphasizing the importance to resist it, see Lee Edelman, *No Future: Queer Theory and the Death Drive* (Durham, NC: Duke University Press, 2004), especially chapter 1. My present analysis is inspired in part by Edelman's work.

9. Derrida, "Deconstruction of Actuality," 104/70.

10. Ibid., 105–6/71.

11. Jacques Derrida, "Structure, Sign, and Play in the Discourse of the Human Sciences," in *Writing and Difference*, 293, originally published as "La structure, le signe et le jeu dans le discours des sciences humaines," in *L'écriture et la différence*, 427–28.

12. Ibid., 291/425–26.

13. Claude Lévi-Strauss, *Introduction to the Work of Marcel Mauss*, trans. Felicity Baker (London: Routledge and Kegan Paul, 1987), 59. Cited in Derrida, "Structure, Sign, and Play," 291/426. I

have quoted Bass's translation of this passage as it appears in Derrida's essay, since the published English translation of Lévi-Strauss's *Introduction* omits the explicit reference to birth, translating "*n'a pu naître que*" as "can only have arisen." The original sentence is found in Claude Lévi-Strauss, "Introduction à l'oeuvre de Marcel Mauss," in *Sociologie et anthropologie*, by Marcel Mauss, 4th ed. (Paris: PUF, 1968), xlvii.

14. Derrida, "Structure, Sign, and Play," 292/426.

15. Bennington draws attention to this strangeness, and underlines the way birth here stands for contingency in the future, in his *Interrupting Derrida*, 64–67. Bennington's reading complicates the scene further, since he suggests it is unclear whether the others are indeed avoiding looking at the monstrous or not (presumably they could be turning away toward the monstrous). I'm not convinced that one ought to read the passage in the way here intimated—from what then are they turning away?—but doing so would provide further support for the second interpretation I favor below.

It is also worth noting that one possible source for the imagery in addition to that of birth that Derrida here uses may be the following passage from Husserl's *Formal and Transcendental Logic*, which Derrida cites in a different context in "Violence and Metaphysics," 131–32/193. Speaking of the necessity of starting from one's own subjectivity, Husserl writes: "Whether convenient or inconvenient, and even though (because no matter what prejudices) it may sound monstrous to me, it is the *primal matter-of-fact to which I must hold fast*, which I, as a philosopher, must not disregard for a single instant. For children in philosophy, this may be a dark corner haunted by the spectres of solipsism and, perhaps, of psychologism, of relativism. The true philosopher, instead of running away, will prefer to fill the dark corner with light" (Edmund Husserl, *Formal and Transcendental Logic*, trans. Dorian Cairns [The Hague: Martinus Nijhoff, 1969], 237).

16. Derrida, *Of Grammatology*, 4–5/14. I have modified the translation to conform to Bass's rendering of the corresponding paragraph in "Structure, Sign, and Play," so as to better represent these passages' shared vocabulary in the original French.

17. This phrase can be connected to Eugen Fink's description of the basic problem of phenomenology as "the origin of the world," in his "The Phenomenological Philosophy of Edmund Husserl and Contemporary Criticism," in *The Phenomenology of Husserl: Selected Critical Readings*, ed. and trans. R. O. Elveton (Chicago: Quadrangle Books, 1970). For an account of Fink's essay emphasizing its importance for Derrida's early reading of Husserl, see Leonard Lawlor, *Derrida and Husserl: The Basic Problem of Phenomenology* (Bloomington: Indiana University Press, 2002), 11–23. This notion of "the origin of the world" also plays a crucial role in "Violence and Metaphysics," where Derrida argues against Levinas's understanding of the Face as this origin. In that essay, there is a fleeting reference to birth in Derrida's critique of Levinas's recourse to the spatial figure of exteriority. Contra Levinas, Derrida characterizes space as "the wound and finitude of birth (of *the* birth) [*finitude de naissance (de la naissance)*] without which one could not even open language, one would not even have a true or false exteriority to speak of" (Derrida, "Violence and Metaphysics," 132/166). If one were pursue this line of thought further, it could also be related to the way Derrida differentiates his understanding of the trace from that of Levinas in *Of Grammatology*. See in particular the remark that "archi-writing, at first the possibility of the spoken word, then of the '*graphie*' in the narrow sense, the birthplace [*lieu natal*] of 'usurpation,' denounced from Plato to Saussure, this trace is the opening of the first exteriority in general, the enigmatic relation of the living to its other and of an inside to an outside: spacing" (*Of Grammatology*, 70/103). Also relevant are Derrida's descriptions of the trace made in the context of his discussion of Saussure, when he writes that "the absence of *another* here-and-now, of another transcendental present, of *another* origin of the world appearing as such, presenting itself as irreducible absence within the presence of the trace, is not a metaphysical formula substituted for a scientific concept of writing" (ibid., 47/68).

18. Derrida, *Chaque fois unique*, 9.

19. Ibid., 11. I should also note that Derrida discusses Celan's line several times in his final seminar. There his interpretation follows closely the one given in "Rams" that I articulate below, repeatedly emphasizing its connotation of birth. Interestingly, in the one moment in these discussions where the phrase "the origin of the world" appears, it refers to the mother who is carrying the child: "Well, still beyond all the imports I've already tried to count here or there of this unheard-of proposition, of this performative lodged like a pearl in the oyster of the constative, like a still unborn child, to be born, to be carried to term in the uterus of the origin of the world as it is, there would be today the import of a declaration of love or of peace at the moment of a declaration of war" (Derrida, *Beast and the Sovereign*, 2:259/358).

20. Derrida, "Rams," 140/23.

21. This link is also made in *The Work of Mourning* in a piece written immediately after Louis Althusser's death in 1990, where Derrida states the following: "What is coming to an end, what Louis is taking away with him, is not only something or other that we would have shared at some point or another, in one place or another, but the world itself, a certain origin of the world—his origin, no doubt, but also that of the world in which I lived, in which we lived a unique story. It is a story that is, in any case, irreplaceable, and it will have had one meaning or another for the two of us, even if this meaning could not have been the same, and not even the same just for him. It is a world that is for us the whole world, the only world, and it sinks into an abyss from which no memory—even if we keep the memory, and we will keep it—can save it" (Derrida, *The Work of Mourning*, 115/146). However, in stating that "it is *a* world that is *for us* the whole world" (my emphasis), it seems that in this earlier text Derrida has not yet conceived of "the end of the world" in the radicality expressed in *Chaque fois unique*'s preface and "Rams" (both written in 2003).

22. Derrida, "Rams," 159/72.

23. Ibid.

24. Jacques Derrida, "The Night Watch (over 'the book of himself')," trans. Pascale-Anne Brault and Michael Naas, in *Derrida and Joyce: Texts and Contexts*, ed. Andrew J. Mitchell and Sam Slote (Albany: State University of New York Press, 2013), originally published as "La veilleuse ('. . . au livre de lui-même')," preface to *James Joyce ou l'écriture matricide*, by Jacques Trilling (Belfort: Circé, 2001). Hereafter referred to as NW/LV. Trilling's essay was first published in 1973. I am grateful to Pascale-Anne Brault and Michael Naas for sharing with me their English translation of this text in advance of its publication. This translation helped me interpret the text's dense polysemy, a polysemy beginning with the title, which Brault and Naas explain as follows: "Capitalized in the Trilling text that Derrida is prefacing, the feminine noun suggests first of all a woman who keeps watch, who remains vigilant, who holds vigil—a 'Nightwatchwoman' or 'Waking woman.' But a *veilleuse* is also a little candle or light that in certain Jewish families is kept lit for seven days after the death of a loved one. In other contexts, a *veilleuse* is a light or lamp that dimly lights a child's room at night—a nightlight. One also speaks of the *veilleuse* of an appliance, a pilot light, for example, which remains lit even when an appliance is off, or else of an appliance being *en veilleuse*, that is, illuminated or turned on but not fully functioning, in 'standby mode.' From these various contexts, we can see that the semantic kernel of the word suggests a keeping watch, a standing by, a remaining awake or vigilant when everyone else has forgotten or gone to sleep, a remaining lit or illuminated when all other lights have been extinguished" (NW, 103n1).

25. For Trilling, "matricide" is to be understood as primarily referring to the person who kills a mother, rather than the act of killing. This is signaled in the footnote he attaches to his title: "Rare. A person who has killed his mother. See parricide (*Robert*)." Jacques Trilling, *James Joyce ou l'écriture matricide* (Belfort: Circé, 2001), 33. In Trilling's French text the gender of the matricide is not always specified (as it is not in this citation), but Derrida suggests that throughout Trilling is speaking only of sons (NW, 93/LV, 15–16).

26. Montaigne, "On Affectionate Relationships," 207, 212.

27. Deutscher, "Derrida's Impossible Genealogies," 27.

28. I should note that Derrida breaks this pattern in another late text, *Prégnances: Lavis de Colette Deblé. Peintures* (Mont-de-Marsan: L'Atelier des Brisants, 2004). There he interprets Colette Deblé's paintings as engaged in acts of inheritance, through images of pregnancy, and so positions her firmly as both heir and legatee. However, here Deutscher's critique concerning the absence of negativity applies, since Derrida quite clearly casts Deblé's work as a positive improvement on the patriarchal Western tradition, an instance of perfectibility without perversion: "The grand and venerable history of painting *appears better*, henceforth, it is born [*elle voit le jour*], not wounded but finally vulnerable" (11). Deblé's work itself would thus be only a chance for the future, not a threat. Relatedly, there is no aggression in Derrida's own inheritance from Deblé—he does not point out inadequacies in her work or reveal any aporetic structure that she has attempted to avoid. Which is to say Derrida does not inherit Deblé's work in the same way he inherits the work of philosophers. This absence of negativity is the reason I have not devoted more attention to *Prégnances* in the present analysis, which one might have thought perfect for examining the subject of birth in Derrida's writings. I read it as just another example of Derrida figuring birth in purely positive terms, akin to the images I discussed at the beginning of this chapter, offering very little to the more complex notion I am attempting to develop. That said, *Prégnances* is not an easy text, and it may be that others are able to draw more from it on this theme than I.

29. For an excellent discussion and critique of the saturation of violent images in recent Continental philosophy, see Ann V. Murphy, *Violence and the Philosophical Imaginary* (Albany: State University of New York Press, 2012).

30. Trilling, *James Joyce*, 93. First cited by Derrida on NW, 91/LV, 12.

31. As Derrida notes, Trilling does not mention Job (NW, 91/LV, 13). But Trilling does cite Silenus's curse against one's own birth as it is expressed in Nietzsche's *The Birth of Tragedy* (Trilling, *James Joyce*, 119). Since Job's words are uttered specifically against the womb, focusing on this curse rather than Silenus's allows Derrida to more directly link the wish never to have been born to the matricidal desire.

32. Derrida is here capitalizing on the aural proximity of "*naître*" and "*être*" in French, the only difference being the "*n*" that suggests the negation carried in the curse against one's own birth. This is made fully explicit in the next sentence when Derrida evokes the two questions of "to be or not to be [*être ou ne pas être*]" and "to be born or not to be born [*naître ou ne pas naître*]." This allusion to Hamlet also heralds the imminent arrival of the specter in the text.

33. The citation "father and son of his works" is from Trilling, *James Joyce*, 48.

34. See Jacques Derrida, *Memoirs of the Blind: The Self-Portrait and Other Ruins*, trans. Pascale-Anne Brault and Michael Naas (Chicago: University of Chicago Press, 1993), 87–88, originally published as *Mémoires d'aveugle: L'autoportrait et autres ruines* (Paris: Réunion des Musées nationaux, 1991), 91–92.

35. Jacques Derrida, "Psychoanalysis Searches the States of Its Soul: The Impossible Beyond of a Sovereign Cruelty," in *Without Alibi*, trans. Peggy Kamuf (Stanford: Stanford University Press, 2002), originally published as *États d'âme de la psychanalyse* (Paris: Galilée, 2000).

Conclusion: Inheriting Derrida's Legacies

1. For an analysis that takes a first step in this direction, applying a somewhat simpler understanding of the Derridean conception of birth to the phenomenon of multiple citizenship, see Samir Haddad, "Citizenship and the Ambivalence of Birth," *Derrida Today* 4, no. 2 (2011).

Works Cited

Abeysekara, Ananda. *The Politics of Postsecular Religion: Mourning Secular Futures*. New York: Columbia University Press, 2008.

Balibar, Etienne. "Eschatology versus Teleology: The Suspended Dialogue between Derrida and Althusser." In *Derrida and the Time of the Political*, edited by Pheng Cheah and Suzanne Guerlac, 57–73. Durham, NC: Duke University Press, 2009.

Beardsworth, Richard. *Derrida and the Political*. New York: Routledge, 1996.

Bennington, Geoffrey. *Interrupting Derrida*. New York: Routledge, 2000.

Butler, Judith. "Finishing, Starting." In *Derrida and the Time of the Political*, edited by Pheng Cheah and Suzanne Guerlac, 291–306. Durham, NC: Duke University Press, 2009.

Cheah, Pheng. "The Untimely Secret of Democracy." In *Derrida and the Time of the Political*, edited by Pheng Cheah and Suzanne Guerlac, 74–96. Durham NC: Duke University Press, 2009.

Custer, O. "Making Sense of Derrida's Aporetic Hospitality." In *Jacques Derrida: Critical Assessments of Leading Philosophers*, edited by Zeynep Direck and Leonard Lawlor, 199–219. New York: Routledge, 2002.

Derrida, Jacques. *Adieu to Emmanuel Levinas*. Translated by Pascale-Anne Brault and Michael Naas. Stanford: Stanford University Press, 1999. Originally published as *Adieu à Emmanuel Lévinas* (Paris: Galilée, 1997).

———. *The Animal That Therefore I Am*. Translated by David Wills. New York: Fordham University Press, 2008. Originally published as *L'animal que donc je suis* (Paris: Galilée, 2006).

———. *Aporias: Dying—Awaiting (One Another at) the "Limits of Truth."* Translated by Thomas Dutoit. Stanford: Stanford University Press, 1993. Published in French as *Apories* (Paris: Galilée, 1996).

———. *Archive Fever: A Freudian Impression*. Translated by Eric Prenowitz. Chicago: University of Chicago Press, 1996. Originally published as *Mal d'archive* (Paris: Galilée, 1995).

———. "As If It Were Possible, 'Within Such Limits.'" In *Paper Machine*, 73–99. Translated by Rachel Bowlby. Stanford: Stanford University Press, 2005. Originally published as "Comme si c'était possible, 'within such limits' . . . ," in *Papier machine* (Paris: Galilée, 2001), 283–319.

———. "Autoimmunity: Real and Symbolic Suicides." Translated by Pascale-Anne Brault and Michael Naas. In *Philosophy in a Time of Terror: Dialogues with Jürgen Habermas and Jacques Derrida*, edited by Giovanna Borradori, 85–136. Chicago: University of Chicago Press, 2003. Published in French as "Auto-immunités: suicides réels et symboliques," in Jacques Derrida and Jürgen Habermas, *Le concept du 11 septembre: Dialogues à New York (octobre–décembre 2001) avec Giovanna Borradori* (Paris: Galilée, 2004), 133–96.

———. "Avances." Preface to Serge Margel, *Le tombeau du dieu artisan—sur Platon*, 9–43. Paris: Minuit, 1995.

——. *The Beast and the Sovereign.* Vol. 1. Translated by Geoffrey Bennington. Chicago: University of Chicago Press, 2009. Originally published as *Séminaire: La bête et le souverain volume I (2001–2002)* (Paris: Galilée, 2008).

——. *The Beast and the Sovereign.* Vol. 2. Translated by Geoffrey Bennington. Chicago: University of Chicago Press, 2011. Originally published as *Séminaire: La bête et le souverain volume II (2002–2003)* (Paris: Galilée, 2010).

——. "Before the Law." Translated by Avital Ronell. In *Acts of Literature*, edited by Derek Attridge, 181–220. New York: Routledge, 1992. Originally published as "Devant la loi," in Jacques Derrida et al., *La faculté de juger* (Paris: Minuit, 1985), 87–139.

——. *Chaque fois unique, la fin du monde.* Paris: Galilée, 2003.

——. "The Deconstruction of Actuality." Translated by Elizabeth Rottenberg. In *Negotiations: Interventions and Interviews, 1971–2001*, edited by Elizabeth Rottenberg, 85–116. Stanford: Stanford University Press, 2002. Originally published as "La deconstruction de l'actualité," *Passages* 57 (1993): 60–75.

——. "Derelictions of the Right to Justice (But What Are the 'Sans-Papiers' Lacking?)." Translated by Elizabeth Rottenberg. In *Negotiations: Interventions and Interviews, 1971–2001*, edited by Elizabeth Rottenberg, 133–44. Stanford: Stanford University Press, 2002.

——. "Ethics and Politics Today." Translated by Elizabeth Rottenberg. In *Negotiations: Interventions and Interviews, 1971–2001*, edited by Elizabeth Rottenberg, 295–314. Stanford: Stanford University Press, 2002.

——. "A Europe of Hope." Translated by Pleshette DeArmitt, Justine Malle, and Kas Saghafi. *Epoché* 10, no. 2 (2006): 407–12. Originally published as "Une Europe de l'espoir," *Le Monde Diplomatique*, November 2004, 3.

——. "Faith and Knowledge: The Two Sources of 'Religion' at the Limits of Reason Alone." Translated by Samuel Weber. In *Acts of Religion*, edited by Gil Anidjar, 42–101. New York: Routledge, 2002. Originally published as "Foi et savoir," in *Foi et savoir, suivi de Le siècle et le pardon* (Paris: Le Seuil, 2000), 9–100.

——. "For a Justice to Come: An Interview with Jacques Derrida." In *The Derrida-Habermas Reader*, edited by Lasse Thomassen, 259–69. Chicago: University of Chicago Press, 2006.

——. "Force of Law: The 'Mystical Foundation of Authority.'" Translated by Mary Quaintance. In *Acts of Religion*, edited by Gil Anidjar, 230–98. New York: Routledge, 2002. Originally published as *Force de loi* (Paris: Galilée, 1994).

——. "Freud and the Scene of Writing." In *Writing and Difference*, 196–231. Translated by Alan Bass. Chicago: University of Chicago Press, 1978. Originally published as "Freud et la scène de l'écriture," in *L'écriture et la différence* (Paris: Minuit, 1967), 293–340.

——. *Given Time: I. Counterfeit Money.* Translated by Peggy Kamuf. Chicago: University of Chicago Press, 1992. Originally published as *Donner le temps. 1: La fausse monnaie* (Paris: Galilée, 1991).

——. "Hospitality, Justice and Responsibility." In *Questioning Ethics: Contemporary Debates in Philosophy*, edited by Richard Kearney and Mark Dooley, 65–83. New York: Routledge, 1999.

——. "Hostipitality [Seminar]." Translated by Gil Anidjar. In *Acts of Religion*, edited by Gil Anidjar, 358–420. New York: Routledge, 2002.

——. "Hostipitality [Talk]." Translated by Barry Stocker with Forbes Morlock. *Angelaki* 5, no. 3 (2000): 3–18. Originally published as "Hostipitalité," in *Pera Peras Poros*, edited by Ferda Keskin and Önay Sözer (Istanbul: Yapi Kredi Yatinlari, 1999), 17–44.

———. *Learning to Live Finally*. Translated by Pascale-Anne Brault and Michael Naas. Hoboken, NJ: Melville House, 2007. Originally published as *Apprendre à vivre enfin* (Paris: Galilée, 2005).

———. *Limited Inc*. Translated by Samuel Weber. Evanston, IL: Northwestern University Press, 1988. Published in French as *Limited Inc*. (Paris: Galilée, 1990).

———. "Marx & Sons." Translated by G. M. Goshgarian. In *Ghostly Demarcations: A Symposium on Jacques Derrida's* Specters of Marx, edited by Michael Sprinker, 213–69. London: Verso, 1999. Published in French as *Marx & Sons* (Paris: PUF/Galilée, 2002).

———. *Memoirs of the Blind: The Self-Portrait and Other Ruins*. Translated by Pascale-Anne Brault and Michael Naas. Chicago: University of Chicago Press, 1993. Originally published as *Mémoires d'aveugle: L'autoportrait et autres ruines* (Paris: Réunion des Musées nationaux, 1991).

———. "Nietzsche and the Machine." Translated by Richard Beardsworth. In *Negotiations: Interventions and Interviews, 1971–2001*, edited by Elizabeth Rottenberg, 215–56. Stanford: Stanford University Press, 2002.

———. "The Night Watch (over 'the book of himself')." Translated by Pascale-Anne Brault and Michael Naas. In *Derrida and Joyce: Texts and Contexts*, edited by Andrew J. Mitchell and Sam Slote, 87–108. Albany: State University of New York Press, 2013. Originally published as "La veilleuse ('. . . au livre de lui-même')," preface to *James Joyce ou l'écriture matricide*, by Jacques Trilling (Belfort: Circé, 2001), 7–32.

———. "No Apocalypse, Not Now: Full Speed Ahead, Seven Missiles, Seven Missives." Translated by Catherine Porter and Philip Lewis. In *Psyche: Inventions of the Other*, 1:387–409. Stanford: Stanford University Press, 2007. Originally published as "*No apocalypse, not now*: à toute vitesse, sept missiles, sept missives," in *Psyché: Inventions de l'autre*, 2nd ed. (Paris: Galilée, 1998), 1:395–418.

———. "Not Utopia, the Im-possible." In *Paper Machine*, 121–35. Translated by Rachel Bowlby. Stanford: Stanford University Press, 2005. Originally published as "Non l'utopie, l'impossible," in *Papier machine* (Paris: Galilée, 2001), 349–66.

———. *Of Grammatology*. Translated by Gayatri Chakravorty Spivak. Baltimore: Johns Hopkins University Press, 1976. Originally published as *De la grammatologie* (Paris: Minuit, 1967).

———. "On Cosmopolitanism." Translated by Mark Dooley. In *On Cosmopolitanism and Forgiveness*, 3–24. New York: Routledge, 2002. Originally published as *Cosmopolites de tous les pays, encore un effort!* (Paris: Galilée, 1997).

———. "On Forgiveness." Translated by Michael Hughes. In *On Cosmopolitanism and Forgiveness*, 27–60. New York: Routledge, 2002. Originally published as "Le siècle et le pardon," in *Foi et savoir, suivi de Le siècle et le pardon* (Paris: Le Seuil, 2000), 103–33.

———. "On a Newly Arisen Apocalyptic Tone in Philosophy." Translated by John Leavey Jr. In *Raising the Tone of Philosophy*, edited by Peter Fenves, 117–71. Baltimore: Johns Hopkins University Press, 1993. Originally published as *D'un ton apocalyptique adopté naguère en philosophie* (Paris: Galilée, 1983).

———. *The Other Heading: Reflections on Today's Europe*. Translated by Pascale-Anne Brault and Michael Naas. Bloomington: Indiana University Press, 1992. Originally published as *L'autre cap* (Paris: Minuit, 1991).

———. "Others Are Secret because They Are Other." In *Paper Machine*, 136–63. Translated by Rachel Bowlby. Stanford: Stanford University Press, 2005. Originally published as "Autrui est secret parce qu'il est autre," in *Papier machine* (Paris: Galilée, 2001), 367–98.

———. "*Ousia* and *Grammē*: Note on a Note from *Being and Time*." In *Margins of Philosophy*, 29–67. Translated by Alan Bass. Chicago: University of Chicago Press, 1982. Originally published as "Ousia et grammè: Note sur une note de Sein und Zeit," in *Marges de la philosophie* (Paris: Minuit, 1972), 31–78.

———. "Passions: 'An Oblique Offering.'" Translated by David Wood. In *On the Name*, edited by Thomas Dutoit, 3–31. Stanford: Stanford University Press, 1995. Originally published as *Passions* (Paris: Galilée, 1993).

———. "Plato's Pharmacy." In *Dissemination*, 61–171. Translated by Barbara Johnson. Chicago: University of Chicago Press, 1981. Originally published as "La pharmacie de Platon," in *Dissemination* (Paris: Seuil, 1972), 77–213.

———. "Politics and Friendship." Translated by Robert Harvey. In *Negotiations: Interventions and Interviews, 1971–2001*, edited by Elizabeth Rottenberg, 147–98. Stanford: Stanford University Press, 2002.

———. *Politics of Friendship*. Translated by George Collins. London: Verso, 1997. Originally published as *Politiques de l'amitié* (Paris: Galilée, 1994).

———. *Prégnances: Lavis de Colette Deblé. Peintures*. Mont-de-Marsan: L'Atelier des Brisants, 2004.

———. "The Principle of Hospitality." In *Paper Machine*, 66–69. Translated by Rachel Bowlby. Stanford: Stanford University Press, 2005. Originally published as "Le principe d'hospitalité," in *Papier machine* (Paris: Galilée, 2001), 273–77.

———. "Privilege: Justificatory Title and Introductory Remarks." In *Who's Afraid of Philosophy? Right to Philosophy I*, 1–66. Translated by Jan Plug. Stanford: Stanford University Press, 2002. Originally published as "Privilège: Titre justificatif et remarques introductives," in *Du droit à la philosophie* (Paris: Galilée, 1990), 9–108.

———. "Psychoanalysis Searches the States of Its Soul: The Impossible Beyond of a Sovereign Cruelty." In *Without Alibi*, 238–80. Translated by Peggy Kamuf. Stanford: Stanford University Press, 2002. Originally published as *États d'âme de la psychanalyse* (Paris: Galilée, 2000).

———. "Rams: Uninterrupted Dialogue—Between Two Infinities, the Poem." Translated by Thomas Dutoit and Philippe Romanski. In *Sovereignties in Question: The Poetics of Paul Celan*, 135–63. New York: Fordham University Press, 2005. Originally published as *Béliers: Le dialogue ininterrompu: Entre deux infinis, le poème* (Paris: Galilée, 2003).

———. "The Reason of the Strongest (Are There Rogues States?)" Translated by Pascale-Anne Brault and Michael Naas. In *Rogues: Two Essays on Reason*, 1–114. Stanford: Stanford University Press, 2005. Originally published as "La Raison du Plus Fort (Y a-t-il des États Voyous?)," in *Voyous: Deux essais sur la raison* (Paris: Galilée, 2003), 17–161.

———. "Responsabilité et Hospitalité." In *Manifeste pour l'hospitalité*, edited by Mohammed Seffahi, 111–24. Grigny: Paroles d'aube, 1999.

———. *Rogues: Two Essays on Reason*. Translated by Pascale-Anne Brault and Michael Naas. Stanford: Stanford University Press, 2005. Originally published as *Voyous: Deux essais sur la raison* (Paris: Galilée, 2003).

———. "Sauf le nom (Post-Scriptum)." Translated by John P. Leavey Jr. In *On the Name*, edited by Thomas Dutoit, 33–85. Stanford: Stanford University Press, 1995. Originally published as *Sauf le nom* (Paris: Galilée, 1993).

———. "Signature Event Context." In *Margins of Philosophy*, 307–30. Translated by Alan Bass. Chicago: University of Chicago Press, 1982. Originally published as "Signature Evénement Contexte," in *Marges de la philosophie* (Paris: Minuit, 1972), 365–93.

———. *Specters of Marx: The State of the Debt, the Work of Mourning, and the New International.* Translated by Peggy Kamuf. New York: Routledge, 1994. Originally published as *Spectres de Marx: L'état de la dette, le travail du deuil et la Nouvelle Internationale* (Paris: Galilée, 1993).

———. *Speech and Phenomena and Other Essays on Husserl's Theory of Time.* Translated by David B. Allison. Evanston, IL: Northwestern University Press, 1973. Originally published as *La voix et le phénomène* (Paris: PUF, 1967).

———. "Structure, Sign, and Play in the Discourse of the Human Sciences." In *Writing and Difference*, 278–93. Translated by Alan Bass. Chicago: University of Chicago Press, 1978. Originally published as "La structure, le signe et le jeu dans le discours des sciences humaines," in *L'écriture et la différence* (Paris: Seuil, 1967), 409–28.

———. "Typewriter Ribbon: Limited Ink (2)." In *Without Alibi*, 71–160. Translated by Peggy Kamuf. Stanford: Stanford University Press, 2002. Originally published as "Le ruban de machine à écrire: *Limited Ink II*," in *Papier machine* (Paris: Galilée, 2001), 33–147.

———. "Une hospitalité à l'infini." In *Manifeste pour l'hospitalité*, edited by Mohammed Seffahi, 97–106. Grigny: Paroles d'aube, 1999.

———. "The University without Condition." In *Without Alibi*, 202–37. Translated by Peggy Kamuf. Stanford: Stanford University Press, 2002. Originally published as *L'université sans condition* (Paris: Galilée, 2001).

———. "Violence and Metaphysics: An Essay on the Thought of Emmanuel Levinas." In *Writing and Difference*, 79–153. Translated by Alan Bass. Chicago: University of Chicago Press, 1978. Originally published as "Violence et métaphysique: Essai sur la pensée d'Emmanuel Levinas," in *L'écriture et la différence* (Paris: Seuil, 1967), 117–228.

———. "What Does It Mean to Be a French Philosopher Today?" In *Paper Machine*, 112–20. Translated by Rachel Bowlby. Stanford: Stanford University Press, 2005. Originally published as "Qu'est-ce que cela veut dire d'être un philosophe français aujourd'hui?" In *Papier machine* (Paris: Galilée, 2001), 337–47.

———. *Without Alibi*, Translated by Peggy Kamuf. Stanford: Stanford University Press, 2002.

———. *The Work of Mourning.* Edited and translated by Michael Naas and Pascale-Anne Brault. Chicago: University of Chicago Press, 2001. Published in French as *Chaque fois unique, la fin du monde* (Paris: Galilée, 2003).

———. "The 'World' of the Enlightenment to Come (Exception, Calculation, and Sovereignty)." Translated by Pascale-Anne Brault and Michael Naas. In *Rogues: Two Essays on Reason*, 115–59. Stanford: Stanford University Press, 2005. Originally published as "Le 'Monde' des Lumières à Venir (Exception, Calcul, et Souveraineté)," in *Voyous: Deux essais sur la raison* (Paris: Galilée, 2003), 163–217.

Derrida, Jacques, and Anne Dufourmantelle. *Of Hospitality.* Translated by Rachel Bowlby. Stanford: Stanford University Press, 2000. Originally published as *De l'hospitalité* (Paris: Calmann-Levy, 1997).

Derrida, Jacques, and Elisabeth Roudinesco. *For What Tomorrow . . . : A Dialogue.* Translated by Jeff Fort. Stanford: Stanford University Press, 2004. Originally published as *De quoi demain . . . : Dialogue* (Paris: Fayard/Galilée, 2001).

Deutscher, Penelope. "Derrida's Impossible Genealogies." *Theory and Event* 8, no. 1 (2005).

———. "'Women, and So On': *Rogues* and the Autoimmunity of Feminism." *Symposium: Canadian Journal of Continental Philosophy* 11, no. 1 (2007): 101–19.

Dick, Kirby, and Amy Ziering Kofman. *Derrida: Screenplay and Essays on the Film.* New York: Routledge, 2005.

Diogenes Laertius. *Lives of Eminent Philosophers*. Vol. 1. Translated by R. D. Hicks. Loeb Classical Library. Cambridge, MA: Harvard University Press, 1925.

Eagleton, Terry. "Marxism without Marxism." In *Ghostly Demarcations: A Symposium on Jacques Derrida's* Specters of Marx, edited by Michael Sprinker, 83–87. London: Verso, 1999.

Edelman, Lee. *No Future: Queer Theory and the Death Drive*. Durham, NC: Duke University Press, 2004.

Ferry, Luc, and Alain Renaut. *French Philosophy of the Sixties: An Essay on Antihumanism*. Translated by Mary S. Cattani. Amherst: University of Massachusetts Press, 1990.

Fink, Eugen. "The Phenomenological Philosophy of Edmund Husserl and Contemporary Criticism." In *The Phenomenology of Husserl: Selected Critical Readings*, edited and translated by R. O. Elveton, 73–147. Chicago: Quadrangle Books, 1970.

Fritsch, Matthias. "Derrida's Democracy to Come." *Constellations* 9, no. 4 (2002): 574–97.

———. *The Promise of Memory: History and Politics in Marx, Benjamin, and Derrida*. Albany: State University of New York Press, 2005.

Gasché, Rodolphe. "European Memories: Jan Patočka and Jacques Derrida on Responsibility." In *Derrida and the Time of the Political*, edited by Pheng Cheah and Suzanne Guerlac, 135–57. Durham NC: Duke University Press, 2009.

Gratton, Peter. "Questioning Freedom in the Later Work of Derrida." *Philosophy Today* 50, supp., (2006): 133–38.

Guenther, Lisa. *The Gift of the Other: Levinas and the Politics of Reproduction*. Albany: State University of New York Press, 2006.

Habermas, Jürgen. *The Philosophical Discourse of Modernity: Twelve Lectures*. Translated by Frederick Lawrence. Cambridge, MA: MIT Press, 1987.

Haddad, Samir. "Citizenship and the Ambivalence of Birth." *Derrida Today* 4, no. 2 (2011): 173–93.

———. "A Genealogy of Violence, from Light to the Autoimmune." *Diacritics* 38, nos. 1–2 (2008): 121–42.

———. "Language Remains." *CR: The New Centennial Review* 9, no. 1 (2009): 127–46.

———. "Reading Derrida Reading Derrida: Deconstruction as Self-Inheritance." *International Journal of Philosophical Studies* 14, no. 4 (2006): 505–20.

Hägglund, Martin. "The Challenge of Radical Atheism: A Response." *CR: The New Centennial Review* 9, no. 1 (2009): 227–52.

———. *Radical Atheism: Derrida and the Time of Life*. Stanford: Stanford University Press, 2008.

———. "The Radical Evil of Deconstruction: A Reply to John Caputo." *Journal for Cultural and Religious Theory* 11, no. 2 (2011): 126–50.

Haverkamp, Anselm, ed. *Deconstruction is/in America*. New York: New York University Press, 1995.

Honig, Bonnie. *Democracy and the Foreigner*. Princeton: Princeton University Press, 2001.

Husserl, Edmund. *Formal and Transcendental Logic*. Translated by Dorian Cairns. The Hague: Martinus Nijhoff, 1969.

Kant, Immanuel. "Toward Perpetual Peace." In *Practical Philosophy*, translated and edited by Mary Gregor, 317–51. Cambridge: Cambridge University Press, 1996.

Kearney, Richard. "Desire of God." In *God, the Gift, and Postmodernism*, edited by John D. Caputo and Michael J. Scanlon, 112–45. Bloomington: Indiana University Press, 1999.

Klossowski, Pierre. *Les lois de l'hospitalité*. Paris: Gallimard, 1965.

La Caze, Marguerite. "Not Just Visitors: Cosmopolitanism, Hospitality, and Refugees." *Philosophy Today* 48, no. 3 (2004): 313–24.

Lawlor, Leonard. *Derrida and Husserl: The Basic Problem of Phenomenology*. Bloomington: Indiana University Press, 2002.

———. "Jacques Derrida." *Stanford Encyclopedia of Philosophy*. http://plato.stanford.edu/entries/derrida/.

———. *This Is Not Sufficient: An Essay on Animality and Human Nature in Derrida*. New York: Columbia University Press, 2007.

Lefort, Claude. "La question de la démocratie." In *Le retrait du politique*, by Philippe Lacoue-Labarthe, Jean-Luc Nancy, et al., 71–88. Paris: Galilée, 1983.

———. "The Question of Democracy." In *Democracy and Political Theory*, 9–20. Translated by David Macey. Minneapolis: University of Minnesota Press, 1988.

Lévi-Strauss, Claude. "Introduction à l'oeuvre de Marcel Mauss." In *Sociologie et anthropologie*, by Marcel Mauss, ix–lii. 4th ed. Paris: PUF, 1968.

———. *Introduction to the Work of Marcel Mauss*. Translated by Felicity Baker. London: Routledge and Kegan Paul, 1987.

Levinas, Emmanuel. *Totality and Infinity*. Translated by Alphonso Lingis. Pittsburgh: Duquesne University Press, 1969.

Montaigne, Michel de. "On Affectionate Relationships." In *The Complete Essays*, 205–19. Translated by M. A. Screech. London: Allen Lane, Penguin Press, 1991.

Murphy, Ann V. *Violence and the Philosophical Imaginary*. Albany: State University of New York Press, 2012.

Naas, Michael. *Derrida from Now On*. New York: Fordham University Press, 2008.

———. *Taking on the Tradition: Jacques Derrida and the Legacies of Deconstruction*. Stanford: Stanford University Press, 2003.

Nancy, Jean-Luc. *The Experience of Freedom*. Translated by Bridget McDonald. Stanford: Stanford University Press, 1993.

Norval, Aletta J. *Aversive Democracy: Inheritance and Originality in the Democratic Tradition*. Cambridge: Cambridge University Press, 2007.

O'Byrne, Anne. *Natality and Finitude*. Bloomington: Indiana University Press, 2010.

Rousseau, Jean-Jacques. *On the Social Contract*. In *The Basic Political Writings*, 139–227. Translated by Donald A. Cress. Indianapolis: Hackett, 1987.

Seffahi, Mohammed, ed. *Manifeste pour l'hospitalité*. Grigny: Paroles d'aube, 1999.

Thomson, A. J. P. *Deconstruction and Democracy: Derrida's Politics of Friendship*. London: Continuum, 2005.

———. "Derrida's *Rogues*: Islam and the Futures of Deconstruction." In *Derrida: Negotiating the Legacy*, edited by Madeleine Fagan et al., 66–79. Edinburgh: Edinburgh University Press, 2007.

Trilling, Jacques. *James Joyce ou l'écriture matricide*. Belfort: Circé, 2001.

Weber, Samuel. "Rogue Democracy." *Diacritics* 38, nos. 1–2 (2008): 104–20.

———. "La Surenchère—(Upping the Ante)." In *Le Passage des frontières*, 141–49. Paris: Galilée, 1994.

Index

SAMIR HADDAD is Assistant Professor of Philosophy at Fordham University.

CPSIA information can be obtained at www.ICGtesting.com
Printed in the USA
LVOW080926020513

331976LV00002B/2/P